Postmodern Worship & The Arts

Edited by
Doug Adams and Michael E. Moynahan, SJ

Resource Publications, Inc.
San Jose, California

Reprint Department
Resource Publications, Inc.
160 E. Virginia #290
San Jose, California 95112-5876
(408) 286-8505 voice
(408) 287-8748 fax

Library of Congress Cataloging-in-Publication Data
Postmodern worship & the arts / edited by Doug Adams and Michael E. Moynahan.
        p.   cm.
Includes bibliographical references.
ISBN 0-89390-546-1
1. Worship 2. Christian art and symbolism. I. Title: Postmodern worship and the arts.
II. Adams, Doug, 1945- III. Moynahan, Michael E.

BV10 .P67 2002

2001059431

Printed in the United States of America.
02 03 04 05 06 | 5 4 3 2 1

Editorial director: Nick Wagner
Production coordinator: Romina Saha
Copyeditor: Tricia Joerger
Cover design: Nelson Estarija
Cover photo: Ruben Alfaro

Contents

Introduction

*P*ostmodern worship engages the whole body: the eye and the ear, the body, and the mind. The chapters in this book lead us beyond modern worship, which in the last few centuries communicated primarily to the ear and mind through words of sermons, prayer texts, and hymns but rarely reached the rest of the body. Postmodern worship not only gives us eyes to see and ears to hear but also a sense of wholeness or, as the poet Theodore Roethke said, "eyes that hear and ears that see." Such worship with all the arts involves those who remember through hearing and those who remember through seeing and those who remember through eating and dancing. Such worship helps churches grow by bringing together persons of all different ages, races, genders, and classes.

We find ourselves at the dawn of a new millennium. This involves both an ending and a new beginning, a death, and a new birth. The poet T. S. Eliot, in his *Four Quartets*, reminds us that what we call the end is really the beginning. "The end is where we start from."

The world seems to be shrinking in many ways. Thanks to the technological advances in transportation (air travel) and electronic communications (e-mail), people don't see large distances necessarily dividing them. Ideas and information are much more easily exchanged than at the beginning of the twentieth century. We still, however, continue to look for those things that both express and nurture a common identity among us such as common beliefs and a common language. These are two things that will mark us irrevocably as one global community. Arts have emerged as the primary languages of our day.

This new millennium breathes renewed hope and new life into many of our interests and endeavors. This volume, *Postmodern Worship & The Arts*, is a book that explores common beliefs (worship) and a common language (the arts). It brings together the work of numerous scholars who work in the areas of worship, education, and the arts. All the authors share one thing in common. They have been students, colleagues, collaborators, and friends of James L. (Jake) Empereur, S.J.

Jake did his doctoral work in worship at the Graduate Theological Union under the renowned Massey Shepherd. Jake spent more than twenty-five years of his life at the GTU. During this time he was a faculty member of the Jesuit School of Theology in Berkeley. He dedicated himself to teaching young theologians preparing for ordination, crafting renewal programs for international ministers from all over the world, directing the work of graduate students at the GTU who explored the relationship of theology and the arts (Area VII of the curriculum), and acting as mentor and spiritual guide to many who sought his wisdom and help as they continued to grow in their theological understanding and in the living of their faith life.

A continuing passion for Jake has been the arts in worship and religious education. He expressed, on more than one occasion, the irony of how easily a group of believers can come together around an art work and in worship but have such difficulty coming together around a doctrine. The existence of such a phenomenon invites the type of investigation that we undertake in this book to honor him.

We believe it is important to consider the future of the arts in worship and education. Our past experience, working in churches throughout North America, Europe, Asia, and Australia, convinces us that the arts are critical in this twenty-first century if we wish to be one in mind and heart and spirit. We have seen churches growing through the arts across divides of race, class, age, gender, and so forth. Some outstanding examples of this would be East Liberty Presbyterian Church in Pittsburgh, Middle Collegiate Church in New York City, Glide United Methodist Church of San Francisco, San Fernando Cathedral in San Antonio, Texas, to name but a few.

The essays in this book are divided into three parts. The first part explores the criteria for artful liturgy (Adams, Walton, Zimmerman, and Larson-Miller). The second part explores particular art forms in relationship to worship (Moynahan, Weil, Hoare, Carter, Seubert, De Sola, Kirk, Foley, and Baldovin). The third part examines a variety of important implications of artful liturgy (Fernandez, Martin, Splain, and Rodriguez). The book concludes by allowing the man we honor to have the last word. For many years as editor of *Modern Liturgy* magazine, Jake Empereur offered an almost monthly column entitled "Rite On" in which he reflected on the topic of a particular issue. In this "Rite On" reprise, Jake examines how the church can worship in postmodern times. All of these essays will offer challenge and thoughtful help to those who are curious and concerned about the future of the arts and worship.

Throughout his life as a liturgist, teacher, speaker, mentor, writer, and spiritual guide, Jake Empereur has always invited us to notice the easily overlooked, to pay attention to the easily dismissed, to regard chaos as well as order as a potentially rich resource since God created out of chaos. Jake has been a model and challenge to us all. He has called us through his theological thinking, his liturgical writings, and ministerial example to find those bridges between liturgy and justice, liturgy and life, liturgy and culture, education and culture, and on and on. Jake's work and his ministry have always pointed others to look to the horizon, to become aware and respond not simply to the here and now but to what an exploring faith, a resilient hope, and a compassionate imagination can bring into being. It is our strong hope that *Postmodern Worship & The Arts* will act as our collective "thanks" and "yes" to the challenging and life-giving road that Jake Empereur has shown us through the witness of his life and ministry.

Doug Adams (Berkeley, Calif.)
Mike Moynahan, SJ (Firenze, Italia)

Part 1

Ambiguity As a Gift of Arts to Formation of Inclusive Community

Doug Adams

Arts in worship renew a church's vision, membership, and mission by providing communication able to draw together people of different races, ages, genders, and economic classes. Robert Chestnut's *Transforming the Mainline Church* (Louisville: Geneva Press, 2000) details how the East Liberty Presbyterian Church of Pittsburgh uses arts in that way. Similar growth is evident in the work of Cecil Williams at Glide Memorial United Methodist Church in San Francisco, Gordon Dragt at Middle Collegiate Church in the East Village of Manhattan in New York City, and Jake Empereur at San Fernando Cathedral in San Antonio. The arts help these churches and many others in cities and suburbs and towns to grow dramatically from small,

dying, nearly all white, elderly congregations to thriving congregations with people of all colors, ages, genders, and most remarkably all classes together. The key in each case is ample use of a wide range of musical, visual, dance, and dramatic arts in worship. Hundreds of persons are drawn into their worship by gospel choirs and jazz bands or orchestras with musicians aged eight to eighty, by video and slide projections and art exhibitions in the chancel or sanctuary, and by intergenerational dance and drama companies. These arts open many windows and doors of interpretations through which the diversity of peoples may enter.

My close friend Jake Empereur, SJ, is fond of saying that "the problem with fundamentalists is that they have only one window." There are fundamentalists of the left as well as of the right. Having taught in Berkeley for twenty-five years, I know much about fundamentalists of the left. On what issues are you and I fundamentalists with just one point of view? There is nothing wrong with our one window which may allow an important perspective on an issue, but the danger of having only one window is that we see only one side of an issue. Also, someone may build next door and block our one view. Having a house with many windows on all sides allows us to see more and allows our vision to survive the blocking of any one window. Such a place may become a home for people with differing views. The church is fortunate to have at least four Gospels to welcome home persons of some different perspectives.

In an age when our single-issue mentalities threaten to destroy any possibility of broad community, I believe that ambiguity is a major gift of the fine arts through worship to formation of a healthy inclusive community (whether it is an historic or an emerging community). The ambiguity in fine art helps us see the flaws in our heroes and the redeeming qualities in our enemies; and so such art allows us to love our enemies and include them in our life which then develops wider visions of community while we see also the need for ourselves and even our favorite leaders to confess sins that we or they commit. In Jesus' parable of the Good Samaritan, there is no help from either the Jewish priest or the Levite, but help comes from the Samaritan, whom Jewish listeners considered an enemy because Samaritans centuries before had cooperated with an invader who exiled faithful Jews and gave their land to Samaritans. If Jesus had told the story with the Samaritan passing by and not helping and the priest stopping to help, he would have been like a propagandist pandering to the prejudices of his listeners. Art without ambiguity slips into propaganda merely confirming our prejudices that we are the good guys and our enemies are the bad guys.

"Ambiguity" is a Latin derivative from the Greek "amphibolia" which described the military predicament of being attacked from two sides simultaneously as art historian Leo Steinberg notes in his insightful multiple interpretations of Leonardo's "Last Supper." (See "The Seven Functions of the Hands of Christ: Aspects of Leonardo's Last Supper," *Art, Creativity, and the Sacred: An Anthology in Religion and Art*, edited by Diane Apostolos-Cappadona [New York: Continuum, 1995] 40.) Ambiguity required a military leader to give attention to two different directions at once rather than focusing all of his attention in one direction. Art historian Jo Milgrom taught me that the opposite of ambiguity is idolatry which mistakes our part for the whole and excludes from our attention other equally important parts.

In Leonardo's "Last Supper" (figure 1), the figures ambiguously present not only a scene we associate with the institution of communion on Holy Thursday before the crucifixion but also scenes helping us remember postresurrection appearances of Jesus and also much later martyrdom of the disciples themselves. The disciples to Jesus' right are crowded together in constricted positions suggestive of how they were to die years later. The youthful John, who died in his sleep in old age, slumbers peacefully. (His sleeping also reminds us that he would go to sleep later that night in the garden.) An old balding Peter, whom church tradition says was crucified upside down, extends himself horizontally toward Jesus and appears as close to being upended as possible while still being visible above the table. Andrew holds up both hands so that his arms and hands diagonally form an X reminiscent of his crucifixion diagonally in the shape we call the St. Andrew's cross. In front of Andrew, Peter's hand holds a knife pointing toward the end of the table where we see the standing figure of Bartholomew, whom church tradition says was martyred by flaying.

In contrast, to the left of Jesus more expansive figures remind us of his appearances to them after the resurrection. Several disciples are grouped in positions with arms outstretched in surprise or in prayer. Such positions are reminiscent of their bodies in art works rendering their response to recognizing Jesus in his breaking of bread at Emmaus. Poignantly, only Thomas' head and hand with finger extended appear next to Jesus reminding us of the disciple who doubted and was invited to place his finger in the wounds of the resurrected Jesus on yet another occasion. Rather than being a snapshot of one Scripture verse, this great art work is more like a film including many episodes of Jesus ministry,

Fig. 1. Raphael Morghen after Leonardo da Vinci, *The Last Supper* (engraving, 1800).

crucifixion, and resurrection as well as his disciples' later lives and deaths.

Each of Jesus' parables is ambiguous and so gives birth to hundreds of different sermons. (In contrast, we can think of some poor stories from which one cannot squeeze anything but one pathetic sermon if that.) In noting that Jesus' parables are polyvalent, scholars are pointing to multiple interpretations, multiple perspectives, and multiple valences which such parables offer: that is, a Jesus parable has many windows. The humor of a Jesus parable is in such ambiguity of each character who is neither good nor bad but a complex mix of good and bad.[1]

To develop wider appreciation of ambiguity in worship and education, see *Spaces for Faith: Stephen De Staebler's Winged Figures*. De Staebler's sculpture at the heart of Graduate Theological Union Library in Berkeley, California, and his other winged figures in Houston, New Harmony, Indiana, and elsewhere elicit different perceptions among those who experience his work. I once asked De Staebler why he became a sculptor rather than a painter. He responded, "Because I had been a basketball player."

Seeing that I did not understand, he explained that in basketball one relies on peripheral vision as one may pass or receive the ball to or from those on either side or even behind. (This is one reason that television has a much harder time following a basketball game than a football game.) A sculptor needs far more peripheral vision than a painter; for in sculpting, one must be aware simultaneously of the many sides of a sculpture. I remember reading Bill Bradley's description of his developing peripheral vision by walking through downtown Princeton and trying to look into the shop windows on both sides of the street at once. They said of Boston Celtics' player Bob Cousy that he could look east and enjoy the sunset. Such developed peripheral vision helped make Bradley a fine basketball player and a most insightful political leader who appreciates ambiguity.

One slide does not do justice to a sculpture. One needs to take many slides from many perspectives to present what a sculpture offers to viewers who walk around it. People of different views may gather around a sculpture and all appreciate it from their own perspectives. It is less likely that a diverse group could gather around a doctrine unless we learn to appreciate doctrines as poetry rather than as polemics.

Nineteenth-century Methodist preacher Peter Cartwright used the art of humor to put down the idolatry of doctrinal education when his sermon was interrupted by a prominent highly educated Presbyterian who sarcastically asked, "How is it that you have no doctors of divinity in your denomination?" Cartwright responded, "Our divinity is not sick and don't need doctoring." Henry Ward Beecher (in a series of sermons supporting teaching of evolution in the pubic schools in the 1870s) noted that the fundamentalist attempt to turn the book of Genesis into a book of geology is like trying to turn his father's fiddle into a washboard. It won't wash and it ruins the music. He also noted, "I'd as leave be descended from a monkey as from some men I know."[2]

Free standing sculpture invites viewers to see many different perspectives; and such sculpture posed a problem for some church officials who wanted believers to see everything the same way. By prohibiting free standing sculptures or placing them high up in niches of church walls, such officials have eliminated the perceptions of ambiguity and reduced the multiple perspectives of believers. I appreciate more the suggestion of liturgical artist Susan Edenborough who has created some surprising banners. Some were in the shape of columns and standing in the aisles. To reward the most curious of children, she would suspend interesting objects inside the column so they would be seen only by those children who got down on their hands and knees on the floor and looked up inside the column.

De Staebler's "Winged Figure" (figures 2, 3, 4, and 5) may be seen as masculine when viewed from the front but as feminine when viewed from the rear. Rising from a column buried six feet in the bedrock below the library, the figure may appear as crucified or suffering in its incompletion with only one leg and one arm. Others see that the figure rises upward and forward in resurrection. The concave shaped wing which surrounds the shoulders was formed on the belly of a pregnant woman and may be seen as a womb from which the figure emerges like a child from a mother or a Jesus from a Mary, but pietà possibilities are suggested as well where the Christ figure stands with a supportive mother behind him such as Michelangelo's Rondanini "Pietà" which inspired De Staebler's "Pietà" in New Harmony, Indiana. The foregoing are perceptions which occur to those with Christian expectations.

The sculpture has qualities like Henry Nouwen's idea of a wounded healer; De Staebler notes that recognition of the figure's incompleteness helps us recognize our own incompleteness and makes possible empathy with others. De Staebler likens the frontality of the figure to the frontality of conversation at the dinner table which invites deeper engagement than the chatter of a cocktail party when we usually stand at oblique angles to each other so as not to become committed and to be able to slip away if we see someone more interesting.

From Jewish perceptions, Jo Milgrom sees the "Winged Figure" embodying many qualities seen in the first chapter of Genesis in which neither the birds of the air nor humankind are considered finished in contrast to the animals. She does a careful linguistic analysis noting that "and it was so" (which has the root meaning of fixed or set or established) climaxes the creations of many of the days but not when the birds and humankind are created. She sees the sculpture, too, as not finished but fragilely free with the power of transformation which is called turning in Judaism.

From Buddhist perspectives, Ron Nakasone helps us see how "Winged Figure" shapes space in a creative process to reveal the beauty of the formless self. He found a viewing of the figure from the ground floor most exciting. He writes that the sculpture "suggests a transformation of the human and the divine, and seems suspended between the timeless and time. The single tiptoeing leg emerging from the polished perpendicular column seems to indicate that 'Winged Figure' is leaping from the formless metal block. On the other hand, the formless mass that envelopes the top left shoulder, and encircles the back that merges into a shield, suggests that 'Winged Figure' is devolving from the divine to the human. Formlessness reveals itself in form. Is 'Winged Figure' shedding its wings or is humanity becoming transcendent? Is the figure descending from the eternal into time? Is it ascending to the eternal from time? Is the divine becoming human or is the human becoming divine?" The foregoing obser-

vations and questions and many more result from sharing our perceptions of "Winged Figure" with others and from hearing their perceptions which enlarge our vision.

In visual art courses in both the seminaries and in churches, I use the following strategies to develop appreciation for ambiguity. I require students to spend an hour with a different art work every two weeks and then to write up a brief two pages detailing multiple perceptions they have gained from approaching the art work.[3]

In class sessions, students share their papers with five other students who have chosen the same art work for viewing. (In each two week sequence, we have listed five art works in museums or on campus from which students choose; so, there are usually a half dozen students in each of the five discussion groups in a class of thirty students.) In the discussion groups, students hear how other students have perceptions which differ from their own; so the polyvalency or ambiguity of the art work becomes evident. In the course of a semester, a student goes through this process six different times.

At first, some students try to maintain only one point of view; for all of us tend initially to see what we expect to see and obliterate other possibilities. Halfway through the semester, most students are beginning to see more easily multiple perspectives in their hour with the art work and look forward to learning even more perspectives which others in their discussion groups have discovered. As students learn to transcend their own viewpoints and to appreciate the viewpoints of others, a healthy community develops in the classroom. In such transcendence, we experience a gift of the arts to community.

In churches, we integrate into worship such learnings from church school classes taught intergenerationally with the method detailed in the previous paragraphs. The art used may be an exhibition set up in the worship setting or in the narthex or in the fellowship hall. One art work is taken from the exhibition and placed on an easel by the pulpit or by the altar table. The persons who have spent an hour with the art work then share their different insights during the sermon time. We find that the finer the art work the wider the range of possible different interpretations. In more informal worship services, we have many art works related to the biblical text and

Fig. 2. Stephen de Staebler, *Winged Figure*, 1993, Hewlett Library, Graduate Theological Union. Front view.

Fig. 3. Stephen de Staebler, *Winged Figure*, 1993, Hewlett Library, Graduate Theological Union. View from right.

Fig. 5. Stephen de Staebler, *Winged Figure,* 1993, Hewlett Library, Graduate Theological Union. View from left.

Fig. 4. Stephen de Staebler, *Winged Figure,* 1993, Hewlett Library, Graduate Theological Union. Back view.

place those art works (or reproductions of them) on the walls of the worship space. All in the congregation are urged to look at the different art works and then stand by the work which is most interesting. People then share with others who are standing by the same work why they chose that art.

The exhibitions may be set up in the narthex (a different artist featured each month as at Church of the Beatitudes in Phoenix) or in the sanctuary for the weeks of Lent. In the Presbyterian Church in San Anselmo, California, the themes of those lenten weeks are announced six months earlier for a juried art exhibition; and more than two hundred art works are usually submitted from people in the wider community and some sixty selected for exhibition in the sanctuary.

With film having become the primary language of our time and with children raised on television, sixty percent of the population now remember primarily by what they see and not by what they hear. Only twenty percent of the population, mostly over sixty and raised on radio, remember primarily by what they hear; and the other twenty percent remember kinesthetically by movement. In their worship, fast growing churches use film and video and slide projections on screens at the front of the chancel or through a TV monitor set up next to the pulpit. If you find dying churches with few people under age sixty, it is easy to see why. Such dying churches usually offer nothing significant for the eye. If there is nothing to see, then there is not memorable worship for sixty percent of the population. Most churches are reaching the twenty percent of the population who were raised on radio and who remember by what they hear; but most churches are failing to reach the majority of the population raised on television and who remember by what they see. Much as we have learned to use the language of the people in preaching and worship (that is English or Spanish instead of Latin) so now we need to learn to use the language of the majority of the people in this increasingly visual culture (that is film).

I often use excerpts from major films when they are running in the theaters or rerunning on television. Films like *Forrest Gump* or *Dead Poets Society* or *E.T.* are thinly disguised renderings of the Jesus story; but one may use films which contrast with the Jesus story so the preacher may point out how the

biblical story differs from the film plot. I find many TV commercials are suitable to include in preaching; and they have the virtue of being brief like a Jesus parable. In a sermon on the parable of the wise and foolish virgins, I have integrated two TV commercials for a chewing gum. In one commercial, a woman has waited for years to see a rare whale leap from the ocean. She is chewing a gum which has lost its flavor. As she turns her eyes to look down into her purse to find a fresh piece of chewing gum, the whale leaps from the ocean and then disappears back into the water before the woman looks up again. In the next scene, those who saw the whale are celebrating at one end of the boat while she sits dejectedly at the other end. In another ad for the same gum, a man waits at an observatory to see a comet which comes into view briefly only once every seventy-five years. As he waits, his gum loses flavor and he looks down to unwrap another piece of gum from his pocket. Just at that moment, the comet streaks by overhead; and while the others enjoy the sight, he fails to see it and later appears dejected. In a sermon on Jesus' parable of the pearl of great price, I use a commercial for Sprint telephone service. In the backseat of a limo moving through Wall Street, a wealthy man talks on the phone with his stock broker and suddenly says, "Sell everything and buy the ranch ... with horsies."[4]

I find our own church members of all ages to be remarkably insightful about the most meaningful parts of a film or TV show. I urge church members to tape their favorite films and shows and loan me those videos which contain parts they identify as tacitly relating to biblical or theological ideas. To save time, I ask the church member to have the video forwarded to the part of the show he or she wants me to see. When using such a video clip, I usually credit the church member who has called it to my attention if she or he gives me permission to do so.[5]

The younger son (who had gone away and lived a loose life) returns and is embraced by his father who rushes to embrace him. That son enjoys the party his father gives at their home, but the elder son does not come to the party. The father and the elder son later quarrel. Does this story sound familiar? It was the plot of the first episode of the prime time TV CBS show *Orleans* starring Larry Hagman as the father who is a judge named Luther Charbonnet with a younger son named Jesse. Unlike Jesus' parable of the prodigal son which ends unresolved with the elder son and father arguing in the courtyard, that first episode of *Orleans* ends in a church worship service with all singing "O God Our Help In Ages Past." The second episode dealt with just and unjust judges. The third episode began with a discussion of quoting from the Bible about Eve, dealt with death (one man who was thought dead returned to life and another man who was thought alive was dead), and ended with an informal memorial service. Television and movies have come home to biblical stories and the church. The question is "Will the church embrace these prodigal media and include them in our party of worship and preaching?"

Notes

1. I have detailed the ambiguity of each parable in my recent book *The Prostitute in the Family Tree: Discovering Humor and Irony in the Bible* (Louisville: Westminster/John Knox Press, 1997). In a semester length course "Bringing Biblical Humor To Life," I help students develop a sense of biblical humor and how to dramatize the humor in worship. Those many methods of dramatic arts are detailed in that book. I help students to develop abilities to perceive ambiguity in semester length visual art courses such as "Spirituality in 20th century American Art" which methods I discuss toward the end of this chapter. Such methods are applicable in teaching at schools and churches and introducing arts in worship.

2. For these and many other examples of using humor in preaching to lay low American idolatries of power, wisdom, and wealth, see my book *Humor in the American Pulpit from George Whitfield through Henry Ward Beecher* (Austin: The Sharing Company, 1975).

3. For a detailed process, see the multiple methods I detail in my book *Eyes To See Wholeness: Visual Arts Informing Biblical and Theological Studies in Education and Worship through the Church Year* (Prescott: Educational Ministries, Inc., 1995).

4. For ways of meaningfully integrating brief clips from recent films and from television programs into sermons and other parts of worship, see my article "Embracing the Prodigal Media of Popular Films, TV Shows, and Commercials in Preaching," *Academy Accents* (Spring 1997), 1–4.

Edward McNulty insightfully details which segments of modern popular films are theologically significant for preaching in *Praying the Movies: Sitting in the Dark While Looking for the Light* (Louisville: Westminster/John Knox, 2000). McNulty's monthly magazine *Visual Parables* reviews the most current movies. (For that, write Dr. Edward McNulty, 63 Booke Lake, Walton, KY 41094.)

5. Much as churches buy music licenses, they may purchase a film license. For $75 a year, my seminary buys such a license which allows any teacher or student to use videos of most films in preaching and teaching. (Write to Motion Picture Licensing Corporation, 13315 Washington Blvd., 3rd Floor, Los Angeles, CA 90066-5145.)

DOUG ADAMS is professor of Christianity and the arts at Pacific School of Religion and serves on the core doctoral faculty in history of art and religion at The Graduate Theological Union, Berkeley. His eight books include: *Transcendence with the Human Body in Art: Segal, De Staebler, Johns, and Christo* and *Eyes to See Wholeness: Visual Arts Informing Biblical and Theological Studies in Education and Worship through the Church Year*.

Liturgy That Does Justice

Acts of Imagination, Courage, Curiosity

Janet Walton

When, therefore, we seek liturgy which fosters justice, we are confronted with an immense challenge—celebrating liturgy which challenges not only the hearts of worshipers but, through them, the way the world—and the church—are organized and function.[1]

The Sunday liturgy in San Fernando Cathedral in San Antonio, Texas, had begun only five minutes earlier when suddenly a man walked down the center aisle. At first, he walked only part of the way to the front of the church. He seemed unsure about whether he should keep going. A few minutes later he began the trek again, this time with more determination. He reached the steps that separate the leaders from the congregation, hesitated a bit, and then proceeded into the center of the space, near the altar. He knelt to pray. He needed something and he needed it now.

The assembly of professional liturgists who had gathered for their annual meeting continued their worship as scripted. After some time, Jake Empereur, the host of the gathering, slowly moved from his place in the assembly and walked toward the man. At first, he just stood next to him. Then, he put his arm around him. Finally, he spoke with him. After some minutes, both walked to the side of the sanctuary. The man, then, left our view. Jake Empereur returned to his seat in the assembly.

Street dwellers and other people often not welcomed in public gatherings are surprising in religious places, even during public worship. Though many in this assembly probably have had experiences like this one, every such event also has its own distinctiveness. The question raised each time is how to include the person in a setting in which the prepared script may not provide room for spontaneous responses.

Jake Empereur is known among the professional liturgists who were gathered in the San Fernando Cathedral as one who regularly raises questions about the importance of worship that does justice. But rarely has there been an occasion for us to see such a visible expression of his commitment. What moved me most on this occasion was the expression of reverence toward this man. He obviously wanted something from this place, from this group of people, from God, whatever the order. Though the script, carefully prepared and rehearsed, did not anticipate such a disruption, to provide for his need was easily accommodated. Empereur acted for all of us, waiting, touching, speaking, listening, and walking with him. He did not rush. He was not embarrassed. Jake Empereur attended to him; he *made space* for him. In so doing he also expanded the liturgical space for all of us. Whatever our need, it, too, was welcome. *Making space* is an essential component of liturgy that does justice. To do it requires imagination, courage, curiosity, and practice.

Imagination

In his own way, the unexpected guest at the liturgy described above asked the community to notice him and to support him.

Often, people do not ask for what they need, or when they do, they stop at the first hint of resistance particularly when institutional leaders or other congregants say no. So most people presume they have to leave much of themselves at the door when they come to our churches or synagogues, especially their pain, vulnerability, shame, failure, worries, and differences. There is minimal space for anything that challenges comfortable norms, those invisible standards set by what is imagined to be correct, most often by what people regularly experience. To *make space* is to expand these boundaries with incomplete circles in which there is always room for what is new or unpredicted, in which persons know that whatever they are experiencing has a place in the liturgy. Particular circumstances like this uninvited guest often provide a situation to challenge a community to take another step.

For one woman, her needs and feelings were welcomed at her death. Miriam Frank's sister had lived all her life struggling with depression. When she died, Dr. Frank and Rabbi Wenig decided to break the traditional silence about mental illness. They wanted to provide an opportunity to speak publicly of the intense pain of chronic depression that Miriam Frank's sister had endured, to give it a rightful place in her memorial liturgy. So instead of proceeding with the traditional pattern, they stretched its boundaries. The liturgy began with a time of prayer and study, using contemporary readings about mental illness interspersed with psalmody and readings from the Torah. A more formal memorial liturgy followed that also included texts about experiences of mental illness. This time, Miriam's sister's story was not left at the door. Rather it became a pivotal part of the life of the community. Her pain shaped the community's prayer. The invitation to pray, to listen, to speak, to touch one another, indeed, to walk with each other, had flesh. To include this story made space not only for Miriam and her sister but for an unpredictable number of others. Pain, mental illness, chronic depression is the stuff of real life. It belongs in our liturgies if they are to connect with what we are and do in any real way. To plan a memorial service with this kind of integrity required imagination.

"To tap into the imagination," says Maxine Greene, "is to become able to break with what is supposedly fixed and finished. ... to become freed to glimpse what might be ... and to remain in touch with what presumably is." She refers to Wallace Steven's poem "The Man with the Blue Guitar":

> They said, "you have a blue guitar,
> You do not play things as they are."
> The man replied, "Things as they are
> Are changed upon the blue guitar."
> And they said then, "but play,
>   you must,"
> A tune beyond us, yet ourselves,
> A tune upon the blue guitar
> Of things exactly as they are.[2]

A blue guitar, imagination, *making space* for what seems, at first, to be incongruous is the task of worship that does justice. An assembly sees something about itself in a man who walks unexpectedly into the church; the congregation hears reverberations of their own experiences in a woman's struggle with mental illness. The blue guitar, the unexpected, the truthtelling invites a widening of parameters of the script, whether it be texts, sounds, smells, gestures, or environment. Connections breathe in the moment, from people's realities in time. They offer fresh metaphors, incisive critiques; they express present hungers. Our memories evoked by the script, our connections rooted by a script, offer references against which emerging links are shaped and tested. A blue guitar. An interruption. A public telling of a secret struggle. Quests for dignity. Dreams of justice.

Courage

Suppose the man who entered the San Fernando Cathedral had begun cursing, cursing the government, cursing people who had denied him freedom, cursing the church, maybe even cursing God, how would the assembly have made space for him in the community's prayer? Would he have been ushered out as quickly as possible?

"Blessing and cursing," says Adrienne Rich, "are born as twins and separated at birth to meet again in mourning."[3] In a world in which many people "live trapped in pain," in a world in which all of us who are citizens "wrestle for our own beings, and for the soul of this country,"[4] perhaps we need to provide a place for cursing alongside blessing in our liturgies.

"Where are we moored? What are the bindings? What behooves us?"[5] Rich asks us. Liturgical actions intend to provide an answer: a way of life that responds to human need, every kind of need. We come together as worshiping communities, not because we are perfect but precisely because we are not. So, week after week, we gather to "draw the holy into life."[6] We expect to hear, to taste, to see, to touch, to remember, and to imagine God in our lives. We await God; we want to grasp an ever-unfolding vision that challenges evil with goodness. We anticipate healing, yes, and also the strength to take our place in the world as a holy people, citizens determined to right injustices. This time in history, a world fragmented and torn up, requires expressions of rage, of frustration, and of anger. We need to make space to name evil and to claim the power as people who believe in God to rid ourselves of evil. The time calls for cursing.

Cursing is not ordinarily a part of regular liturgical experiences though some denominations use cursing during excommunications or exorcisms. Excommunications publicly segregate a person from the community because of actions or statements that are incongruent with the rules of the community. Exorcisms intend to cleanse, to call out evil from a person, in order to make the person fit for inclusion in the community. These public rituals of excommunication and exorcism are exceptional, rarely experienced by most people.

What *is* common in our liturgical assemblies is the claiming of our sinfulness. However, collective action that expects the power to rid ourselves of evil is most often considered off limits. It has not always been so. There is liturgical precedent for cursing in the liturgical history of the Roman Catholic Church. In *The Consecration of Virgins in the 1950 Roman Pontifical*, there is a time for cursing as well as a time for blessing. The cursing applied to anyone who attempted to rob these consecrated virgins of their property.

> If anyone presume to attempt this he
> shall be cursed at home and abroad,
> cursed in the city and in the country,
> cursed whether awake or asleep, cursed
> in eating or drinking, cursed in walking
> or sitting; cursed be his flesh and his
> bones, and from the sole of his foot to
> the top of his head let there be no
> health in him.[7]

And there is an even more ancient precedent for cursing. The playwright, Aeschylus, too, identified the need. In the Greek tragedy, *Eumenides*, he calls upon the Furies to speak of the unspeakable deeds against humankind, and to act against them with censure and punishment.

> Now then upon this sacrifice
> Here is a song, driving him mad,
> wrecking his mind with derangement,
> chanted with no note of lyre,
> chaining mind and sense, the hymn
> Furies chant to wither men (328 ff.).

No reticence here. Evil is named. Curses are in order when innocent people are harmed. Nothing is spared to punish the perpetrator. The curses are expected to enact what they say. This gathering community through its choice to participate in the occasion had accepted the responsibility to accompany these women in their lives. At times this task would require blessing and at times, cursing. In the *Roman Pontifical*, the location of cursing action right after the blessing of the women is also instructive. Here, in Rich's words, blessing and cursing are side by side, seen as "twins."

Marjorie Procter-Smith argues that "when a curse arises out of justified anger, the energy it embodies can bring about well-being and, ultimately, blessing."[8] She points to the story in Alice Walker's *The Color Purple* when Celie curses her husband for his years of abuse. The cursing, the naming of evil, says Procter-Smith, brings about his redemption.

Several years ago in a class entitled "Women's Experiences: A Resource for Worship" Delores Williams and I, the co-teachers, planned a liturgy that included blessing and cursing. Our intention was to experiment with forms that expressed a wide spectrum of human need especially within women whose experiences were often, "left at the door." We chose actions of blessing and cursing because they are liturgical forms that presume action, that is, when we say the words and use the gestures we anticipate an actual experience of that power. When the time came to express curses and blessings none of the students was able to curse, only the teachers.

Making space for cursing takes courage. In a world in which unspeakable evil exists, such courage is demanded. Cursed be those societies in which children murder children! Cursed be those persons who bomb wantonly! Cursed be those who randomly dispose of chemicals that cause the deaths of innumerable generations of people! Cursed be those who rape and ravage another's body. Cursed be those who deny freedom to others. To identify evil in our liturgical assemblies with emotion, energy, and power assumes that our action, as part of God's actions, can enact change and thus be redemptive. Cursing is an ingredient of worship that does justice.

Curiosity

The uninvited man in the San Fernando Cathedral had been here before. He knew what to expect.

Perhaps, at first, curiosity as a characteristic of worship that does justice may seem quite unusual. The word typically conjures up the meanings of intrusiveness or meddlesomeness. But, I am not referring to that definition. Rather, I am using the word to convey an active interaction with another, a curiosity that leads a person to want to know another. Liturgy that is "an act of communication and communion"[9] requires this kind of curiosity.

The story of Ralph Eugene Meatyard offers a poignant example. By profession, Mr. Meatyard was a lens grinder; he was also a skilled photographer. Writer Guy Davenport describes Gene Meatyard as a man who had "a curiosity that went all the way." When he met someone he wanted to know more about this person. To learn more was for Gene Meatyard "a deep sense of courtesy."[10] Meatyard made remarkable efforts to find out more about a person, to read books if the person was a writer, to look at paintings if the person was a painter, that is, to attempt see the person through her or his own particular lens. This curiosity was not about fact finding. Rather it was a quest to understand the essence of the person.

Imagine a worshiping community characterized by a similar deep sense of learning about each other's cultures and backgrounds, even to trying to speak and understand new languages. It would be no surprise to hear a variety of religious texts or to see multiple expressions of symbols that represented the particularities of the identities represented in the community. In this congregation, one would expect to hear young people's music, old people's music, sounds that expressed racial and ethnic heritages alongside of and mixed with traditional cultic sounds. This spirit of curiosity would also encourage members to seek out people whose lifestyle or choices were quite different from their own. Like Gene Meatyard, they would want to know what matters most to others. They would want to affirm and cherish it within the worshiping practices of the community so they could avoid the habit of anyone leaving important aspects of one's life "at the door." These narratives are the "hidden, fragmented, diverse traces of the Word of God," says David Power in which "the promise resides, that the power of living in hope can be accessed."[11]

Practice

Worship that does justice happens over time. It takes years of trying: fits and starts, repetition, frustration, success, starting over, and more of the same. The objective is to acquire new habits, to "try on" an imaginative, courageous, courteous pattern of living within the safety of a community intent on similar goals in order to also do it when we leave. From this ever-enlarging vision of drawing "the holy into life" we have the courage to speak out when silence is cowardly, to keep silent when to speak spreads lies, to try something with no proof of success or not to try when doing represents only a superficial commitment, to sing loud and passionately when the music seems hard and even harsh if the singing represents a respect for those rarely heard. We have the strength to ask questions when the answers will lead to changing comfortable patterns, and always to advocate for the people rarely heard from, rarely seen, rarely touched. Worship that does justice is active work; there is no sitting back and waiting. Every member of the community is responsible for drawing out expressions of justice in others. Each person helps another. No one person can make it happen. And no one presumes it will be easy; what is easy is to return to what is familiar.

At that Sunday liturgy in the San Fernando Cathedral something quite magical happened. Not scripted, not even predicted, an uninvited man issued an invitation to us. He reminded us to notice those who are ordinarily left at the door.

Jake Empereur did what he usually does, responded in the moment. We watched. Maybe some of us caught a spark from the uninvited man. Maybe for a moment we felt what it is like to be marginalized, rejected, or unclean. Maybe we felt empowered to pray differently. Maybe we felt commissioned to act with courage, imagination, and curiosity on behalf of this man and others in arenas outside this cathedral. The uninvited guest invited us to make space. The rest was up to us.

Notes

1. James L. Empereur, S.J, and Christopher G. Kiesling, OP, *The Liturgy That Does Justice* (Collegeville, Minn.: The Liturgical Press, A Michael Glazier Book, 1990), 8.

2. Wallace Stevens, "The Man with the Blue Guitar," *The Collected Poems of Wallace Stevens* (1937; reprint, New York: Knopf, 1964).

3. Adrienne Rich, *An Atlas of The Difficult World* (New York: W.W. Norton & Company, 1991), 23.

4. Ibid.

5. Ibid.

6. David Power, "Liturgy As An Act of Communication and Communion: Cultural and Practical Implications In An Age Becoming Digital" (Catholic University of America, n.d.)

7. *The Consecration of Virgins According to the Roman Pontifical* (Clyde, Missouri: Benedictine Convent of Perpetual Adoration, 1952), 21.

8. Marjorie Procter-Smith, *Praying With Our Eyes Open: Engendering Feminist Liturgical Prayer* (Nashville: Abingdon Press, 1995), 51.

9. Power.

10. Guy Davenport, *The Geography of the Imagination* (San Francisco: North Point Press, 1981), 371.

11. Power 17.

JANET WALTON is professor of worship at Union Theological Seminary in New York. She is author of *Feminist Liturgy: A Matter of Justice* and *Art and Worship: A Vital Connection*.

Beauty and the Beast

Criteria for Artful Liturgy

Joyce Ann Zimmerman, CPPS

Beauty—although not entirely subjective—is surely capricious. What may be beautiful to one—a modern sculpture, for example—might be beastly to another. What may be beastly to one—French Gothic style of architecture, for example—might be beautiful to another. A professional artist knows certain basic principles govern the production of art; at the same time artists freely choose to produce innovative, fresh expressions of beauty, taking us in new directions that the acceptable principles would seem to preclude.

The beauty so essential to good liturgy is no stranger to subjective caveats. What may be beautiful to some—chasing, twinkling lights nestled in ropes of artificial greens rising 200 feet adorning a gothic arch, for example—might be garishly beastly and distracting to others. What may be beastly to some and barely feeding religious affectivity—the simplicity of a monastic liturgy, for example—might be beautiful, inspiring, and deeply moving to others. Careful attention to the repetition of ritual action might be freeing for some but confiningly boring for others. Incense might pique some but be discomforting for others. Some prefer traditional music with organ while others favor recently composed music sung to the accompaniment of a variety of instruments. For some, liturgical garb for presider and other ministers is festive while for others it sets them apart and sometimes even alienates.

It would be easy if liturgy's requirement for beauty could be discharged simply by recognizing diversity of preferences. We could merely offer different styles of liturgy so that all might be satisfied according to like tastes. Indeed, already in many parishes differing styles are clearly evident and consistent at certain liturgies, and rightly so. Yet we also know the real beauty of liturgy is not so easily measured nor so easily satisfying. Herein lies the substantive challenge. Many ritual elements are not often enough given sufficient attention when preparing and measuring the beauty, quality, and fruitfulness of liturgy. Such elements include:

- gesture
- largeness of symbol use
- silences
- postures

☙ pacing
☙ vocal control
☙ assembly's dress
☙ types of eye contact
☙ configuration of participants and liturgical spaces
☙ preparedness of ministers and their ease of ministry
☙ gathering and dismissal customs
☙ quality of accouterments
☙ rhythm within ritual as well as between the liturgical seasons
☙ inclusivity

We are usually even more inattentive to other less tangible ritual elements when considering the beauty and artfulness of liturgy:

☙ sense of solidarity in the Body of Christ
☙ communion of the saints
☙ awareness of the unity of all liturgy
☙ marriage of the earthly and heavenly liturgy
☙ presences of Christ, Trinitarian, and Marian dimensions
☙ play of transcendence and immanence
☙ cognizance of Mystery
☙ notion of celebration
☙ immersion in liturgical time

The question "What makes liturgy beautiful?" is analogous to the question "When is liturgy *good* liturgy?" Two other questions loom large when responding to these two: "What is the essential purpose of liturgy?" and "What is the participants' role?" A certain subjectivity is not only consistent with but essential for beautiful and artful liturgy. But here subjectivity does not mean personal preference or tastes; rather, it means that the beauty and artfulness of liturgy redounds to the subject, who it is who celebrates liturgy.[1] In this context, a kind of objectivity with respect to the beauty and artfulness of liturgy can be posited; that is, liturgy's beauty and artfulness is measured by the realization of its purpose in those who celebrate. Criteria for the artfulness of liturgy, then, are not generated out of *individual* tastes or needs but are generated out of a determination of what really happens (or supposed to happen) at liturgy.

These remarks guide the organization of this chapter into three parts. The first part explores theories of beauty and art in order to draw an analogy between the nature of aesthetics and liturgical action. The second part explores a theory of imagination in order to advance the subject's role in liturgical fruitfulness. The final part of the chapter puts forth ten criteria for preparing and evaluating artful liturgy.

Beauty and Art

Aesthetics is the theory of beauty and art and how beauty and art are produced from nature and taste. An attempt at even a reasonably complete historical survey of aesthetics would necessarily be quite technical, take us well beyond the scope of this chapter, and is not absolutely essential for addressing our concern. Our concern is the very basic question of subjectivity and objectivity related to liturgical matters.

Objectivity and Subjectivity

Basic to the questions, "What is beautiful? or "What is art? is the issue of whether beauty or art is found in reality (in things themselves apart from any evaluation of them) or only in our experience (residing in ourselves as subject and dependent on our estimation or evaluation). Hence, objectivists are concerned with the question, "Where does beauty or art reside?" and argue that beauty is in the thing itself and not dependent upon a subject's taste or pleasure for its existence. Subjectivists, on the other hand, argue that beauty resides in the taste or pleasure of the subject and not in the thing itself. The former position permits a certain objectivity with respect to beauty or art and more easily allows for universal criteria for judging beauty or art. The latter position accounts for the role of the subject in the aesthetic experience and allows for a certain mutability with respect to beauty or art. The distinction between whether liturgy is beautiful in itself or whether its aesthetic value is the result of the assembly's estimation or evaluation raises a significant liturgical question. We will examine nine thinkers who are either objectivist or subjectivist. However, our point here is not to promote one or other position.[2] Both objectivist and subjectivist views have something to contribute to an understanding of liturgical aesthetics.

Plato: Plato attempted to reconcile Heraclitus' world of change and Parmenides' world of being and in so doing he juxtaposes them and presents a two-world philosophy: the world of ideas (unchangeable, eternal) and the world of the sensible (changeable, finite). For Plato, the world of the sensible is a reflection or imitation of the world of ideas.[3] Since art is a making, it is an imitation, too, because it belongs to and imitates the sensible world. But, further, the sensible world is an imitation of the world of ideas, and so art is an imitation of an imitation. Ultimately, for Plato, to become beautiful is to become god-like:[4] the most beautiful art is that for which the imitation comes closest to the eternal idea.

Plato's evaluation of art depends upon his notion of the measure of excess and defect. Art is good art if the imitation is measured to lie in the mean (neither excess nor defect), if the imitation is true, and if the execution of the imitation is good and worthy.[5] Further, since Plato's overriding concern was for the good order of the state, an important issue is the role that art plays in the life of citizens and its effect on their characters and so this political aspect plays an important part in Plato's evaluation of art.

Aristotle: Aristotle rejects Plato's two-world view and places the idea within the thing itself. He follows Plato in that art is a production that imitates its various subject matters. He considers art as a certain disposition (habit) concerned with right-reasoned plan and process of making.[6] Since a habit allows us to proceed with ease and facility and with little or almost no effort, art should also proceed with ease. The material used must have the potency to be made into art, and the thing to be made must exist (at least conceptually) in the mind of the artist. For Aristotle, art completes what nature left unfinished.[7] For example, we might have a block of marble, a product of nature which the artist makes into a statue. The statue is more beautiful and pleasing to us as art than the block of marble given us by nature. The artist proceeds with right reason (that is, possesses conceptually the potency to produce the piece of art according to laws of measure and proportion); nature does not proceed with right reason but from an intrinsic principle and built-in direction to an end (the form) which is not conscious. Art is the product of human making.

Aristotle follows Plato in espousing the doctrine of the means in his evaluation of art: the beautiful is that which is equidistant from the extremes of excess or defect.[8] Additionally, beauty lies in order, symmetry, and definiteness.[9] He also mentions the fittingness of beauty and that it is different at different times of our lives.[10]

Plotinus: Plotinus, considered the founder of neo-Platonism, gave us a philosophy of emanation: from the One (the good, the supreme) emanates the mind (the intellect, a duality of subject and object); from the mind emanates soul (first a world soul, then a multiplicity of souls); and from the soul emanates matter. The One, the mind, and the soul are perfecting principles; matter is a limiting, imperfecting principle. The two kinds of beauty in Plotinus' view are intellectual or spiritual beauty which mirrors the One, and sensible beauty which reflects matter. All beauty participates in and is derived from the beauty of the One. The more removed beauty is from the sensible, the more perfect is that beauty.[11] Beauty is in a thing to the extent that symmetry or pattern (by reason) brings matter to yield in all respects to the ideal form.[12] Plotinus presents an ascetical doctrine urging us to transcend sensible beauty and move toward the more perfect beauty of ideas and through them to the One. Plotinus' theory—especially his mystical approach—is important in the Christian philosophy of Augustine and later on in the German idealists.

For Plotinus, ultimate perfection is found in unity and there is a dilution or degradation in each succeeding degree of emanation. A key evaluative criterion is symmetry or pattern, in which all parts must be pleasingly ordered toward the whole.[13]

Augustine: Augustine believed that the world of ideas exists in the mind of God and is not distinct from it; all other things (the sensible world) are distinct from it (the mind of God). God is the "beauty of all things beautiful."[14] There is only one beauty and everything else participates in (imitates) it. Beauty is based on the notion of number[15] and its purpose is to approach the unity of the Divine. Influenced greatly by Plotinus, Augustine holds that number and proportion are measured with respect to unity, the basic perfection. Beauty is the conformation of the mind to the eternal. For Augustine, everything has a natural proportion and rhythm. If a thing is to be beautiful it must easily exhibit this natural rhythm and proportion and only to this extent can it approach the unity of the Divine. Augustine asks, in his *Confessions*, "What is beauty?" and answers his question by offering two criteria: wholeness and fitness (by which he means that each part contributes harmoniously to the whole).[16]

Aquinas: Aquinas held (following Aristotle) that ideal forms are immanent in the empirical world. He allowed for an objectivity to beauty at the same time that he posited that the contemplation of beauty gives pleasure to the subject.[17] Also following Aristotle, Aquinas held that art imitates nature.[18] In the line of the classical Greeks, art is a rational capacity resulting from the intellect.[19] For Aquinas, too, the beautiful participates in Divine beauty.[20] Aquinas sets out several criteria for judging beauty: integrity or perfection, due proportion or harmony, and brilliance.[21]

All of the above writers posit a certain objectivity with respect to beauty and art; that is, beauty resides in the thing, which works on the knower to bring pleasure. Although they may express it differently, all these writers also view beauty and art as imitation of the ideal. We now make a radical shift and turn to four thinkers who hold subjectivist positions in which beauty and art are *expressions* of the knower.

Kant: Kant may be considered the first of the modern philosophers of art. His concern was to go beyond empirical analysis and locate aesthetics as a domain of human experience, the critique of which is equal in dignity to the cognitive and the moral domains of human experience. For Kant, the judgment of the aesthetic must be universal and so there must be some a priori common to all human experience which he identified as the form and not the sensations of the thing of beauty.[22] He held that beauty is expressed when form causes a harmonious interplay between imagination and understanding, when beauty pleases immediately, and when it pleases apart from any interest.[23]

Kant proposes that the artist produces a work of art for the purpose of submitting it to the aesthetic judgment, and thereby satisfying taste. Kant held four moments in the judgment of taste: judgment about quality, in which he stresses that the judgment of taste is disinterested; judgment about quantity, which stresses the universality of the judgment;

judgment about relation, which stresses the direction or purpose of the judgment; and modality, which stresses the uniqueness of the judgment (different from theoretical or moral judgments).[24]

Croce: Perhaps the most extreme subjectivist position is held by Benedetto Croce who maintained that everything is an activity of the mind; art exists in the mind of the artist, so physical things are not art. For Croce intuition and expression are identical, and the art object itself is of little consequence.[25] The externalization of intuition in a work of art is secondary to its appearance in the consciousness of the artist. The content of intuitions, however, is derived from practical life. For Croce, intuition is the first step in any critical thinking and so, in this sense, everyone is an artist since everyone has intuitions. He also differs from others we have briefly examined in that he places aesthetics within the domain of general linguistics and emphasizes art as expression or communication. Intuitions which make up the artist's consciousness are products of feeling; intuition and feeling are brought together and fused in the unity of expression. Art, therefore, is a symbol of feeling.[26]

Bell: Clive Bell insists that art should be pure, isolated aestheticism; it is not something we rationalize about, analyze, or describe.[27] Art is something that we can only *experience*; good art evokes a unique (singular, unrepeatable) aesthetic emotion that approaches—if not achieves—ecstacy. Bell distinguishes between significant form, the property that makes certain works of art valuable,[28] and aesthetic emotion, that which occurs when someone is aware of significant form. Art both *represents* reality (and so is descriptive) and it *expresses* emotion (and so it is intuitive). In contemplating a work of art, then, the beholder appreciates a certain vision of reality created by the artist. A good artist is one who is able to see objects as pure form. Finally, Bell suggests this pure form will henceforth not be expressed in visuals easily identified with reality, but in certain combinations of lines and colors suggesting the emotion the artist is purporting to capture and communicate.[29] Bell is ultimately concerned with the relationship of art and life, and parallels a heightened production of good art with a rise in religious fervor.[30] For Bell, the same renewal of spirit which is able to produce the aesthetic ecstacy of the artist envelopes the contemplation of the mystic. Things contemplated—for both the mystic and the artist—are ends in themselves, not means to ends. In contemplation we become lost in the form. Bell cautions us against equating this religious spirit with any kind of formalized doctrine, and charges that when we become over concerned with dogmatic formulae our real religious fervor wanes.

Langer: Susanne Langer propounded a theory of symbolic transformation[31] whereby she holds that the human intellect not only has the power to store and transmit symbols but it also has the power to transform the experiential data into endless varieties of more or less creative and spontaneous ideas. It is this symbolic transformation that allows us to take ridiculous and non-purposive behavior and find a deeper significance. Thus, for example, ritual is important not merely for the external expression of frenzy or the release of a particular and overpowering religious sentiment. Ritual also denotes deep (and usually religious) significance for those actions. She suggested that works of art symbolize states of the mind (feelings) but the relation between a work of art and the feelings it produces is not to be explained in terms of any rule of reference such as that which operates in language. For her, symbol and object are related in that they possess the same logical form. In analyzing art within the context of symbolic transformation, the artistic inspiration of the creator can be more easily understood. Through symbols we see significance and relationships in things long before they need be understood. We cannot create significance from nothing; we need only *find* it, then transform it through symbol. The content of art, then, is verbally ineffable but not symbolically inexpressible. Art can give expression when words fail.

Some Remarks Germane to Liturgy

The differing positions of the objectivists and the subjectivists alert us to liturgy's dialectic between its own objective content (the paschal mystery) and the appropriation of the content in the lives of the celebrating community. Other specific elements point to weighty implications for those concerned with good liturgy.

Two philosophers so widely separated by time and culture and philosophical presuppositions as

Plato and Bell share in common an interest in the relationship of art and human living. Plato was concerned with art's affect on citizens and, consequently, on the civil state and Bell observed the relationship of art and religious fervor. This suggests to those of us concerned with good liturgy that if beauty and art are not attended to carefully by the liturgical assembly, relating liturgy to the experience of that assembly is at least more difficult, if not impossible. Beauty and art, then, are not something *added to* the liturgy but are an essential element of it. If liturgy is life, then beauty and art are liturgy's lifeblood.

Objectivists deal with beauty as approaching the godlike, and within this context focus on the contemplative or mystical aspects of beauty and art. Beauty and art usher us into the transcendent. Pastoral reflection on this point could bear much fruit. When liturgy is too close to the mundane—whether in posture, attire, environment, attitude, music, and so forth—it loses power to communicate divine presence. It also loses its God-centeredness, and might quickly become narrowly focused on us and our concerns (legitimate as those might be). When our celebrations are largely devoid of beauty with little stimulation for the senses—for example, auditorium-type buildings with no sacred adornment or music that emulates a local radio station's fare—we run a high risk of substituting other elements for what is missed.[32] Liturgies lacking that beauty that stimulates a sense of the transcendent might also promote the substitution of commonplace elements for sacred elements (for example, substituting poetry for sacred Scripture or popular songs for required service music). Perhaps the most important consequence of the relationship of beauty and the divine is the potential breakdown of the pervasive dualism between the secular and the sacred.

The notion of imitation is fundamental in the Greek approach to art and for those following upon it. First of all, the symbol functions in liturgy as our sensible entry into the nonsensible or spiritual or invisible realm.[33] A pastoral implication is that the symbols used in the celebration of sacraments must play on our senses in an inviting and large way if they are to be vehicles of the invisible or sacred. Little dabs or minimalizing the things used so that we must *think about them* in order to grasp their significance gets in the way of the immediacy of how symbols work. Langer, coming from a very different philosophical persuasion, nonetheless strongly makes this same point in her discussion of symbolic transformation: we "see" the significance and relationship of symbols before we understand them. Liturgy *immerses* us in the divine; we do not have to *understand* it before encounter can occur or before liturgy can be fruitful.

Number and unity is another important theme for the objectivists. This reminds us to strive to maintain a rhythm and movement throughout the celebration such that the various elements unfold as a unity rather than as an eclectic conglomeration of elements we pick and choose or emphasize now one element and tomorrow another. The rhythm of liturgy and what is more or less important is determined by its unity of mystery. Similarly, Aristotle's notion of habit—art is a right-reasoned plan and process of making—reminds us that the repetition characteristic of ritual is also part and parcel of its beauty. When we disrupt the ritual pattern we, in effect, transform the beauty into a beast.

The subjectivists convincingly remind us that the beauty of liturgy also must be *experienced* by the worshiping assembly and this involves an act of communication. If art pleases, the liturgy must also please but in the sense that it produces pleasant effects in the celebrating subject. At issue here is the active role of the assembly in the celebration and the requirement that the assembly appropriate the liturgical action within their own experience for living. Perhaps this is where we encounter the crux of the challenge. In order to be experienced, the beauty of liturgy must fall within the realm of the experience of the celebrating assembly. This raises not only inculturation questions, but raises issues about the radically communal nature of liturgy. Since so much of beauty rests in individual taste, we are pastorally tempted to let tastes dictate what makes liturgy beautiful and artful (and fruitful). The subjectivists, nonetheless, maintain some kind of universality to the significant forms (Langer's term) pointing us to the deeper significance of liturgy. Ultimately, liturgy is the act of the whole Body of Christ.

At this point in our discussion we move on to the next major section of the chapter. Here the role of the subject of liturgy is explored in more detail from a particular vantage point, that of imagination.

Imagination

Any number of theories of imagination might help us further our reflection on criteria for artful liturgy, and those from a psychological, sociological, cultural, or philosophical perspective. We choose the latter philosophical perspective from which to explore imagination.

French philosopher Paul Ricoeur's theory of imagination[34] is wrest out of his theory of metaphor[35] and both imagination and metaphor are products of semantic activity. Metaphor, for Ricoeur, is the consequence of a semantic impertinence ("twist") which capitalizes on the juxtaposition of dissimilars, and in that juxtaposition creates new meaning. Two unlikely concepts or images are brought together such that one is predicated of the other. A good metaphor takes one known entity and predicates of it something dissimilar. If we were to make the metaphoric claim that someone is "blind as a bat," we would be applying to "blind" (something we know by a literal meaning) a very dissimilar term, "bat." But we know bats are not blind (at night). At a literal level the statement makes little or no sense. Yet, the statement pushes us toward semantic innovation, a new predication of meaning comprising such images as day and night, light and darkness, controlled ability, and so forth. Ricoeur proposes that imagination is intrinsic to the production of metaphoric meaning and is the semantic activity that enables the shift from literal incongruence to metaphoric congruence.

Like so many other terms, "imagination" conjures up many meanings. In the popular mind probably most of them are pejorative, often equivalent to empty daydreaming. One of Ricoeur's concerns is to rescue imagination from this personal, psychological, largely unreal realm and move it to a semantic approach that actually shows imagination to be connected to the real, to what is. He outlines three steps in the shift from a psychology of imagination to a semantics of metaphor dependent on a semantics of imagination.

First, imagination is a "seeing as." It is imagination that enables us to see likeness in differences, the conflict between previous dissimilarity and a new congruence or similarity. Imagination functions in spite of and through the differences, enabling a gain in meaning. It brings together disparate concepts or images, and precisely in overcoming the distance between the literal meaning of the disparate elements is any similarity grasped. Imagination enables us to let go of the literal meaning in order to know a deeper meaning that discloses a congruence between the two elements brought together. To take as an example a classic Christian metaphor, that of the Pauline body of Christ: the dissimilar entities are the glorified body of the risen Christ and our own mortal bodies. To remain at a literal level provides no gain in meaning because the gulf between Christ's body and our own, between the divine and the human seems insurmountable. Christian imagination, however, predicates of baptized persons a unique relationship with the risen life of the divine. The congruence that imagination constructs out of these dissimilars is a predication of identity of life, a "seeing as."

Second, the images of our imagination are not representations of something (a substitute and weakened sensorial impression for something absent or unreal); rather, imagination displays relations so that a "new intended connection is grasped as what the icon describes or depicts."[36] But we apply the linguistic term "image" to a range of possibilities, from schematization without full blown images (for example, a model of an atom) to "wild images" that distract more than instruct (for example, much of daydreaming). Ricoeur suggests semantic innovation occurs as "bound images," something midway on the image range. Bound images are "concrete representations aroused by the verbal element and controlled by it."[37] In other words, bound images are connected to our experience of the real and are controlled by it. To again take up our body of Christ metaphor, the image range for Christian imagination might include the schematization of the institutional church, on the one side, to the "wild image" of physical "look alikes"—complete with limpid eyes and beard—of the historical Jesus.[38] A bound image of the body of Christ is the carefully constructed yet innovative image of the relationship of identity that is possible between ourselves as baptized Christians and the risen Christ. This bound image never quite loses sight of our own imperfect human nature and singular bodies at the same time that it enables us to

perceive ourselves as the real presence of the risen Christ for those we encounter.

Third, the image brings a moment of suspension or negativity. Here Ricoeur's notion of "split reference" is helpful. The ordinary reference of an image ("blind" means, literally, sightlessness) is suspended in favor of a deeper reference ("blind" implies not physical sightlessness but inability or unwillingness to "see"). If the literal reference is not suspended, there can be no new or radical way of looking at things. Out of the ruins of the literal sense a new semantic congruence is born and new meaning is constructed. The body of Christ metaphor asks that we suspend our perception of "body" as organic relationship and go deeper into the mystery toward the grace-filled, personal, intimate relationship of shared life that God offers us through Christ.

Imagination "sees as" bound images that suspend literal meaning and thereby enable innovation in meaning. The function of imagination, according to Ricoeur, is to schematize—give an image—to the suspension proper to split reference.[39] It is a necessary step for the construction of new meaning and is the condition for the projection of new possibilities for redescribing the world. Without imagination we would be unable to move beyond the literal. We would be unable to see congruence in incongruence, similarity in dissimilarity. We would be unable to be novel and creative. Rather than a mere residue of perception, imagination is a critical element in the constitution of meaning. Its schematization of possibilities opens up new meanings to be appropriated. In this sense imagination has something to do with the way we live.

So far, this is only half our analysis. We have briefly focused on the semantics of imagination and underscored the essential (institutive) role imagination plays in the construction of new meaning. Ricoeur, however, goes one step further. To these three moments of imagination ("seeing as," bound images, and split reference), he parallels three moments of feeling[40] which moves the discussion toward a consideration of human action and opens up ethical and (for our purposes) liturgical questions.

First, the instantaneous grasping of new congruence is "felt" as well as seen. In other words, the semantic or linguistic dimension has a counterpart in terms of the very being of the subject who creates or disengages the semantic innovation. This is a moment that includes the subject in the metaphoric process. To "feel" is to appropriate *for self* the dissimilarities as similar and to abolish the distance between the knower and the known. Feeling is "thought made ours."[41] The "feeling" aspect of the body of Christ metaphor unfolds as an appropriation of a new identity, *in persona Christi*, so real that we live out of this identity unto new life.

Second, feelings have a parallel to the bound images of picturing relationships; "pictured" feelings are "moods" (moods are different from an emotional state of "moodiness" which comes out of a more psychological point of view). Although we underscore our earlier distinction between feelings and emotions, feelings do have a disclosure in terms of human action. If semantic congruence is disclosed in images, then congruence in human action is disclosed in feelings. Moods as pictured feelings are what move us to concrete human action. From the perspective of our body of Christ metaphor, moods are the step toward actually living Gospel values. To be the body of Christ is to live as Jesus lived.

Third, feelings, too, have their own split structure. Bodily emotions (the "literal" expression of feelings) are suspended so that a poetic transposition can happen. In this, the subject is "attuned to" new aspects of reality which can be appropriated for new possibilities of human action. Feelings move us toward an integration of action just as imagination integrates disparate elements. As we live the identity of the body of Christ, feelings integrate us with the whole. They preclude against "emotionalism" and open us to genuine religious affectivity.[42]

Ricoeur holds imagination and feeling in a dialectical relationship, the former disclosing the sense component of meaning and the latter the reference component.[43] Imagination belongs to the semantics of discourse and feeling belongs to the semantics of action. Ricoeur's analysis of imagination and feeling points to a dynamic, creative tension between a semantics of discourse and human action.

We can relate this discussion of imagination to artful liturgy in at least two ways. First, imagination—imaging—is a necessary activity on the part of each member of the celebrating assembly in order to juxtapose the familiar (the symbols) and the unfa-

miliar (the divine order, the paschal mystery). The fruitfulness of liturgy hardly just happens. Active participation of the assembly in the making of liturgy's meaning is absolutely required. Moreover, imagination and metaphor-making promise no end of creative possibilities for entering into and living liturgy's dialectic of sacred word and transforming divine action.

Second, our discussion of imagination addresses squarely the question of feelings and liturgy and transposes it out of psychologism to another realm.[44] Feelings are essential if liturgy is to have an effect on the living of the worshiper because feelings draw us to operate at a deeper level of significance. Feelings always lead to human action.

When beauty or artfulness of liturgy impinges on our experience of celebration, it becomes a powerful means to effect the transformation of self proper to ritual. Beauty entices us to surrender ourselves to the ritual action so that the realm of the sacred is at hand. This is no small measure at stake.

Criteria for Artful Liturgy

The preceding extended remarks on aesthetics and imagination help us generate criteria for artful liturgy. We list ten such criteria here with brief commentary.[45]

1. Strive for balance in liturgy; either excess or defect diminishes its artfulness. An example of an excess is a liturgy so overloaded with music (even if it is very fine music) that the ritual pattern is disrupted. An example of a defect is pouring a few drops of water at the baptismal rite rather than full immersion. Other balances command our attention; for example, too many words and explanations vs. sixteen minute "quickies," utter casualness vs. stuffy formality, rubricism vs. anything goes. The point to balance is not mediocrity. Balance assures that all ritual elements receive their just due so the integrity of the rite is not compromised. Only in this way can liturgy fulfill its command to "Do this in memory of me."

2. Recognize a liturgy's fittingness. Not every celebration and certainly not every liturgical season calls for the same style of celebration. The vigil Mass for Sunday held on Saturday afternoon or evening is stylistically different from the Sunday mid-morning liturgy. School Masses differ from Sunday parish celebrations. Different celebrations, too, call for a reflection on the liturgy's fittingness; for example, the baptism of infants is necessarily quite a different liturgy from that of older children, adolescents, or adults. Every liturgical community also recognizes subgroups that would benefit from a well thought-through style. A children's Mass (at which almost all participants are children) is different from a family Mass is different from a Mass in an auditorium accommodating an overflow assembly. Implementation of art and beauty must vary according to time, season, and assembly. At all times, however, good taste is in order.

3. Achieve a liturgical rhythm so the ritual unfolds with ease and unity. The predictability of ritual is intended to be a freeing structure. It is beastly and devastating when we get caught up in individual elements and lose the rhythm that draws the many elements into one. When ritual is predictable, we are able to surrender with ease to liturgy's demands. Rather than paying attention to what is happening—a reflective, cognitive activity—we are able to enter into the deeper significance of the mystery. Paying attention to the dynamics of liturgical rhythm promotes an artful liturgy insofar as unity is pleasing.

4. Respect liturgy's symmetry and ritual patterns. Criteria 3 addresses the issue of liturgical rhythm. Here we address the issue of rhythm *within* the celebration. Not all liturgical elements are equal. Some are preparatory. Some are transitory. Some are central. We must understand the individual ritual elements so that we can pace our celebrations accordingly: more time and care given to central elements, other elements dispatched expediently (but not without care and never in a hurried manner). The largest and most important symmetry of elements is between word and sacrament. Additionally, care must be given to the patterns of silence and utterance, stillness and movement, individual and community.

5. Be careful that all accouterments are worthy of the sacredness of what is being celebrated and are true to their form and function. Sacraments use familiar, everyday things as symbols: water, oil, bread, touch, and so forth. They are the "stuff" of our world. However, the objects and gestures must be worthy, beautiful, lavish if they are to move us to mystery. Chipped communion vessels, dirty or unkempt vestments, bread that barely feels or looks or tastes like bread, a sip of wine so small it is barely tasted and need not even be swallowed, oil that cannot be seen or smelled or felt, incense that is not abundant, liturgies timed to parking lot filling and emptying, and on and on bespeak an attitude of unimportance, insignificance, indifference. Great care with the things of liturgy makes visible liturgy's priority in our lives as well as calls us to prioritize the things and events of our lives.

6. Do not explain away the actions, symbols, incongruences, impertinences. If liturgy is to open up space for us to encounter mystery, then we must allow unknowns to challenge us exactly at that level: the unknown. The more we try to explain all the ritual mysteries, mystery itself is more and more difficult to face and is greatly compromised. The biggest risk here is that we make liturgy our own and shackle it for our own purposes.[46] Liturgy is always God's proffer of self to us.

7. Use silence as a way to create space for the imagination to work. Silence is less a time for reflection than it is a "time out" to encounter. It is a time for us to become conscious of our experience and feelings so that God's beauty might be recognized. Silence is a time for creating the alternative worlds in our imaginations that we appropriate in order to transform the real world in which we live and have our being.

8. Respect the assembly's ability to "see as," that is, to construct metaphors. This criterion helps us measure our ability to hear, appropriate, and live with incongruences so that the freshness of the Spirit might lead us to alternative ways to embrace Gospel living. "Seeing as" shakes us out of what we know and what is comfortable and enables us to enter into radically alternative worlds in which we are able to see likeness in differences. "Seeing as" helps us relate doing justice and caring for others to the shared identity we enjoy as the Body of Christ. "Seeing as" helps us move from being to action. Ultimately, "seeing as" is the condition for the transformation of ourselves into ever more perfect images of the Body of Christ which is the prophetic challenge of liturgy as well as its fruit.

9. Maximize the "bound images" inherent in liturgy so that semantic innovation is fostered. The images conjured by the incongruences of liturgy are bound by liturgy's adeptness for making present the paschal mystery. Any semantic innovation, then, is bound by this mystery. All innovation draws us deeper into this mystery, or it is merely novelty. The radically alternate world of our bound images helps us move from ritual to appropriate actions, from liturgy to life. In this, liturgy is freed from ritual confines and becomes a way of life, a spirituality to be lived. Any sense of "attending" Mass and "leaving," having fulfilled our "duty" as Christians, is precluded in the demands for appropriation of liturgy's transformative power into our everyday lives.

10. Implement ritual so rich that bodily emotions are unleashed, then create the silent space for these bodily emotions to be suspended so poetic transposition can happen. Ritual must unfold in such a way that it intersects with our own experience. That recognition of God impinging on us helps well up within an insatiable desire for union with God and unfettered joy in the experience of our God choosing to be present to us. Poetic transposition is nothing less than the divinization of ourselves and our world. Although the fruitfulness of liturgy is not measured by the good feelings ("moods") it precipitates, feelings are, nonetheless, not inappropriate.[47] But these feelings come from the deeper space of our encounter with God's mystery, not from a human production that is pleasing to our tastes.

By now, it should be quite clear that artful liturgy means much more than lush environment and use of visual arts, graceful movement and dance, festive attire, engaging proclamation, and wonderful music, although all of these elements are essential and should be done to the very best of the assembly's ability.[48] The deeper significance of the integral use of all of these elements and other less tangible ones—silence, rhythm, appropriation of meaning, mission, and so forth—is that we strive (dare) to approach the mystery of divine presence and in that presence we are transformed. Artful liturgy is—literally—life-threatening, for in our surrender to the ineffable attraction of divine beauty we lose ourselves—die to self—so that we might find a new life beyond that which even our wild images could muster. For, ultimately, liturgy transforms us so that our world can be transformed. In that God's reign is spread. The most profound artfulness of liturgy is that beauty which empowers us to make the hills to be made low and the valleys to be raised up; is that beauty which empowers us to raise up the lowly and bring low the mighty; is that beauty which empowers us to receive each and every one we encounter as sister or brother in Christ. With artful liturgy, the beast is slain: God's effulgence dispels the darkness of sin and death; the word's dwelling is truly within each of us; the Spirit's creativity builds with us a new heaven and earth.

Notes

1. On the subject of liturgy, see my "Liturgical Assembly: Who Is the Subject of Liturgy?" *Liturgical Ministry* 3 (1994): 41–51.

2. To promote one or other position would require a much more in-depth and thorough study not only of these thinkers but also of others not included here who have contributed more or less significantly to the discussion of aesthetics. Since this can only be a brief survey limited to this point, the selection is restricted to and guided by those in my estimation who can give us insights pertinent to art and liturgy.

3. See Book X of *The Republic* for Plato's response to the question "What is imitation?" See also *Sophist 267.*

4. See *Symposium* 212.

5. On the important notion of measure, see Plato's *Statesmen* 283–285; on the notion of mean, see 284. In his treatise *Laws* Plato mentions the traits of the one who judges art: Know of what the imitation is, know that it is true, and know that it has been well executed (see *Laws* II: 669).

6. See Aristotle's *Nicomachean Ethics* VI: 1140a, 5.

7. See *Physics* II: 199b, 15.

8. See *Nichomachean Ethics* II: 1160a, 30.

9. See *Metaphysics* XIII: 1078b, 5.

10. See *Rhetoric* I: 1361b, 2–15. He says that young men are beauteous if their bodies are fit for running and contests of strength; men in their prime are beauteous if they have a pleasant but formidable countenance because they must be fit for warfare;

and old men are beauteous if they have sufficient strength to perform such tasks as they must and are free from deformities of old age which are unpleasant for others.

11. Note the similarity here with Plato's notion that beauty helps us become godlike.

12. See Plotinus' *Ennead I, Sixth Tractate* 2. Notice the similarities in this thought to Hegel, who understood the whole purpose of art to be the mastery of spirit over matter.

13. See his *Ennead I, Sixth Tractate* 1.

14. See *Confessions* III: ch. 6, 10.

15. The term "number" may mean proportion, rhythm, fittingness of parts to whole, or the unity of the Divine. See *De Musica*, book VI: xiii, 30; see also xvii: 56–57.

16. See *Confessions* IV: ch. 23, 20.

17. See *Ennead I, Sixth Tractate*: I, 5, 4, reply to obj. 1 and I–II, 27, 1, reply to obj. 3.

18. See *Exposition of Aristotle's Politics* I: Lecture 1.

19. See *Ennead I, Sixth Tractate*: I–II, 57, 4.

20. See *Exposition of Dionysius on the Divine Names*, ch. 4, Lecture 5–6.

21. See *Ennead I, Sixth Tractate*: I, 39, 8; I–II, 145, 2; I–II, 180,2, reply to obj. 3.

22. See Immanuel Kant, "Critique of the Aesthetical Judgment" in *Critique of Judgment*, first book, §§ 1 and 12. Because aesthetical judgment is not a cognitive but aesthetical judgment, Kant says that this judgment must be subjective.

23. In his notion of interest or disinterest, Kant's subjectivity really comes to the fore. He argues that a judgment about beauty cannot be concerned with the thing itself and its purpose but is only concerned with the satisfaction produced within the subject. He uses the example of a palace: My judgment of beauty has only to do with my satisfaction and nothing to do with the function of the building, the sweat of those who built it, and so forth.

24. See Kant, "Critique of the Aesthetical Judgment" in *Critique of Judgment*, first book, first moment, §§ 1–22.

25. It is for this radical position that he has been most criticized. Croce wrote a four-volume work *Philosophy of Spirit*, the first volume of which is on aesthetics (1902).

26. This is a position which we will see again in Langer.

27. See Clive Bell, *Art* (New York: Frederick A. Stokes Company, Publishers, 1913), especially Chapter 1, "What Is Art?"

28. The kernel of Bell's philosophy of art lies in his conviction that all good works of art—these works are able to evoke aesthetic ecstacy—have some quality in common; this is what he calls significant form.

29. It is easy to see why Bell's theory paves the way for the styles of modern art characterized by forms rather than representations of reality.

30. *Art* ch. 2.

31. See Chapter 2, "Symbolic Transformation" in her *Philosophy in a New Key* (New York: Mentor Paperback Books, 1951).

32. The effect of this might be undue clutter in the worship space (addition of tacky banners with themes written on them or an excess of green plants that emulates the local shopping mall) or an emphasis on devotional elements to the detriment of liturgy's objective to make present the paschal mystery.

33. The scholastic understanding of a sacrament is that it is a visible sign of an invisible reality; cf. Sixth Tractate: III, 60, 2. See also Sixth Tractate: III, 60, 4: sacramental signs consist in sensible things.

34. I am summarizing the theory in two of Ricoeur's works in particular for this theoretical section. See "The Metaphorical Process as Cognition, Imagination, and Feeling," *Critical Inquiry* 5 (1978): 143–159 and "Imagination in Discourse and Action," *Analecta Husserliana* 7 (1978): 3–22.

35. Ricoeur's works on metaphor abound; his seminal work on metaphor is the classic *The Rule of Metaphor: Multidisciplinary Studies of the Creation of Meaning in Language*, trans. Robert Czerny with Kathleen McLaughlin and John Costello, SJ (Toronto, Buffalo, London: University of Toronto Press, 1977).

36. Ricoeur, "The Metaphorical Process," 148.

37. Ibid. This is particularly interesting for popular devotions. Unhealthy devotion or piety is founded on "wild images" rather than "bound images." For example, the instructions formerly given to first communicants not to "chew Jesus so we don't hurt him" is a good example of a bound image gone wild. The bound image is the body of Christ as food. It goes "wild" when we fail to escape the literal meaning to see the congruence—and innovation in meaning—in the dissimilarity. I believe much of the popular devotions abound in wild images—a good reason why they are so suspect, but also why they are so appealing.

38. I suggest one of the main arguments against women's ordination—an *alter Christus* must have the gender identity of the historical Jesus—is really a "wild" image.

39. Our Christian imagination enables us to grasp "body" as organic relationship not as the piece of bread but rather as a complex of relating that extends vertically toward God and horizontally toward each other.

40. Ricoeur contrasts "feeling" with "emotion": "Indeed our natural inclination is to speak of feeling in terms appropriate to emotion, that is, to affections conceived as (1) inwardly directed states of mind, and (2) mental experiences closely tied to bodily disturbances, as in the case of fear, anger, pleasure, and pain. In fact both traits come together. To the extent that in emotion we are, so to speak, under the spell of our body, we are delivered to mental states with little intentionality, as though in emotion we

'lived' our body in a more intense way. Genuine feelings are not emotions ..." ("The Metaphorical Process," 154–155). Don E. Saliers uses "religious affections" in a similarly restricted way: "The concept of affection ["feeling" for Ricoeur] designates a basic attunement which lies at the heart of a person's way of being and acting. In quite specific ways, our affections qualify our perceptions, our fundamental attitudes, and our behavior; yet affections cannot be reduced to feelings ["emotions" for Ricoeur], perceptions, or attitudes" (*The Soul in Paraphrase: Prayer and the Religious Affections* [New York: The Seabury Press/A Crossroad Book, 1980], 7).

41. Ricoeur, "The Metaphorical Process" 154.

42. Cf. Don E. Saliers' discussion of the chief Christian affections (gratitude, giving thanks, holy fear, repentance, joy and suffering, love of God and neighbor) that liturgy promotes (*The Soul in Paraphrase 50–73*).

43. Ricoeur defines meaning as a dialectic between sense and reference (see his *Interpretation Theory: Discourse and the Surplus of Meaning* [Fort Worth: The Texas Christian University Press, 1976], 19–22).

44. When we speak of liturgy giving us good "feelings," we really mean "mood" in the sense discussed here. There is nothing objectionable in having liturgy precipitate good feelings or moods; we must understand, though, that this is neither the end of liturgy nor the criteria for evaluating good, artful liturgy.

45. Obviously, these are not the only criteria for artful liturgy, but they are pivotal ones that follow from our discussion. Questions not addressed in this chapter are, for example, "Who is responsible for evaluating liturgy's artfulness?" and "How is this task implemented?"

46. This is always the danger of "theme" Masses.

47. See note 44.

48. Many of these elements are the topic of other chapters in this volume, which attests to the fact that they cannot be taken for granted nor left to the discretion of a few individuals.

JOYCE ANN ZIMMERMAN, CPPS, is director of the Institute for Liturgical Ministry in Dayton, Ohio, and the founding editor of *Liturgical Ministry*. Among her many publications are *Liturgy and Hermeneutics* and the annual volume *Living Liturgy: Spirituality, Celebration, and Catechesis for Sundays and Solemnities*.

Hierarchy and Liturgical Space

Lizette Larson-Miller

Like many forays into academic research, this one began with a variety of pastoral experiences and questions which prompted a desire for some logical context, if not answers. The first question arose from a recurring experience at liturgy in which invitations to prayer were couched in the language of "let us turn to God in prayer." My immediate response is always a desire to raise my hand and ask "where"? In a post-Vatican II church which appears to have renounced any physical expressions of the symbolic importance of orientation, how does directionality of prayer and arrangement of liturgical space replace the orientation of buildings, of prayer, and indeed, of the whole dispensation of liturgical space? The second experience, which led to the following research, is a sense of bewilderment in seeing fairly new churches deliberately built or adapted to include tabernacles in a central place and even communion rails reincorporated as fences around altars. Why was a "holy of holies" seen as desirable, in spite of legislation and catechesis to the contrary? Why, if given a choice, would people prefer a cultic "temple" arrangement rather than a unitive inclusive space?

The final piece of the puzzle represented below is a continuing personal interest in issues of authority, priesthood, hierarchy, and ecclesiology which has become something of a research mandate as I have moved into teaching sacramental theology.

What I hope to propose in this article is a biblical, liturgical, and theological check to a current concept of hierarchy which has essentially become a synonym for abuse of power, patriarchy, and non-collegiality. This ecclesiologically informed view of hierarchy will in turn suggest a theologically based proposal for liturgical space. This thesis is presented by first reviewing the early church development of liturgical space which functions as an icon of changing views of clergy, authority, and relationality in liturgy; second, by suggesting ecclesiologically an alternative to popular views of hierarchy and community; and finally, by proposing an alternative to a liturgical space conceived of as a temple space.

From Domus Ecclesiae to Domus Dei Revisited

The history of Christian architecture reveals a progression from a house for the church to a building functioning as a temple, which parallels a liturgical development toward a temple cult in which the holiest people function as mediators for the other members in a space strictly divided into progressive gradations of holiness.[1] In spite of differences in naming the stages and articulating geographical differences, scholars of ecclesial architecture agree that the most momentous changes occurred within the first six centuries of this era. We could broadly summarize these stages of development by dividing them into four categories, each with important liturgical and theological ramifications.[2]

The House Church

The first two centuries of Christianity have left us no archeological remains to collaborate or illuminate the literary accounts of the gathering together of the followers of Jesus to remember, to pray, and to celebrate the breaking of the bread. The frequent references in the New Testament (and in the *Didache*) suggest to us a eucharistic celebration in the context of a full meal, which was held in a domestic setting and, most logically, in the actual dining room of moderate to large private homes. The most extensive information regarding these communities comes from the apostle Paul whose letters reveal a network of house churches. Because there is no written or physical evidence of a desire for an articulated or adapted space until the third century, we may presume that these earlier spaces served the community's gathering in much the same way that a formal dining room served any meal event with more than the usual household in attendance. "The extension of hospitality through the meal setting was the central act that served to define the worshiping community, the church (*ekklesia*) in household assembly."[3] This is truly, therefore, the era of identifying "the church—the gathering" solely with the people and not with any physical space.

The House for the Church

In the third century we have both archeological and literary evidence which signals a shift in the place where the church gathered for communal prayer. This shift is one of adaptation to existing domestic or other places, in which the given space, as it was inherited, was perceived to need some architectural change to accommodate the Christian gathering. The earliest archeological evidence of a house adapted for the church is the famous example of Dura-Europos on the far eastern border of the Roman Empire. The house was renovated in 240–241 primarily by means of enlarging the dining room, adding a raised platform at the end of the rectangular space (roughly to the east), and creating a distinct baptismal space from a separate room in the house.[4] These adaptations are partially explainable by the shifts occurring in the late second/early third century in the communities and liturgies, in which the growth in numbers of Christians and the separation of Eucharist from the *agápe* necessitated a space and an arrangement in which larger groups could participate. There is evidence of third-century shifts, however, which are not simply attributable to growth in numbers, most notably the inclusion of a raised platform in the gathering room, the elaboration of baptismal space, and the addition of ancillary spaces for other uses (such as catechumens?). Other archeological remains possibly dating from this same century[5] reveal three characteristics of the *domus ecclesiae*:

- The "house for the church" phase is distinguished from the house church by "spatial articulation"[6] in which the gathering space is enlarged and adaptations for liturgical reasons, such as the raised platform on the eastern end of the room (in some cases), are added.
- These adapted spaces include a division between the "public" parts of the house for the church and the remaining private domestic spaces (and in some cases, the ceasing of any domestic use of the space).
- A recognition (particularly by non-Christians) that these buildings functioned as meeting places for the Christian cult,[7] a reminder that

public knowledge of Christianity was widespread prior to the peace of Constantine.

The Aula Ecclesiae[8]

This stage of Christian architecture must not be taken as a mid-stage between the *domus ecclesiae* and the basilica. It is simply a useful way to categorize a more ambitious adaptation to domestic structures for the church in some places and in others, structures built specifically for the worship of the church. It existed side by side with simpler house churches and endured well into the era of monumental Constantinian basilicas. Many of the foregoing "houses for the church" (see note 5) go through this stage also as adaptation to space continued to meet the changing liturgical requirements of the community.

The best examples of these "very adapted spaces" are some of the literary descriptions of worship space which give us insight into how early the space is delineated toward the cultic temple design described in the introduction. From Cyprian of Carthage in 250 we have a stunning example of symbolic architectural inculturation in which Cyprian borrows freely from the civil Roman architecture around him to define a space for the clergy separate from that of the laity. In a letter describing the ordination of the confessor Celerinus to the office of reader, he uses the technical Roman architectural term *pulpitum* (tribunal, raised platform) to describe the place of the clergy:

> When this man came to us, beloved brethren, with such honor of the Lord ... what else was there to do than to place him upon the pulpit, that is, upon the tribunal of the church, so that, propped up in the place of highest elevation and conspicuous to the entire congregation for the fame of his honor, he may read the precepts and Gospels of the Lord which he follows with such courage and faith?

Regarding Celerinus and Aurelius later in the same letter:

> I have established their glorious faces in the higher place where, being observed by all those who stand around them, they may give an incitement of glory to all who see. Moreover, know that we have already designated the honor of the presbytery for them, that they may be honored with the same gifts as the presbyters and be recipients of the monthly divisions in equal proportion, to sit with us regularly in their advanced and strengthened years."[9]

Cyprian even uses this "pulpit" or tribunal as a technical term to describe ordination, in which the act of ordination is called *ad pulpitum venire* ("to come to the pulpit").[10] When Cyprian's description of the area set aside for clergy (and ambo?) is put together with the earliest architectural knowledge we have of North African churches,[11] one might hypothesize that this raised platform is the eastern apse area (which served as a burial place for martyrs too). The unique African placement of the altar (toward the middle of the nave)[12] created an interesting arrangement in which the *pulpitum* was not inclusive of the altar, and therefore the call to the presbyterate was perhaps a call primarily to witness to Christ through proclamation and preaching (and martyrdom).

From another major Christian city of the early church, Antioch, comes a similar image of the space reserved for the clergy. Preserved by Eusebius, the ouster of the "heretic" Paul of Samasota from the episcopal seat in Antioch in 270 contains a criticism of Paul for some architectural adaptations which he made (and which were removed at his departure).

> Nor [did we base our decision] on the trickery in the ecclesiastical assemblies which he devised, courting popular opinion and personal appearance and astonishing the minds of the simpler people by means of the *bema* and the lofty throne which he had built for himself, not as a disciple of Christ but like the ruler of the world,

and with a *secretum* which he has and
even calls it.[13]

Paul's *bema* is undoubtedly a borrowed Roman
tribunal like that of Cyprian's because it has added
to it another structure, the *secretum,* which is a technical Roman civil architectural term for the magistrate's chamber often built on the tribunal (and to
which a magistrate could retire between cases).[14]
The use of the transliterated term from civil architecture also makes it more likely that this is an apsidal
or eastern end *bema* rather than the classic cen-
ter-of-the-nave *bema* found in later Syrian basilicas
(mostly East Syrian).[15] This raises the intriguing
question as to whether Paul of Samasota had an early
iconostasis of sorts, blocking the apsidal area from
view. Regardless of exactly where the *bema* had been
in the building, it was apparent that Paul had
reserved an area for himself as bishop which was
raised and hidden from view, and by calling it a
secretum, he implied for himself the trappings of
power and authority due to the civil magistrate.

The Fourth-Century Basilica

When we move to the fourth stage of architectural
style, the era of the Constantinian basilica (and all of
its countless imitations), we arrive at shifts on several fronts. First, while the domestic and adapted
spaces of earlier centuries certainly continue
throughout and beyond the fourth century (clearly in
the outlying rural areas), we have, for the first time in
our extant evidence, buildings of monumental proportion which publicly declare the triumph of Christianity. Their scale alone changes the character of
these buildings away from any association with
domestic structures. Second, the triumphalistic
nature of some of these buildings finds two
ready-made sources for interpreting the meaning of
the interior arrangement: one is the civil basilica, the
public space *par excellence,* the other is the language
of the shattered Jewish temple. The latter is
nowhere more apparent than in Eusebius' description of Paulinus' new basilica in Tyre, in which the
comparison of the rebuilt basilica with the rebuilt
temple is the primary metaphor:

Why need I now describe in detail his
guidance of the wise and skillful
architectural arrangements and the
surpassing beauty of each part, since
the testimony of these leaves no room
for instruction through the ears? But,
verily, having thus completed the
temple he also adorned it with very lofty
thrones in honor of the presidents and,
moreover, with benches arranged
throughout in accord with propriety,
and finally, he set in (their) midst the
altar, the holy of holies. Once again,
then, so that they might be inaccessible
to the masses, he fenced around them
with wooden latticework, adorned with
the craftsman's utmost artistry so as to
present a wonderful scene to the
beholder.[16]

This space for the clergy has now taken on the
added importance of housing the altar, "the holy of
holies," and the whole complex of clergy and altar
has been made "inaccessible to the masses." This
delineation of space is a ranking of space—it seems
first dictated by the presence of the bishop and pres-
byters, and secondarily by the presence of the altar
(the placement of the ambo can only be speculated,
the raised platform would help acoustically but it is
not clear that that is the actual reason for the "lofty"
area).

With the fourth-century victory of Christianity,
the adoption of Jewish cultic language and images
becomes more pronounced[17] and the use of these
images are certainly aided by the parallel shifts in the
place for the clergy and the changing understanding
of how those ordained leaders functioned in relation
to the rest of the community. These developments
contributed to the symbolic shift of space and the ritual use of those spaces which in turn shifted the theology of Eucharist itself:

The early church's worship places
unwittingly evolved from buildings
which housed the Christian liturgical
communities into sacred buildings
which functioned as temples.
Hand-in-glove with these developments

is the evolution of the presbyter
and bishop into a sacerdos,
a priest-mediator.[18]

Hierarchy: Inclusive or Exclusive?

The most common misunderstandings of the meaning of church are probably that it refers to the building only or, if referring to people, to the ordained clergy who then alone constitute the church. Very closely related to this is an understanding of the term "hierarchy" as referring solely to the clergy, whose position in society and in the eyes of God constitutes a holier status or calling. Both issues, ecclesiology and hierarchy, have benefited from theological reflection at and after the Second Vatican Council.

One of the great contextual shifts of Vatican II was its return to a sense of church as both the sacrament of Christ and inclusive of all the baptized. Regarding the former, the church as sacrament finds its new beginnings in several documents of the council. In the *Constitution on the Sacred Liturgy* it is "the wondrous sacrament of the whole Church" coming from the side of Christ in his death[19] and the "sacrament of unity."[20] In the *Dogmatic Constitution on the Church,* the Church is "in Christ, a kind of sacrament, i.e., sign and instrument of intimate union with God and of the unity of the whole human race."[21] The restoration of church as foundational sacrament gives it an authentic dynamism in the economy of salvation:

> Modern Catholic theology describes the
> Church as sacrament of salvation ...
> [b]ut the Church is a kind of sacrament
> only in dependence on Christ. It is not
> a new social sacrament that substitutes
> for the primordial sacrament, Jesus
> Christ. Rather the Church has a role to
> play in the economy of salvation, which
> is analogous to that which Christ
> exercised during his earthly life. The
> dependence of the Church on Christ is
> expressed by the Pauline imagery of
> head and body.[22]

When the restored image of the church as sacrament is united to the sense of the church as the whole "People of God"[23] and "a chosen race, a royal priesthood, a holy nation"[24] we move away from the sense of the ordained functioning to the exclusion of any active role of the laity. It is the whole church, the whole people of God who together are and who together do.

If we assume that Vatican II was an articulate summation of preceding work but not the last word on ecclesiology, we can turn to the developments of the past thirty years in which there is a discernable trend toward the East. As Western Christians increasingly draw on the common stock of early Christianity that was both East and West, part of this reintroduction to the theology as preserved in several Eastern Christian communities has found fruition in what is commonly known as "communion ecclesiology." This term represents a shift in Western thinking that moves the primary image of church away from that of "a legal institution" to one that is "ultimately a web of interwoven relationships of love"[25] perhaps best captured in the biblical word *koinonia,* fellowship. "Essentially 'communion' is a shared life with God and with one another ... rooted in the life we share with Christ and in his Spirit."[26] The phrase can mean different things, however, and it is perhaps most clearly categorized as having an external and an internal dimension. Externally, communion ecclesiology can be a vehicle for reconciling differences between the *locus* of ecclesiology as local or universal and in ecumenical dialogue. "[O]ne of the key advantages to communion ecclesiology is its ability to reconcile diversity and unity. It gives us models for talking about how a deep sense of oneness can be cultivated without losing respect for differences."[27]

Internally, communion ecclesiology can function as a context for understanding issues of hierarchy and authority. In contrasting two different approaches to authority within the Roman Catholic Church today, retired Archbishop John Quinn of San Francisco summarized them this way:

> The fundamental concern of the
> political model is order and therefore
> control. The fundamental concern of
> the ecclesial model is communion and

therefore discernment in faith of the diversity of the gifts and works of the Spirit.[28]

It is this idea of diversity of gifts that connects communion ecclesiology and hierarchy: "The hierarchy is only for communion in the church,"[29] in other words, the primary function of hierarchy is to represent and support this diversification of charisms through which communion in the church is constituted and maintained.

The word hierarchy itself, from *hiereus* (priest, sphere of the holy) and *arche* (rule, order), would seem to lend itself to the sections of *Lumen Gentium* which differentiate between laity and hierarchy, implying the former are not part of the latter. There is another way to approach this, however, which can do justice to communion ecclesiology and the inheritance of the early church. If we return to the recurring phrase from 1 Peter 2:9–10, which describes the baptized as "a chosen race, a royal priesthood, a holy nation," baptism is clearly entry into this "royal priesthood." Perhaps what would be more appropriate is to recognize that there are actually no non-ordained Christians, and that, therefore, the hierarchy is inclusive of all the baptized.[30] All the baptized have entered into an order, the first, most fundamental, and most important being the order of the baptized.

> Baptism and especially confirmation (or chrismation) as an inseparable aspect of the mystery of Christian initiation involves a "laying on of hands." The theological significance of this lies in the fact that it reveals the nature of baptism and confirmation as being essentially an ordination ... the immediate and inevitable result of baptism and confirmation was that the newly baptized would take his particular 'place' in the eucharistic assembly.[31]

If the whole hierarchy is for communion, then it is also intimately bound up with the premiere manifestation of communion, the Eucharist, which "makes the church as a communion ordained to love, where each one accepts to receive and hand over his [or her] life."[32]

The problem which needs reconciling in many people's minds, however, is not the inclusion of ranks or orders as a concept, but that the ranks are perceived as different and therefore unequal. Particularly for Americans, hierarchy and democracy are utterly incompatible: Democracy attempts to guarantee equality; hierarchy, in concrete historical examples, has often proved to be clearly opposed to equality. Theologically, though, hierarchy's differentiation of charism actually means equal and different. The Pauline theology of the church as the Body of Christ, in which the apostle pleads for a recognition of the diversity and the equality of all true gifts used for the community, is set in a critical place between a presentation on the Eucharist and the famous presentation on the ultimate context for all gifts, "So faith, hope, love abide, these three; but the greatest of these is love" (1 Cor 11:17—13:13). The body cannot function if there are only hands; the church cannot function if there are only prophets, the Eucharist cannot function if there are only cantors. It is only in the God-given differentiation of charisms that the parts together form a whole, and the primary action of the Eucharist, the gathering in communion, expresses most completely what the church is always becoming. One of the many paradoxes of the church is that the Spirit unites by means of this differentiation, by dividing. "We find it natural to speak of the community first as a unity and then as a diversity of ministries. But in a pneumatologically conditioned ontology the fact is that the Holy Spirit unites only by dividing (1 Cor 12:11)."[33]

When all the baptized are part of the differentiation of charisms in the hierarchy, no one is indispensable. All participate, all make the church which makes the Eucharist which makes the church. Even one of the earliest "hierarchical" descriptions of a Christian assembly in a building, Chapter XII of the *Didascalia Apostolorum*, with its detailed instructions for the bishop on where each rank or order of Christian goes, can really be interpreted best through the beginning of Chapter XIII:

> Now when you teach, again command and warn the people to persevere in the

assembly of the church, and not to be
stopped but constantly to be assembled
that no one diminish the church by not
assembling, and cause the body of
Christ to be smaller by a member.[34]

A theological recapturing of the concept of hierarchy as inclusive and constitutive of communion within the church leads us to reevaluate the liturgical space in which this inclusive hierarchy celebrates the "source and summit" of its being.

Both Mystery and Hospitality: A Place for the Church

The diversity of gifts and the differentiation of roles in the liturgy are the means by which the Spirit makes of us a communion. By extension, a differentiation of roles would imply a differentiation of liturgical space to house the liturgy. But, can the space be differentiated without the linear progression of holiness which has often carried the assumptions that the people in each of those spaces are themselves progressively holier? I would propose a future liturgical space by discerning a non-temple differentiation of space through the issues of directionality, movement, and mystery, or the importance of sacred space.

Directionality

Directionality has much to do with the understanding of progressive holiness in a church building. When oriented prayer ritually symbolized the expansive role that orientation played theologically and liturgically, the eastern end of an oriented building would, by its very placement, be a logical focal point. This is so because the East is cosmologically significant (the "sun and the stars begin their course from the East"); christologically significant ("Christ, the Sun of justice"); eschatologically significant ("The primordial Paradise of the first parents [to the East] is viewed also as the eschatological Paradise of our expectation"); and soteriologically significant ("Paradise, the place of our fall, becomes the place of our salvation too").[35]

This clarity of focus contributed to an understanding that as one moved through the space in an eastern direction, one crossed through increasingly holy areas. While this same liturgical schema is found in both eastern and western Christianity, it is really theologically developed in the East to a greater degree. For example, in a Byzantine synthesis of the theology of space, the three-part division of space carries tremendous theological weight, both spatially and temporally:

> The narthex is considered
> representative of the world which has
> not yet received salvation and is thus
> the location of penitential services
> and pre-baptismal exorcisms. The nave,
> which is also called the "church
> of the faithful" symbolizes the world
> redeemed, the partially realized
> Kingdom of God, the mystical body
> of Christ dominated by the main dome
> of the church with its icon of the
> Pantocrator. The third section ... the
> sanctuary, represents heaven itself,
> the fulfillment of the Kingdom. The
> three sections of the church are distinct
> because they represent different planes
> of reality. They are walled off from each
> other, but these walls are pierced by
> doors: the doors of repentance and the
> gates of paradise. The tripartite
> Byzantine church encompasses the idea
> of the flow of salvation history toward
> its ultimate consummation: the
> "already-but-not-yet" Kingdom.
> The "not yet" demands a separation
> of congregational and altar spaces.[36]

The symbolic division of these spaces also carries with it a separation of the ranks of the baptized, with only the ordained traditionally entering into the sanctuary that lies beyond the iconostasis. The almost inevitable result is that many Christians understand the progression of holy spaces as paralleled by a progression of holier people.[37]

With the loss of orientation as a significant factor in most western Christian communions and with the move toward viewing the centrality of the assembly as primary liturgical symbol,[38] the theology of liturgical space has also shifted. The issues of directionality and differentiation of space replace the tripartite symbolism of progressive holiness because the understanding of spatial focus is different. In general, what we have ritually is "the Liturgy of the Word ... directed at the assembly of believers, while the Liturgy of the Eucharist is directed at God in his paradise, located meta-spatially in the East."[39] In other words, we have two very different focal points for the two primary parts of any given eucharistic liturgy. This would seem to imply by its nature two different types of space, which focus respectively out toward the assembly (aurally) and then in toward the action of the Eucharist (visually and kinetically). The placement of a "meta-spatial East" is the more difficult concept unless one uses the primacy of the assembly as symbol to replace orientation. The visual focus at the Liturgy of the Eucharist proper is the altar, but that directionality seems best situated in the midst of the assembly. This arrangement does not compromise the action of the Eucharist or the sacrality of the table. The altar is holy because of what it symbolizes and because of what takes place at it. That alone differentiates its place in the building, it needs no separation by "latticework" or fence—an arrangement consistent with the Byzantine/Syrian theology of temporal cosmic unity in differentiation not commonly held in western Christian communions.

By extension, the differentiation of roles is apparent in the action of the Eucharist itself—there is one presider and as many celebrants as there are baptized in the room. The presider need not be relegated to a more sacred space, the exercise of that particular charism differentiates sufficiently. This bipartite space[40] still needs to be imagined through the lens of the assembly however, which implies the movement of the assembly so that the division of space does not become understood as progressive temple space.

Movement

One of the fundamental and traditional elements of liturgy is procession. The legacy of stational liturgy, the theology of procession as symbolic of the journey of Christian life, the movement of drawing near to God in communion, the inheritance of the cult of saints, the penitential pilgrimage, the dance of creation, and the movement of the Spirit over sacramental elements have all contributed to our understanding of the dynamic and incarnational quality of liturgy. It is this sense of the meaning of movement through a building toward the East and toward the holy which greatly contributed to the placement of altar and relics in medieval Western Christian architecture. In sixth-century Tours, the church dedicated to St. Martin contained inscriptions which led the faithful from the western entrance of the church to the eastern apse as if following the very path of Martin himself toward heaven:

> As you enter the church, look upwards, because a lofty faith admires the excellent entranceways ... this tower is security for the timid but an obstacle to the proud; it excludes proud hearts and protects the weak. The tower [over the altar and tomb] is higher. Famous for its starry roads, it has led St. Martin to the citadel of heaven. From there he who has already journeyed to the rewards of Christ calls people; having gone on already, he has sanctified this journey through the stars.[41]

The replacement of orientation with a flexible directionality, however, also has historical and theological precedence. The most enduring name given to the church is also a job description, *ekklesia*, the gathered, those duly summoned. Eucharist is first and foremost an action of corporate gathering. Hospitality is essentially about invitation and creating an environment in which relationships can be made and maintained. If hospitality is a liturgical virtue, then the spatial direction of this is in—we invite and gather in. Rather than conceiving of this movement as a movement toward the east, just as traditional and biblical would be the movement in toward the middle. Theologically this has been a hallmark of Eastern Christian eschatological understanding particularly in the realm of apostolic succession. The apostles are understood as a college, not so much as individuals, who are gathered in more than sent out. Likewise, their convocation is a symbol of how the church gathering around Christ, liturgically (*circumstantes*) and eschatologically functions: "Mission requires *sending* to the ends of the earth [as individuals], whereas the eschata imply the *convocation* of the dispersed people of God from the ends of the earth to one place."[42]

What would this look like with regard to liturgy and liturgical space? First, procession is something that everyone in the liturgy does (rather than a parade in which some process for the many). Second, to prevent our imaginary bipartite space from becoming two separate spaces for two separate groups of people requires the procession of everyone in the liturgy from one space to another at the appropriate time.[43] Third, the theological dimension of the Eucharist as a gathering, symbolizing the eschatological fulfillment of the ingathering of all people, seems best symbolized by the centrality of the altar in the midst of the gathered people for the Liturgy of the Eucharist and the centrality of the ambo toward the gathered people for the Liturgy of the Word.

When other important focal points of a church building are included in this picture, the theological movement in toward gathering becomes even more pronounced. The preference for placing the baptismal font near the entrance or gathering areas,[44] together with the stational design of the baptismal rite, of the marriage rite, and of funerals all beginning at the threshold, ritually and spatially express this movement from liminality to fulfillment achieved by gathering into the Body of Christ.

Mystery

The most frequent complaint against renovated spaces with an emphasis on the assembly is that the cost of a hospitable space has been the loss of transcendence, of the sacred and thus of a sense of mystery.[45] In a temple space, there is a demarcation of a holy of holies which can function as the sacred focal point in which a holy class of people mediate for the larger group. But is an objective sacredness to a non-temple building theologically desirable or is it holy because of those who gather there and what takes place there? It is the juxtaposition of these two approaches which represents a maturation of reflection on thirty years of liturgical renewal. The answer would have to be a tentative yes to both.

The rise of objective sacrality in Christian church buildings is found very early in the history of the architecture. While the movement toward the adoption of Old Testament temple language and cultic priesthood traced above contributes to this, there are other factors that are just important. One of the most dominant forces toward the understanding of *loca sanctorum* is the cult of martyrs and the intertwining of holy tombs with the place of eucharistic worship. The tomb of the martyr as the "meeting place of heaven and earth"[46] was based on the presence of the martyr in heaven with God while also potently present in the physical relics in the tomb. When, in the Western Christian tradition, the relics are joined to the sacrality of the eucharistic table (already considered holy because it both symbolized Christ and for what took place there), a clear focus for sacred place will dominate over the competing centers. A different approach will contribute to the sense of the holy place in the eastern churches, where as early as the sixth century the *Sogitha* or hymn on the dedication of the cathedral church in Edessa speaks very clearly of the objective holiness of the building itself. What contributes to this sacrality is not the cult of martyrs but the dome which symbolizes the cosmos and by extension, the place and the event of Eucharist as the meeting of heaven and earth. "The imagery of the cosmic temple is very evident in this hymn. The Syriac work *haykla* (temple) is used purposefully to emphasize the building as a holy place, independent of the presence or absence of the congregation."[47]

In the West, the development of the cult of relics will reach its apex in a visually prominent eucharistic reservation which led many to "perceive the sanctuary as more and more holy because Christ dwelt there,"[48] and which, quite literally, turned the house for the church into a *domus Dei*. The reaction against this understanding which came with the Protestant reformation was a fundamental Christian rejection that God could be limited to this building. It was reflected in the mandate to keep churches locked during the week to mitigate against an understanding of church as temple:

> We ... must guard against either taking
> them [church buildings] to be God's
> proper dwelling places, where he may

more nearly incline his ear to us ... or
feigning for them some secret holiness
or other, which would render prayer
more sacred before God. For since we
ourselves are God's true temples, if we
would call upon God in his holy temple,
we must pray within ourselves.[49]

This return to the biblical understanding of the
individual Christian as the temple of God became
fundamental in the renewal of liturgy and space
within Roman Catholicism also:

Having been driven since the Council
of Trent to erect magnificent
warehouses for the sacred, we are now
encouraged to build up a people in
whom God might dwell and to clothe
them in an architectural mantle
of 'noble simplicity.'[50]

At the same time, however, there seems to have
been a return to acknowledging some sense of sacred
space, however dependent upon the understanding
of a gathering of holy people. The 1997 Rite for the
Dedication of a Church contains language which
supports both the primary sense of the holiness of
the people sanctified by the Spirit ("May God, the
Father of mercies, dwell in this house of prayer. May
the grace of the Holy Spirit cleanse us, for we are the
temple of his presence")[51] and a sense of sacred
place ("We now anoint this altar and this building.
May God in his power make them holy, visible signs
of the mystery of Christ and his Church").[52]

With a contemporary willingness to balance the
biblical and theological understanding of personal
sanctification having priority over architectural
sanctification along with the human desire for sacred
space,[53] it remains to question how this can take
concrete form in the liturgy and liturgical space. The
key, in the minds of many scholars of contemporary
church architecture, is beauty.

For the architecture to contribute
sufficiently to the sacred action, it must
already give expression to the
sacredness. It must be ready to receive
and facilitate a ritual that is a sacred

ritual, and sustain that sacredness as a
memory of what has transpired and
what will continue to transpire so long
as the space is a place the community
knows to be home. This is achieved
through the aesthetics of the building.[54]

While beauty ultimately remains "in the eye of the
beholder" certainly the sense of authenticity must be
considered normative. "Our sacramental theology
imposes on us the responsibility of authenticity.
Since the sacraments have entirely to do with God's
disposition to use material things to our good, the
least we can do is to make them available in sufficient physical and symbolic proportions."[55] Another
way to describe this is "quality and appropriateness." "Quality means love and care in the making of
something, honesty and genuineness with any materials used, and the artist's special gift in producing a
harmonious whole, a well-created work."[56] Appropriateness is demanded by the liturgy in two ways:
"it must be capable of bearing the weight of mystery,
awe, reverence, and wonder which the liturgical
action expresses" and "it must clearly serve ritual
action which has its own structure, rhythm and
movement."[57]

Perhaps even more important to understanding
how mystery and transcendence are symbolized in
our liturgical spaces is developing a theology of
beauty. Beauty can "call us into the consciousness
of the transcendent other in whom our faith rests."
And while visual, architectural beauty is not the only
dimension in which the theology of beauty works, it
is key to the spatial discussion of this chapter.

Beauty is the infinitely variable and
permanent mystery. Beauty is the portal
to wonder, and wonder is the proper
human posture in the presence of the
ultimate mystery. Beauty is the only
adequate symbol. Builders who try to
imply the presence of the transcendent
holiness by use of the exotic, the merely
mysterious, or by clever or startling
devices of form or detail are outside the
main tradition.[58]

Developing an understanding of how beauty fits into our liturgical theology, rather than focusing on discrete works of architecture or art which are individually beautiful, may in the long run be a key to restoring an appropriate sense of mystery. Certainly within the vocabulary of liturgical beauty would be issues of light and dark, vertical dimensions of height, relatedness of artistic style in key furnishings, and balance in proportion of space.

A sense of sacred place seems intimately related to the importance of movement and orientation described above. One of the goals of pilgrimage is the arrival at a designated place, usually deemed sacred for various reasons. The other goal of pilgrimage is the journey itself. If we apply these to liturgical space, it seems the parishes which have been most successful in balancing hospitality and mystery have taken these pilgrimage motifs seriously. If the goal is to move toward a sacred place which can bring one to the awareness of the presence of God, and yet we want to claim the assembly space as the sanctuary, then perhaps what we need to recapture is the dimension of pilgrimage into the church proper. If the entry from parking lot to church door through the gathering space to the assembly space is itself a pilgrimage, then having finally arrived in the main body of the church with its centralized orientation will allow the mystery of standing in the presence of God to emerge. If this pilgrimage path to the goal of the sacred assembly place also allows for corporate gathering as well as private devotions, then it would psychologically, as well as theologically, emphasize the assembly place as the symbolic realization of union with God.

All three of these issues—directionality, movement, and mystery—have contributed to an imaginary liturgical space which might better reflect contemporary theological understandings than does a progressive temple space. Upon reflection, however, the space is not just imaginary but a memory of liturgical space which functioned well. It exists in several churches in which I have had the pleasure of worshiping, most notably in the newly constructed space for the parish of St. Gregory of Nyssa in San Francisco. And while the theological construct has taken on concrete form in my mind at least, it need not be limited to any particular communion or geographical location. Attempting to interpret the inheritance of biblical teaching and historical architecture through the lens of liturgical theology, eastern and western, allows for future liturgical space designs to take flesh in countless cultural and linguistic imaginations.

Notes

1. See Joseph Keenan, "Temples and Churches," *Worship* 68 (1994): 222–231: "the history of the changing role of the clergy and the evolution of *domus ecclesiae* to *domus Dei* ... slowly but surely caused the Christian worship environment to function more and more like a temple and the church ministers to function like temple priest-mediators" (223). "Temple" is defined as a place with a "hierarchy of sacredness" and multiple functions: "The temple sacralizes space, spells out creation or new creation motifs, expresses the meaning of the society using it, localizes the presence of God, creates a sense of the sacred" (231).

2. In this section I am indebted to the fine summary of L. Michael White, *The Social Origins of Christian Architecture. Volumes I & II* (Valley Forge, Pa.: Trinity Press International, 1990, 1997).

3. Ibid. I: 109.

4. For the work of excavation, see C. H. Kraeling, *The Christian Building* (Excavations at Dura-Europos, Final Report VIII: 2 [New Haven: Dura-Europos Publications, 1967]).

5. In addition to Dura-Europos, we might add the following archeological sites as probably having late third-early fourth- century evidence: Qirqbize in Syria (G. Tchalenko, *Villages antiques de la Syrie du Nord,* 3 vols. [Paris: J Gabalda, 1953–1958]); the "Julianos' Church" in Umm-el-Jimal, Syria/Arabia (B. De Vries "Research at Umm-el-Jimal, Jordan, 1972-1977, *Biblical Archeologist* 42 [1979], 49–55); the *Titulus Byzantis* of Rome (Richard Krautheimer, "The Beginnings of Early Christian Architecture" *Review of Religion* 3 [1939], 144–151); the *Titulus Clementis* of Rome (Paul Lawlor, *San Clemente: Gli Edifici Romani, La basilica Paleocristiana, e la Fasi Altomedievali* [Rome: Collegio San Clemente, 1992]); the *Titulus Aequitii (or Sylvestri)* of Rome (Richard Krautheimer, *Corpus Basilicarum Christianarum Romae* Vol. 3 [Vatican City: Pontifical Gregorian Institute,

1939–1956], 87–124); the *Titulus Chrysogoni* of Rome (Richard Krautheimer, *Corpus Basilicarum Christianarum Romae*, Vol. 1: 144–164); and the Roman Villa in Lullingstone (Eynsford, Kent) in Britannia (G.W. Meates et al., *The Roman Villa at Lullingstone*, 2 vols. [Chichester: Phillimore, 1979]). See the summary of archeological work in L. Michael White, *The Social Origins of Christian Architecture*, Vol. II: 121–257.

6. L. Michael White, *Social Origins* I: 104.

7. The earliest example seems to be the inclusion in the Edessene Chronicle of 201 which described the destruction of buildings in a flood as including "the temple of the church of the Christians." Cited in L. Michael White, *Social Origins* I: 118. The most striking example has to be the decision of the Emperor Aurelian to hand over a church building in Antioch to the "right Christians" (according to Eusebius): "... after an appeal the Emperor Aurelian made a very just decision concerning the matter. He ordered that the building be made the property of those with whom the bishops of the doctrine in Italy and Rome would communicate in writing." Eusebius, *Historia Ecclesiastica*. Cited in L. Michael White, *Social Origins* I: 87.

8. This is L. Michael White's English-language adaptation of Harnack's *Saalkirchen* to describe a stage prior to the fourth-century basilica. It is a useful term as long as his own caution is taken: "Our term *aula ecclesiae*, however, is not meant to connote any of the technical features of the basilica, save the rectangular plan. It does not suggest a direct line of evolution from house to basilica." Note 49, *Social Origins* I: 155.

9. Cyprian, Epistle 39.4.1, 5.2 (L. Bayard, trans., In *Sources chrétiennes* [Paris: Editions du Cerf, 1974]). Cited in L. Michael White, *Social Origins* I: 68–69.

10. Cyprian, Epistle 38.2. Cited in L. Michael White, *Social Origins* I: 69.

11. While earlier evidence exists, major excavation work cannot be pushed back before the fourth century. The pattern of placing martyr relics under the altar or under (or behind the apse) is attested to in several churches such as Orléansville (324). See the discussion in Richard Krautheimer, *Early Christian and Byzantine Architecture* (Middlesex, England: Penguin Books Ltd, 1986, 4th edition), 187–195 and André Grabar, *Martyrium: Recherches sur le Culte des reliques et l'Art chrétien*, 2 vols. and plates (Paris: College de France, 1946), (reprinted, London: Variorum Reprints, 1972).

12. The African central nave placement is preserved in a famous mosaic of Tabarka, circa 400. See Krautheimer 190.

13. Eusebius, *HE* 7.30.9–11. Cited in L. Michael White, *Social Origins* II: 85–86.

14. While the term *bema* was a Jewish borrowing, the *bema* as such was not the problem for Paul. The innovation of the *secretum* and the throne were apparently what got him into trouble, and these seem to be a direct borrowing from the architecture and imperial trappings of civil government, with all of its associations of power and authority. For the Roman civil terms, see A.G. McKay, *Houses, Villa and Palaces in the Roman World* (London: Thames & Hudson, 1975).

15. See Robert Taft "Some Notes on the Bema in the East and West Syrian Tradition," *Orientalia Christiana Periodica* 34 (1968): 326–359, regarding the development of this liturgical and architectural division between ambo and altar.

16. Eusebius, *HE* 10.3.44. The panegyric was given in 317.

17. This is not to imply that there was no Jewish language or imagery prior to this, but the cultic temple language was either used paradoxically because the associations had been turned on their heads (such as the association of the temple with individual Christians) or applied to Christ himself: "The title *hiereus*—levitical priest, is not applied to officers of the church but it is applied to Christ and to the church itself" in these early centuries. James Burtchaell, *From Synagogue to Church: Public Services and Offices in the Earliest Christian Communities* (Cambridge: University Press, 1992), 322.

18. Keenan, "Temples and Churches," 222.

19. CSL 5.

20. CSL 26.

21. DCC 1, 9. Cited as such in Edward Kilmartin, *Christian Liturgy: Theology*, vol. 1 (New York: Sheed & Ward, 1988), 220.

22. Edward Kilmartin, *Christian Liturgy*, 217–218.

23. The title of Chapter II of *Lumen Gentium*.

24. I Peter 2:9–10 as quoted in LG 9.

25. Dennis M. Doyle, "Communion Ecclesiology," *Church* (1996): 41.

26. Thomas P. Rausch, "The Ecclesiology of Communion," *Chicago Studies* 36 (1997): 282.

27. Doyle 41.

28. John Quinn, "Considering the Papacy," *Origins* 26 (18 July 1996): 123. Cited in Rausch, "The Ecclesiology of Communion," 289.

29. Claude Dagens, "Hierarchy and Communion: The Bases of Authority in the Beginning of the Church," *Communion* 9 (1982): 67.

30. In tracing the continuity of office from Judaism to early Christianity, James Burtchaell sagely points out that the one glaring omission in the borrowing language of office and ordination is "priest." With all the freedom to take on Jewish images, the office of priest, and all that it implies, is deliberately omitted, in spite of the fact that the hereditary Jewish priesthood must have endured in Jewish-Christian families throughout the first century at least. "It is not that there are no longer any priests: there are no longer

any who are not priests. Priesthood is no longer the identity of a clan or a tribe, but the name of an entire people." James Burtchaell, *From Synagogue to Church*, 322.

31. John Zizioulas, *Being As Communion* (Crestwood, N.Y.: St. Vladimir's Seminary Press, 1985), 216.

32. Dagens 73.

33. Zizioulas 217.

34. *The Didascalia Apostolorum in Syriac*, 2 vols., Edited by Arthur Vööbus (Louvain: Secrétariat du Corpus SCO, 1979), II: 130–135.

35. These four dimensions of the significance of orientation summarize the East Syrian view of the importance of oriented buildings and prayer. From the Anonymous Author's *Exposition of the Offices* (a 7th/8th century liturgical commentary most likely by George of Arbela). Cited in Pauly Maniyattu, *Heaven on Earth: The Theology of Liturgical Spacetime in the East Syrian Qurbana* (Rome: Mar Thoma Yogam, 1995), 108–109.

36. Andriy Chirovsky, "Towards a Byzantine Liturgical Architecture," *Diakonia* 18 (1983): 223.

37. While this is the popular interpretation of this type of space (not only from outsiders in western Christianity but also by many eastern Christians themselves), the Byzantine and Syrian emphasis on the differentiation understood temporally rather than just spatially can still lend itself to a hierarchical differentiation of space.

38. "Among the symbols with which liturgy deals, none is more important than this assembly of believers" *Environment and Art in Catholic Worship 28*.

39. Jamie Lara, "*Versus Populum* Revisited," *Worship* 68 (1994): 216.

40. The reality is, of course, that a house for the church has more than just these two primary foci—the baptismal font, the chair, the placement of symbols, the doors, and so forth all diffuse the focus at times to far more than just two possibilities.

41. Cited in Raymond van Dam, *Leadership and Community in Late Antique Gaul* (Berkeley: University of California Press, 1985), 242.

42. Zizioulas 174. Zizioulas further explains that "It is the understanding of eschatology as this kind of presence from beyond history of the Kingdom here and now that requires convocation of the dispersed people of God and of the apostles" (174 note 11).

43. "Special attention must be given to the unity of the entire liturgical space. Before considering the distinction of roles within the liturgy, the space should communicate an integrity (a sense of oneness, of wholeness) and a sense of being the gathering place of the initiated community" (EACW 53).

44. Ibid. 77.

45. As Harold Daniels succinctly states, hospitality creates a tension "between inviting people in and allowing it to be a place of people while avoiding living room coziness in which God is thoroughly domesticated." "Pulpit, Font and Table," *Reformed Liturgy and Music* 16 (1982): 64.

46. See Peter Brown, *The Cult of the Saints: Its Rise and Function in Latin Christianity* (Chicago: University of Chicago Press, 1981).

47. Maniyattu 28.

48. Keenan 229.

49. John Calvin, *Institutes* III:30. Cited in Donald Bruggink, "The Reformation of Liturgical Space," *Reformed Liturgy and Music* 16 (1982): 55.

50. Michael DeSanctis, "Rethinking Catholic Architecture: Part II – Let's Stop Renovating Churches," *Emmanuel* 101 (1995): 142.

51. Rite for the Dedication of a Church 50.

52. Ibid. 64.

53. "While worship's corporate aspect is fundamental, we must not lose the sense of the holy in our zeal to recover a communal sense. To replace the former otherworldliness with mere sociability would be to move from one extreme to another. The church is a community, but it is a community bound together with its Lord. It is the Body of Christ. There needs to be a balance between the sense of community and the sense of the holy" (Daniels 64).

54. Thomas R. Sion, "The House of God and the House of the Church," PhD Dissertation (University of Scranton, 1996). Cited in David Chatford Clark, "In Your Place…," *Liturgical Ministry* 5 (1996): 129.

55. William Seth Adams, "Theology and Liturgical Space," *Liturgy* 6 (1987): 32.

56. EACW 20.

57. Ibid. 21.

58. Edward Sovik, "Elements of the Christian Tradition in Building," *Reformed Liturgy and Music* 16 (1982): 83.

LIZETTE LARSON-MILLER is associate professor of liturgical studies at Church Divinity School of the Pacific and the Graduate Theological Union. She is author of *Annointing of the Sick* and editor of *Medieval Liturgy: A Book of Essays*.

Part 2

New Intelligence for a New Millennium

Drama and Biblical Humor

Michael E. Moynahan, SJ

Articles and books on the topic of "multiple intelligences" appeared increasingly toward the end of the twentieth century. The research of Howard Gardner[1] and his team of Harvard researchers involved in *Ground Zero* postulated that there are many forms of intelligence, many ways by which an individual knows, understands, and learns about the world. There is not simply one way of knowing. Most of these ways of knowing go beyond those that have dominated Western culture and education. Gardner proposes a schema of seven intelligences[2] but suggests that there are probably many others that we have not yet been able to test.

This chapter will examine four of those intelligences and how they are present when we use dramatic forms to uncover the liberating power of biblical humor. Those four "ways of knowing" are: verbal/linguistic intelligence,[3] body/kinesthetic intelligence,[4] interpersonal intelligence,[5] and intra-personal intelligence.[6] Four dramatic forms that both employ these four intelligences as well as uncover humor present in the scriptural texts through the use of the suggested dramatic forms will be discussed. These dramatic forms are (1) Moving Pictures, (2) The Olympic Judges, (3) The Trial, and (4) This Is Your Life.

The Scriptures are the privileged stories of the faith community. They not only express our faith, they deepen and nurture that faith. Often, however, Scriptures poorly proclaimed cannot compete for the attention of "channel surfers"[7] and all those people unfamiliar with their spiritual scriptural heritage. There are similarities between the situation that faced religious educators and worshipers of the eleventh and twelfth centuries and the challenges facing worshipers and religious educators of the twenty-first century. The arts, and eventually biblical drama, became the way of communicating the

"Good News" to people unfamiliar with it. If the Scriptures are not communicated in a way that genuinely engages the audience or congregation, they can have no hope of being the catalyst of conversion that they are intended to be. Let's look, then, at four dramatic forms that employ new kinds of intelligence, are able to communicate scriptural stories in fresh ways, can engage the religious imagination of participants, and have demonstrated an ability to uncover the potential liberating humor of scriptural stories.

Moving Pictures

The first dramatic form is called *Moving Pictures*. I discovered this form of drama over sixteen years ago while working in Australia. While it can be used with any story in Scripture, I have found that it works best with the parables of Jesus. I am presuming that these biblical explorations and use of "multiple intelligences" will be done in the context of a group. The word of God is best explored and broken open in the context of a faith community. So, make sure that your groups are not fewer than six or larger than eight.

This dramatic form involves taking a biblical story and communicating it with six phrases or sounds that are each accompanied by some appropriate action. The biblical story is told gradually through each added part. Each person does his phrase or sound and accompanying action strongly three times so that the audience or congregation can understand it. This person then continues this phrase or sound and accompanying action softly. In this way, the audience or congregation can see the "whole" through its "parts" as well as the "parts" through the "whole." This dramatic method inevitably uncovers humor that is in the biblical story. It is also a wonderfully vibrant way of giving expressive shape to that biblical story in the present. Now let me explain this method step by step and give you a couple examples of what different groups have done.

The first step involves the group together reading aloud the assigned piece of scripture. This scriptural story may be read two or three times by different voices. The different people will automatically emphasize and accentuate different aspects of the story.

The second step consists of inviting the group to brainstorm. Without censoring, have the group members suggest what they consider important dimensions of the story. They eventually have to come up with six phrases or sounds and accompanying actions that will tell this story to the audience or congregation.

The third step entails the group exploring how to communicate their story in the allotted six phrases or sounds and accompanying gestures or movements. The group gradually discusses and selects six. It is important here that the group realize that the phrases or sounds that they use don't have to actually be in the Scripture text. They do, however, have to be suggested and supported by that scriptural text. The following example will help clarify this.

The fourth step consists of the group trying out their selected phrases or sounds with accompanying movements and reacting to them. The group evaluates what they have created and determines whether it actually captures the essential elements and dimensions of their story. Groups will often make changes at this point of the dramatic process. While the limitation of six phrases or sounds and accompanying actions may seem artificial and unfair, experience testifies to the fact that groups can successfully create powerful expressions of their scriptural story working within this limitation. They are able to uncover biblical humor that is often buried in their story. The use of too many words or phrases would only serve to hide, neutralize, or eradicate this life-giving humor.

The fifth step entails the group sharing their "moving picture" interpretation with the audience or congregation. Oftentimes, in a workshop setting, I will give the same piece of Scripture to numerous groups. There are inevitably some similarities but also nuances of interpretation. An example of this process at work follows.

The group was given the story of the call of Jonah[8] from his initial call by God, through his initial refusal and up to the point where the whale spits him up on the beach. Jonah then decides to do what God had asked him to do in the first place. We reproduce this pattern many times in our faith lives. While it may not seem humorous to those who we are going through this, it can provide a great deal of liberating humor to those who view this interaction at a distance, even the distance that time offers us or them.

When the group presented their understanding or interpretation of the "Call of Jonah," they did it with six phrase or sounds and accompanying gestures. They stood in a straight line. The first person said: "Go, Jonah, go!" and used her right arm and "pointer" finger to indicate to the person next to her where Ninevah was. The first person represented God. The second person, after the first person had spoken and gestured three times, responded with "I'll go this way!" and used his left hand and left "pointer" finger to indicate that he would go the opposite way God wanted. The third person, after the second person had spoken and gestured three times, made the following sound: "Blub . . . blub . . . blub ... blub." The third person wiggled his fingers as he gradually descended toward the floor each time he did this series of sounds. Person number three tried to create the impression of someone sinking in water and/or being swallowed by a whale. The fourth person, when it was time for her to come in, clutched her shoulders and communicated fear as she said: "It's dark in here." After she had done this three times, the fifth person said, "I can see the light!" Person number five had excitement in her voice and pointed in a direction just over the heads of the audience or congregation. The sixth person looked and sounded somewhat chastened as he said, "I'll go that way!" He used the thumb of his right hand to indicate the direction that God had initially suggested.

This dramatic form works particularly well with the parables of Jesus. Two such parables that groups work very successfully with are (1) "A Parable on Prayer" which is found in Luke 11:5–9 and (2) "The Parable of the Rich Fool" which is found in Luke 12:16–21. There are many other parables that can present groups with creative opportunities to uncover the liberating power of biblical humor. A few examples are: The Parable of the Rich Man and Lazarus (Lk 16:19–31), The Parable of the Publican and the Pharisee (Lk 18:9–14), The Parable of the Lost Sheep (Lk 15:3–7), The Parable of the Unmerciful Servant (Mt 18:23–35), and The Parable of the Wise and Foolish Bridesmaids (Mt 25:1–13).

The Olympic Judges

For many years, Doug Adams[9] and I have offered a week long workshop on "Bringing to Life Biblical Humor" as part of summer school at the Graduate Theological Union. During one of those summers, which happened to be an Olympic year, a new dramatic form was born.

During one of our sessions, I explored the story of the ten lepers in Luke's Gospel through the use of dramatic improvisation. I asked nine participants to imagine what excuse they would give for not going back to Jesus to give thanks. This imaginative exercise provided some powerful links between the reality of the scriptural story and the reality of our life.

Doug suggested, however, a most important twist. Since it was the Olympic year, he proposed having a panel of "Olympic judges" that would evaluate the excuses of the ungrateful lepers. Each judge was given a series of ten cards marked with the numbers from 1 to 10. After each leper appeared before the panel and offered his or her excuse, the judges would vote. The result was amazing in its insight and humor.

It is very important to interview the judges and ask them to explain the rationale for giving such a high, low, or mediocre mark to a particular leper. A nice touch that Doug added was to have the audience or congregation evaluate the performance of the judges at the end of the process. So let's examine how this dramatic method would unfold.

The first step is to read the passage of Scripture (Lk 17:11–19)[10] to the entire audience or congregation. Then invite all of the audience or congregation to imagine what excuse they would offer for not returning to give thanks to Jesus when they discovered that they were healed of their leprosy.

The second step is to select a panel of five judges. Have them come to the front of the audience or congregation and sit at a special table prepared for them. Give each judge their set of "score cards" and tell them that they are to evaluate the merits of the excuses that they will hear. In selecting the judges be sure and get a variety of perspectives: old and young, male and female, married and single, religious and lay, as well as different cultures. The wider the representation, the more enjoyable and insightful the exchanges.

The third step is to act as the facilitator and announce that you are having a "Leper Reunion" during which the different lepers who failed to return to Jesus will explain their conduct to the panel of Olympic judges. Ask for a volunteer as the first leper.

The fourth step, after the leper has given her excuse, is to invite the judges to evaluate her excuse. A "1" represents the lowest score or "worst" excuse whereas a "10" represents the highest score or "best" excuse. After the judges have held up their cards together (count "one," "two," "three"), begin interviewing the judges and asking them why they gave such a high mark or low mark to this particular leper.

The fifth step, after the nine lepers (or however many you decide to hear) have offered their excuses and been evaluated by the judges, involves turning the tables on the judges. Have the audience evaluate their judging. This last step can be eliminated but adds a further humorous touch to the proceedings.

Key to this dramatic method is the role of the facilitator who keeps the exercise moving and acts as interpreter, interviewer, and commentator. This has proved a most imaginative, entertaining, and insightful way to help participants experience the humor of "making excuses" as well as the "connections" between what is going on in this biblical story and what goes on in our spiritual lives.

The Trial

Perhaps the adjective that best describes our American society is litigious. The United States is a country of lawyers. Some have law degrees. Many more don't. Americans are ready to sue at the least provocation. So why not bring this urge to litigate into our exploration of the Scriptures?

Scripture stories abound in the Hebrew and Christian Scriptures in which one character has a complaint against another. Isaac, in contemporary society, might take his father Abraham to court for attempting to murder him. Jacob steals his brother's birthright. If this isn't grounds for a lawsuit, what is? Joseph's jealous brothers sell him into slavery. Moses is not allowed into the Promised Land. God

might take the Israelites to court for repeatedly breaking the covenant. The Pharisees, on any number of occasions, might sue Jesus for breaking the Sabbath law. And within the parables that Jesus told, material abounds for the lawsuit of one character against another. For our purposes, we will use one such parable to demonstrate this dramatic form.

The parable we will use is "The Vineyard Workers" found in the Gospel of St. Matthew.[11] The owner of a vineyard hires workers at different times during the day but pays them all the same wage at the end of the day. Somehow, according to Jesus, the reign of God is like this. To our American sense of "fair play" and "you get what you work hard for" this simply is no laughing matter. God, however, might look upon this all quite differently. Let's briefly go through the process of this dramatic method.

The first step is to read the Gospel passage to all the participants. Everyone will be involved in this dramatic method. Those participants who don't act as attorneys, defendant, plaintiffs, or witnesses will serve as jurors. This story and this dramatic method can uncover many unconscious prejudices.

The second step is to select a prosecuting attorney and a defense attorney. The defendant will be the owner of the vineyard who is accused of unjust labor practices. The plaintiffs will be those laborers hired the first and second time that the owner went out to hire laborers. Each legal side may call three witnesses. Therefore, six additional members of the group will play the parts of witnesses. The rest of the group will play the role of jurors. A very important role is that of judge. This person moves the proceedings along and makes whatever rulings he wants on motions or objections raised by the prosecuting and defense attorneys.

The third step is to give the prosecution and the defense five minutes to organize their respective cases and witnesses. You can give five more minutes, if you so desire, but a good deal of these dramatic forms draws on improvisation. It is amazing what people say and discover about the scriptural story and themselves through this process.

The fourth step is the actual trial. It should be done in a very quick and efficient manner. There would be no logjam of real court cases if this system were used, for the trial is conducted under the rules for "fast chess."[12] Each attorney has one minute for an opening statement and one minute for a closing statement. Each attorney can call no more than three witnesses. They may ask each witness no more than three questions during the space of no more than one minute. If either attorney exceeds the stated limits they are to be held in contempt of court and ordered by the bench (judge) to watch reruns of Judge Wapner for seventy-two straight hours.

Now the characters go to their respective tables and the case unfolds. The prosecution calls its witnesses first. They may, of course, be cross-examined by the defense but in no more than three questions. Those questions cannot exceed a total of one minute. When the prosecution rests, the defense may call its witnesses. They will, in turn, be cross-examined by the prosecution. When the defense rests, the Judge invites both the prosecuting attorney (first) and the defense attorney (second) to give their closing statement.

The fifth step now begins. This involves the jurors getting together and talking about a verdict. If the jurors cannot reach a unanimous decision, the judge should poll the jury and reveal how each one votes. After polling the jurors, it would be profitable for the judge to go back and interview a couple of the jurors who voted for "conviction" and a couple who voted for "acquittal" to see what their arguments and reasoning were that led them to their decision.

The last step of each of these dramatic methods is to lead the group in a reflection on and discussion of what they experienced through this dramatic process, as well as what they may have discovered about the scriptural story and themselves along the way.

This Is Your Life, Jesus.

In the late 1950s and early 1960s, there was a very popular television show hosted by Ralph Edwards called *This Is Your Life*. Each week some unsuspecting person in the studio audience would discover that his or her life was the subject of the program. Gradually family, friends, former neighbors, and work colleagues would offer verbal clues to the honoree. They would share humorous and moving anecdotes that gave hints about when they interacted with the person whose life was being honored. Some of the guests might be grade school teachers,

classmates who went to school with the honoree, or people who were powerfully influenced by the honoree, even if the honoree was unaware of this. Ralph Edwards opened and closed the evening's program with the line "(Name), *this is your life!*"[13]

There are many characters from the Scriptures that would lend themselves to this type of dramatic process. Abraham, Sarah, Isaac, Jacob, Noah, Joseph, Moses, Miriam, Mary (the Mother of Jesus), St. Peter, Mary Magdalene, and St. Paul are just a few examples of characters you could use as part of this dramatic process.

To illustrate this dramatic form, I will use the character of Jesus. It is important to choose someone to play Jesus who is reasonably familiar with the Gospels.[14] It is quite nice when characters offer Jesus clues about when they interacted with him in his life and he can't quite place them. Those who play the part of Jesus and don't have "total recall" comfort everyone who knows what it feels like to forget someone's name or face. The other key character is the Ralph Edward's persona who moves the process along.

After deciding who will play the part of Jesus, ask this character to please leave the room. Then tell the participants that you want each of them to select a character from the Gospels that was a part of Jesus' life. I usually have prepared some cards or strips of paper with the name of a different character that appeared in Christ's life. Written on each piece of paper are the places in the Scriptures in which this character encounters Jesus. I give the citation of the Scripture location in the Gospels and a brief summary of their interaction.[15]

Whenever possible, give the participants an evening or full day to look up their character in the Gospels and reflect on that character's interaction with Jesus. Participants are not limited to the characters listed on the pieces of paper. They might decide to be "The Woman at the Well" in the fourth chapter of John's Gospel or "The Man Born Blind" in the ninth chapter of John's Gospel. Allow the participants time to reflect on these encounters with Jesus so they can make what they will say to Jesus, by way of clues, their own. Now let's look at this dramatic method.

The first step involves assembling all the participants. The host surprises Jesus[16] by telling him,

"This Is Your Life." After Jesus comes to the front of the room and sits down, the host explains what will happen. Characters from Jesus' life will come up and give Jesus clues about their encounters with him. Jesus will guess their identity. Please note that it is not important for Jesus to correctly guess every character's identity. The host can occasionally help Jesus out or simply come right out and identify the character for Jesus. After the character's identity has been revealed, this character gets to ask Jesus one question. Jesus responds. Then Jesus gets to ask that character one question. The character responds.

The second step is to begin inviting guests up. Each character gives Jesus clues about his identity and how he encountered Jesus in his life. Even if Jesus knows who the character is, it can be a good idea for Jesus to allow the character to give a few more clues for all the members of the audience or congregation to have an opportunity to discover for themselves this character's identity.

The third step comes when Jesus or the host has successfully revealed the identity of the guest. Then that character gets to asks Jesus one question. These questions are another reason to allow the participants time to reflect on their character and what question they would ask Jesus, if they had a chance, for now they do.

The fourth step consists in Jesus asking each character one question. The person who plays Jesus will determine the quality and depth of these questions. What is important to realize is that through these questions that the different characters and Jesus ask, we are enabled to make life-giving connections between the questions of the Scriptures and the questions in our lives, between the challenges of the scriptural stories and the challenges in our lives.

An important element in this dramatic process is that the character Judas comes last. In fact, the host should begin wrapping up the program by thanking the guests for coming and thanking Jesus for being a part of the festivities. The person playing Judas makes his way up to Jesus and says something to the effect, "Do you remember me? I wasn't invited to this but I had to come." The host blusters that his name is not on the official guest list and this is highly irregular. People, including Jesus, catch on quickly to this character's identity. The exchanges between these two characters over the years have been incredible. Perhaps one of the simplest and most profound exchange of questions was when Judas asked: "Can you ever forgive me?" To which Jesus replied: "I can and I do." Then Jesus asked his own question. "Do you believe me?"

The fifth step involves inviting the participants to reflect together and discuss what they learned about their character and what they learned about Jesus through this dramatic process.

Now that you know the process and have a model for giving participants information about their character, try this process with other biblical characters. It is a creative and engaging way to help groups familiarize themselves with important parts of our biblical heritage. While most groups would be comfortable with the story of Jesus in the Gospels, to select a character like Abraham or Joseph or Moses would require us to spend some time familiarizing ourselves with those stories. The rewards make the effort well worth it.

Conclusion

All four intelligences mentioned earlier in this chapter—verbal/linguistic, body/kinesthetic, interpersonal, and intrapersonal—are utilized in each of the four dramatic forms that we examined. These four dramatic forms—Moving Pictures, The Olympic Judges, The Trial, and This Is Your Life—in turn, uncover the liberating humor of the Scriptures.

It is said that the Buddha never attained enlightenment until he left his parents' home, until he got "beyond their gates." Our initial understanding of biblical stories, which is often a literal understanding of them, is like our parents' home. God's word is truth and that truth can set us free. But God's word can only set us free if we get beyond our "gates" of understanding. God's word can only liberate us if we continue to move beyond our initial and literal understanding of the biblical stories so that the Scripture stories can reveal who we are and what we mean. Dramatic forms, and the new intelligences they utilize, prevent us from imprisoning and impoverishing the word of God with our literal mindedness. A new millennium invites us to view familiar realities freshly. Through the use of dramatic forms, we can utilize new intelligence in approaching the Scriptures, in exploring them, and in communicating them in worship and religious education settings.

Notes

1. Howard Gardner, *Frames of Mind: The Theory of Multiple Intelligences* (New York: Harper and Row, 1983).

2. These seven ways of knowing, as summarized by David Lazear in his book *Seven Ways of Teaching: The Artistry of Teaching with Multiple Intelligences* (Palatine, Ill.: Skylight Publishing, 1991) are: (1) Verbal/Linguistic Intelligence; (2) Logical/Mathematical Intelligence; (3) Visual/Spatial Intelligence; (4) Body/Kinesthetic Intelligence; (5) Musical/Rhythmic Intelligence; (6) Interpersonal Intelligence; and (7) Intrapersonal Intelligence.

3. This intelligence "is responsible for the production of language and all the complex possibilities that follow, including poetry, humor, story-telling, grammar, metaphors, similes, abstract reasoning, symbolic thinking, conceptual patterning, reading and writing. This intelligence can be seen in such people as playwrights, story-tellers, novelists, public speakers, and comedians" (Lazear xiv).

4. This intelligence is revealed in "the ability to use the body to express emotion (as in dance and body language), to play a game (as in sports), and to create a new product (as in invention). 'Learning by doing' has long been recognized as an important part of education. Our bodies know things our minds don't and can't know in any other way. For example, it is our bodies that know how to ride a bike, roller skate, type, and parallel park a car. This intelligence can be seen in such people as actors, athletes, mimes (like Marcel Marceau), professional dancers, and inventors" (Lazear xv).

5. This intelligence "involves the ability to work cooperatively with others in a group as well as the ability to communicate, verbally and non-verbally, with other people. It builds on the capacity to notice distinctions among others: for example, contrasts in moods, temperament, motivations, and intentions. In the more advanced forms of this intelligence, one can literally "pass over" into another's perspective and 'read' their intentions and desires. One can have genuine empathy for another's feelings, fears, anticipations, and beliefs. This form of intelligence is usually highly developed in such people as counselors, teachers, therapists, politicians, and religious leaders" (Lazear xvi).

6. This intelligence "involves knowledge of the internal aspects of the self, such as knowledge of feelings, the range of emotional responses, thinking processes, self-reflection, and a sense of or intuition about spiritual realities. Intrapersonal intelligence allows us to be conscious of our consciousness; that is, to step back from ourselves and watch ourselves as an outside observer. It involves our capacity to experience wholeness and unity, to discern patterns of connection with the larger order of things, to perceive higher states of consciousness, to experience the lure of the future, and to dream of and actualize the possible. This intelligence can be seen in such people as philosophers, psychiatrists. spiritual counselors and gurus, and cognitive pattern researchers" (Lazear xvi).

7. Perhaps no image captures our American culture, at the end of the 20th century and beginning of the 21st century, better than a person in front of the television set endlessly switching channels (that is "channel surfing") in the desperate hope that something will leap off of the screen and engage him.

8. Jonah 1:1—2:1, 11,3:1–2.

9. Professor Douglas Adams was a colleague of Jake Empereur. Doug teaches at the Pacific School of Religion in Berkeley, California, and is one of the people responsible for making Area VII (Theology and the Arts) the finest program of its kind in the country. PSR is one of the member schools of the Graduate Theological Union.

10. This dramatic form also works well with stories like the wedding guests who made excuses about why they couldn't come to the Wedding Banquet (Mt 22:1–10 or Lk 14:15–24). You can also use the passage from the book of Exodus where the people are grumbling against God and Moses in the desert. In the first case have the participants explain why they didn't come to the banquet. In the second instance, have the participants explain what the particular focus of their grumble or complaint was.

11. Mt 20:1–16.

12. For an experience of "fast chess" or "speed chess," see the film *Searching for Bobby Fischer* or visit a local park or university student union where one can often find people playing "speed chess." The game is played against a clock. Players have only a certain number of seconds to make a move or they lose a chess piece from the board.

13. The first person I ever saw use this dramatic method was Dr. Norman Fedder of Kansas State University. He briefly described his use of this creative dramatic form with the life of Abraham in an issue *of Modern Liturgy* magazine on "The Miracles of Jesus." The title of his article was "Unstiffening Those

Stiff-necked People: Five Improvisations," *Modern Liturgy* 12:1 (February 1985): 12–14.

14. The most difficult experience of this dramatic process I ever had was with a group of high school students in Australia some sixteen years ago. I did not know any of the students. There was no teacher there to make suggestions. So when I asked for a volunteer to play the part of Jesus, a young man raised his hand and said he would like to play the part. It was clear from the beginning that this choice was a disaster. He didn't know any characters from the Bible. He was uncomfortable playing the part. His responses to the other biblical character's questions were flippant. His own questions to them were trite and unsuccessful attempts to be funny or ridicule them. One of the last characters that came up, a young woman who played Mary Magdalene, redeemed the whole painful process. When Jesus continued to be a first class jerk, Mary Magdalene said to him: "Who are you?" He responded, "Jesus, you idiot." And then she said, "I knew Jesus and he would never treat anyone the way you have treated us. You are simply an imposter!" The young many started to cry and ran out of the room. The whole incident led to some excellent exchanges and conversations among the classmates.

15. Here are some examples.

(1) Mary, the Mother of Jesus:

a. Lk 1:26–38 An angel invited you to become the mother of God.

b. Lk 1:39–56 You visited your cousin who was also pregnant and uttered your Magnificat.

c. Lk 2:1–20 Birth of Jesus and visit of shepherds. You treasured everything in your heart.

d. Jn 2:1–12 The Wedding Feast at Cana. You ask Jesus to save the party and he does.

e. Jn 19:25–27 You had to watch your son die.

(2) John the Baptist:

a. Lk 1:5–25 You were the son of Zechariah and Elizabeth and called the "baptizer."

b. Mt 3:1–17 You appeared in the desert announcing the kingdom and inviting the people to baptism and repentance.

c. Lk 3:19–20 You were imprisoned by Herod because of your public rebukes of his marriage to Herodius.

d. Mt 11:2–6 You sent your disciples to Jesus from your prison cell to ask you the question about your Messiahship directly.

e. Mk 6:17–29 You were finally executed as a result of a foolish pledge made by Herod who had too much to drink.

(3) Anna, a prophetess:

a. Lk 2:36–38 You were a prophetess. You were the daughter of Phanuel of the tribe of Asher. You were eighty-four years old when you first met Jesus in the temple. He was just a baby but

when you saw him, you praised God. You spoke of him to all who looked forward to the deliverance of Jerusalem.

(4) Peter:

a. Mt 4:18–22 You were a fisherman.

b. Mt 8:14 Jesus cured your mother-in-law. You forgave him for this.

c. Mt 4:18–22 Jesus called you along with your brother Andrew to follow him.

d. Mt 14:28–31 You attempted aquambulation (walking on water).

e. Mt 16:22ff. You objected to Jesus' prediction of his passion and he rebuked you sharply.

f . Mt 17:1–8 With James and John you witnessed Jesus' Transfiguration.

g. Jn 13:6–9 You objected when Jesus tried to wash your feet.

h. Jn 18:10 When Jesus was arrested, you assaulted one of the guards with a sword.

i. Mk 14:66–72 During Jesus' passion, you denied him three times.

j. Jn 21:15–23 After his resurrection, Jesus told you to feed his sheep three times.

(5) John:

a. Mt 10:2 You were the son of Zebedee. Your brother was James.

b. Mk 3:17 James and you received the nickname "Boanerges" (sons of thunder) from Jesus.

c. Mt 4:21ff. You called my brother and me from my father's fishing boat to follow you.

d. Mt 20:20–28 Your mother once asked Jesus if James and you could sit on thrones on either side of him.

e. Jn 13:21–30 At the last supper you asked Jesus who would betray him.

f. Jn 20:3–10 After Mary Magdalene brought you news of his resurrection, Peter and you ran to the tomb to see for yourselves. You got there before Peter.

(6) Thomas:

a. Mt 10:3 You were one of the twelve apostles. You were nicknamed "didymus" or the "twin."

b. Jn 11:16 It was you who urged the other apostles to accompany Jesus into Judea and die with him.

c. Jn 20:24–29 You are most remembered for being the disciple who wouldn't believe that Jesus was risen until you saw and touched his wounds. As a result of this you received the nickname "the doubter."

(7) Mary Magdalene

a. Mk 16:9 Jesus expelled seven demons from you.

b. Lk 8:2 You were one of the women who ministered to Jesus' ministerial needs.

c. Mt 27:56 You were a witness at the crucifixion.

d. Jn 20:1–18 Jesus appeared to you after the resurrection. You didn't recognize him at first. Jesus sent you to tell the others. Most Christians identify with you since you were a repentant sinner.

(8) Zaccheus:

a. Lk 19:1–10 You were the chief tax collector of Jericho. You were a Jew who went to see Jesus out of curiosity. Your favorite tree is the sycamore. Randy Newman's song "Short People" describes you. Jesus invited himself to your home for dinner. This moved you to make restitution for all your ill-gotten gains.

(9) The Widow of Nain:

a. Lk 7:11–17 Jesus came to your town of Nain accompanied by his disciples and a great number of people. Jesus raised your only son, who had died, back to life.

(10) Martha and Mary:

a. Lk 10:39–42 Once, when Jesus was visiting you, you got into an argument about who should be doing what.

b. Jn 11:1–57 Jesus raised your brother from the dead.

c. Jn 12:3–8 You (Mary) anointed Jesus' feet at Bethany.

(11) Lazarus:

a. Jn 11:1–57 You were the brother of Martha and Mary. Jesus raised you from the dead.

(12) Pilate:

a. Jn 18–19 You were procurator of Judea when Jesus was executed. You didn't think he was guilty and tried to have him released. Your wife had numerous bad dreams about Jesus. You had Jesus flogged in the hopes that the people would be satisfied with that. They weren't. You asked Jesus the famous question: "What is truth?" You washed your hands in the presence of the people demonstrating that you would not take responsibility for the death of an innocent man.

(13) The Woman with the Hemorrhage:

a. Mk 5:25–34 You suffered from an illness for twelve years. You spent all that you had on treatments but nothing worked. In fact, your condition got worse. You heard about Jesus and thought that if you could just touch a piece of his garment that you would be healed. You did and you were! Jesus told you that your faith had healed you and sent you away in peace.

(14) Bartimaeus:

a. Mk 10:46–52 You met Jesus in Jericho. You heard about him long before you saw him with your own eyes. You were a blind beggar. When you heard Jesus was passing by you cried out to him for help. People tried to shut you up but to no avail. Jesus had you brought to him and asked you what you wanted. Jesus let you see again. You followed him along the road from that day forward.

(15) The Woman Taken in Adultery:

a. Jn 8:–11 You met Jesus in the Temple. The circumstances were very embarrassing for you. Your favorite singing group is the "Rolling Stones." However, you don't like "hard rock." The Scribes and Pharisees tried to get Jesus to condemn you. Jesus outsmarted them. Jesus was gentle, caring, and forgiving. He sent you away and encouraged you to "sin no more."

(16) Judas:

a. Mt 10:4 You were one of the twelve apostles.

b. Jn 12:2–6 When the woman anointed Jesus in Bethany, you complained because you thought the money could be put to better use.

c. Mt 26:14–16 You met with the high priests and agreed to hand over Jesus to them for thirty pieces of silver.

d. Mt 26:20–25 You shared a meal with Jesus the evening you betrayed him.

e. Mt 26:47–56 You led the guards to Jesus in the garden of Gethsemane.

f. Mt 27:3–10 Unable to change what you had done, you took your own life.

16. The part of Jesus has been sensitively and successfully played by both men and women.

MICHAEL E. MOYNAHAN, SJ, is director of Gonzaga University in Florence, Italy. He is the author of many books on liturgical drama and mime including *Once Upon a Mystery*, *Once Upon a Miracle*, and *Once Upon a Parable*.

"Kennst du das Land?"

Comments on the Implications of Diverse Settings of a "Lied" of Goethe As a Source of Insight for the Ordinary of the Mass

Louis Weil

During the past several years a considerable amount of literature has been published on the subject of the relation of the arts to the liturgy. Whereas it is obvious that the arts have always played a significant role in the external framework in which the liturgy has been celebrated, the question has been asked as to whether we should speak of the liturgy itself as being an art form. Both in his teaching and in his publications, James Empereur has made important contributions to this discussion and, in fact, offered readers a very helpful summary of the views of a number of writers.[1] In "Is Liturgy an Art Form?" we find this question discussed from a variety of angles. Perhaps most fruitfully, Empereur links the question to the views on art expressed by Hans-Georg Gadamer in *Truth and Method*.[2] Empereur concludes that liturgy is certainly an art form. But what particularly interests me with regard to the subject of this chapter appears with his enumeration of six ways in which Gadamer's claims about art may be applied equally to the liturgy. After discussing each of these points, Empereur says that "in all these ways art and liturgy proceed along identical lines.[3] The reason that this phrase interests me is that often in my own experience, a work of art—what we would usually call a *secular* work of art in that it had no explicit reference to a religious subject, nor, as in a work of music, was based upon a theological or liturgical text—has been the means by which I have come to some new insight on a specifically religious matter. It was just such a moment of new insight that I want to explore in this chapter.

The title I have given to these observations is indicative of an unusual correspondence of which I became aware through my great love of German *lieder*. Of all forms of music, surely the German *lieder* tradition of the nineteenth century would seem to be among the least likely to offer insight into the musical forms of the Eucharist. The former is based upon the poetry of individual emotion and experience, presented through narrative or dramatic enactment in which strong subjective passions are expressed in words which are then transformed by the composer into musical terms. Not surprisingly, this is music for the solo voice, communicating deeply interior and often private meanings. That would hardly serve as a definition of our goals for the music of the liturgy. I am not, of course, going to suggest that we put aside our priorities for liturgical music, that it be expressive of the corporate and public faith of Christians in forms which are shared by the entire assembly. Nor will I suggest that the musical idiom usually associated with *lieder* would be at all appropriate for use in the liturgy. My concern here is with a certain restrictiveness in the various liturgical traditions with regard to the texts of the western rite which are most generally set to music, that is, the Ordinary of the Mass. Although I have occasionally attended celebrations of the Eucharist in which substitutions have been used, even rather unusual substitutions, for one section of the Ordinary or another, and although as an Anglican I have always been aware that even in the most conservative celebrations of the eucharistic rite of the Book of Common Prayer, "some proper Hymn" (BCP 1928) or "some other song of praise" (BCP 1979) might be used in place of the "Gloria in excelsis," I believe that I am typical in having assumed for many years the absolute priority of the normative texts of the Ordinary, so much so that it was common for most priests to recite those texts when a musical setting was not in the repertory of the parish even if an appropriate hymn might well have been sung in its place.

This issue came into focus for me in an unusual way. Over a period of many years, I have attended many recitals of German *lieder*, and I became aware that one particular text of Johann Wolfgang von Goethe had been set to music by several different composers. At that time, I had no idea how many composers had set the text "Kennst du das Land?" to music, but I did know that the few settings of which I was aware had a profound effect upon the way in which the meaning of the text was conveyed. What intrigued me was how the music became more than merely a setting of the text. It was, in fact, an interpretation of the text. A particular style of musical

setting has the power to transform the meaning of the text and to make it into something other, something greater (or less!) than its initial meaning.

I was awakened to this as I heard Goethe's text in a variety of settings. In the *lieder* repertory, the existence of such a large number of settings of the same text is in itself quite unusual. In fact, this is true of the wider range of musical settings. We normally associate a familiar text with a particular melody. A most obvious example of this would be our national anthem. The words of the anthem are indelibly linked for us with a specific melody. In spite of the great difficulty most of us have in singing that melody because of its very wide range, we would be stunned if someone took the words and set them to another melody. The text and melody are bound together for us. This union of a text with a particular melody is generally true of folk songs, of popular songs, and of many songs in the classical repertory. The text and melody are, as it were, of one piece. But this identification of text and melody is not characteristic of our experience of the familiar texts of the Ordinary of the Mass. In fact, quite the opposite. Most of us are accustomed to a variety of settings of the "Kyrie" or "Gloria in excelsis," for example. We simply take for granted that there are many different musical settings of these texts, often in very different styles. This is why the text of Goethe's "Kennst du das Land?" is so unusual. It offers us an almost unique opportunity to observe how strong an impact a musical setting has upon a text. Over the years I had heard the most familiar settings of the text, those by Beethoven, Schumann, and Hugo Wolf, on many occasions. It was only more recently that I discovered that there are more than fifty known settings of this text.[4] Its popularity among composers is perhaps indicative of its broad emotional potential. The poem appears in Goethe's novel *Wilhelm Meister* as a song sung by the young girl, Mignon, expressing her homesickness for Italy, her native land. It would perhaps be helpful to include the original text and a literal translation at this point.

> Kennst du das Land,
>   wo die Zitronen bluehn,
> Im dunkeln Laub
>   die Goldorangen gluehn,
> Ein sanfter Wind

vom blauen Himmel weht,
Die Myrte still und hoch
  der Lorbeer steht?
Kennst du es wohl?
Dahin! Dahin

Moecht ich mit dir,
  o mein Geliebter, ziehn.
Kennst du das Haus?
  Auf Saeulen ruht sein Dach,
Es glaenzt der Saal,
  es schimmert das Gemach,
Und Marmorbilder stehn
  und sehn mich an:
Was had man dir, du armes Kind,
  getan?
Kennst du es wohl?
Dahin! Dahin
Moecht ich mit dir,
  o mein Beschuetzer, ziehn.
Kennst du den Berg
  und seinen Wolkensteg?
Das Maultier sucht im Nebel
  seinen Weg;
In Hoehlen wohnt der Drachen
  alte Brut,
Es stuerzt der Fels und ueber ihn
  die Flut,
Kennst du es wohl?
Dahin! Dahin
Geht unser weg! O Vater,
  lass uns ziehn!

Do you know the land
  where the lemons bloom,
Where golden oranges glow
  among dark leaves,
Where gentle breezes blow
  from the blue sky,
Where the myrtle stands still,
  the laurel high
Do you know it perchance?
There! there
I want to go with you, O my beloved!
Do you know the house?
Its roof rests on columns,
Its hall sparkles, its chambers gleam,

And marble statues stand and look
  at me:
"What have they done to you,
  poor child?"
Do you know it perchance?
There! there
I want to go with you, O my protector!
Do you know the mountain and its path
  amid the clouds?
The mule seeks its way in the mist;
In caverns dwells the dragons'
  ancient brood,
The cliff plunges down and over it
  the torrent.
Do you know it perchance?
There! there
Leads our way! O father, let us go!

Goethe's own opinion of the role of a composer who would set his texts to music was that the purpose of the music was simply to support the poet's words. His idea was that the setting was a kind of musical illustration in which the composer is a servant to the poet. Not surprisingly, great composers, such as Beethoven, did not take to such a role happily, and Goethe is reported not to have valued Beethoven's setting of the text very highly. For Goethe, the ideal was found in the work of a composer now relegated to virtual oblivion, Carl Friedrich Zelter, who wrote no less than six different settings of "Kennst du das Land?" It seems that at least in his earlier views Goethe was not inclined to favor any musical setting which reflected more on the composer than on the poet. Later in his life, however, Goethe's view shifted. He wrote that "A poem is completed only with the addition of music. When a musician has breathed true life into a song, ... a new poem is created that must surprise even the poet." This latter view can be demonstrated forcibly in a comparison of some of the settings of Goethe's text.[5] It must be admitted from the start that many of the more than fifty known settings of Mignon's song are not easily available to us today and may be presumed without too much arrogance not to be comparable to the settings which have endured.

Some brief observations about three of the settings follow. Among the earliest written, not long after the publication of *Wilhelm Meister*, is that of

Beethoven's. Once you have heard some of the later settings, it is difficult to see how this setting did not meet Goethe's own criterion that the music was merely to support the text. Although a very beautiful setting, Beethoven's seems appropriate to the context in which the text appears, a song of a homesick young girl. Were this the only setting, it would be a valued one in the *lieder* repertory, but certainly not a version characterized by the dramatic intensity of other works by Beethoven. The setting by Robert Schumann was written a little later in the nineteenth century and moves the text into a different emotional framework. In the setting by Schumann, we can scarcely imagine that this is the song of a young girl. The emotional tone is much richer, and we feel moved into the context of a more mature passion. This is a setting of enormous beauty, and at least hints at the view of Goethe in his later years that "a new poem is created." Goethe's text here takes on a richer embodiment which is in effect transformative of the text itself.

It is with the setting by Hugo Wolf, written near the close of the nineteenth century, that we find the tentative emotional leap taken by Schumann enlarged to a dazzling degree. This setting towers over all other musical versions of the text in that it achieves the means of moving the text into an entirely distinct sphere of meaning. From the opening measures we know that we are in a different realm. What Wolf has done with Goethe's poem is to take it from its particular context and to make it into a universal *cri de coeur* of the experience of alienation and loss. It is not my intention to suggest that Wolf's version relegates the versions, for example, of Beethoven or Schumann to the trash. All three settings are superb and worthy of performance. My interest here is to note that by the time we reach the emotional world expressed by Wolf, we must ask ourselves if the text is still experienced as the same text as when a different version is sung. Is it not true that, in Goethe's words, "a new poem is created" with a very different impact upon us? If this is true, as I believe it is, then have we taken seriously enough the impact of the variety of musical settings upon the normative texts of the Ordinary of the Mass? In line with Empereur's words quoted earlier, in this comparison we find that "art and liturgy proceed along identical lines." And so we may ask

the question: Are the texts of the Ordinary "the same" when they are sung and heard in significantly different musical styles? The common view that these texts take a primary place as normative elements in the eucharistic rite must be scrutinized if their meaning is transformed through the type of music to which a text is set.

The title of this chapter suggests that the significant impact of a musical setting upon a text, which I found in listening to several versions of the Goethe text, is, I believe, a source of insight with regard to the Ordinary of the Mass. This insight, I believe, may be found in two important aspects of the normative role of the Ordinary in the structure of the Eucharist. The first concerns what we might call the integrity of the text itself: If its place in the tradition is significant, what does this significance require of us with regard to appropriate musical settings? The second implication is a kind of counterpoint, even a dissonant counterpoint, to the first: Given the extreme diversity of settings of the Ordinary which are the heritage of the contemporary church, and given the suggestion that many of these settings do, within the liturgical experience, transform the meaning of the text, can we continue to think of the Ordinary as a normative model in the same way that it has been seen in the past seven centuries? Let us consider both of these questions.

The first issue has to do specifically with the impact of a particular musical setting upon a text. In recent years, considerable attention has been given by church musicians and liturgists to such concerns as the local culture and the character of the musical resources within the local community. I would be among the first to insist upon the importance of these matters as we become more aware of the imperative that the liturgy not be an official "package" imposed by authority which is removed from the lived reality of the community. During the years since Vatican II there has been remarkable growth not only in the Roman Catholic Church but in other liturgical traditions of the importance of shaping the local celebration to reflect the cultural life and resources of the local community. In the name of that priority, however, musical settings have been used which obscured or even trivialized the sense of the text. If a specific text of the Ordinary has the kind of normative character which official authorization implies, then the trivialization of the text is a serious matter. If the official liturgy is the church's "first theology," as liturgists have been emphatic in proclaiming, and if music is not merely an external decoration but is at the most profound level what I would call an "en-fleshment" of the text, then the impact of a particular musical setting upon a text must be seen as an important concern to those who are responsible for shaping a community's public prayer. We are talking about the primary expression of the church's belief. The words which we sing are the words of faith by which we live. Our participation in regular gatherings of the Christian community is formative of us as a people of faith. In this perspective, it seems to me, the trivialization or sentimentalization of that faith in our liturgical assemblies has far-reaching implications.

Such trivialization is not a new issue. Some people are inclined to think that this problem may be narrowly identified with the emergence of guitar Masses and other forms of folk music celebrations. One example will suffice to show that the trivialization of a text can take place even in the context of well-crafted classical compositions. During the eighteenth century, a custom developed among composers, including such important figures as Franz Joseph Haydn, of meeting the requirement of a musical setting of the Ordinary for a High Mass, and yet avoiding the very lengthy settings used on major occasions by dividing a text so that one section of the choir would sing certain phrases of the text while another section would sing a completely different section of the text. Although the church officially frowned at the use of such settings, they were commonly sung, and were popular because they allowed the length of a celebration of a sung Mass to be pruned to a tolerable length. A well-known example of such a setting is Haydn's "Little Organ Mass" (Missa brevis in honorem Sti. Joannis de Deo, Hob. XXII:7). In this work the technique of setting different phrases of a text simultaneously is carried to such a degree that one commentator refers to it as "a drastic missa brevis." The entire text of the "Gloria in excelsis" takes less than one minute to sing, and half of that time is given to the Amen! It is important to note that this is beautifully crafted and quite lovely music. A composer can trivialize a liturgical text with excellent music. The criterion I am raising is one of the integrity of the text itself. When you listen to the Haydn setting, except for the final Amen, it is almost impossible to understand the rest of the text. In a sense, you could say that the text might just as easily be a grocery list. Only in the most superficial sense could you claim that the text of the "Gloria" is engaged as an integral part of the rite.

My second point will seem to be a strange partner to the first. I want to raise a doubt about the normative character of the Ordinary of the Mass as we have received it. When we look at the new liturgical rites in the various liturgical traditions, we find a very conservative approach to those traditional elements; even in the midst of otherwise substantial reforms, we still seem to see these elements as normative, as having a priority of place within the structure of the eucharistic rite. I am certainly not intending here to suggest that these familiar elements be abolished, but in the light of earlier comments about the impact of setting upon text and acknowledging from experience that a different musical setting does create, as it were, "a new poem," I am suggesting that future liturgical reform might aim at a greater simplification of the essential structure of the eucharistic rite with the expectation that the local community would play an important role in determining how that structure would be "en-fleshed" in their assembly.

Any student of the history of the Eucharist knows that the Ordinary of the Mass may be called an artificial construct. Each section of the Ordinary—Kyrie, Gloria in excelsis, Credo, Sanctus, and Agnus Dei—became a part of the eucharistic rite at a different time, and each has its own unique history.[6] Even after the introduction of a *schola* with its special musical role, the people continued to share in the singing, and musical settings remained simple. Even in the later Middle Ages, manuscripts grouped together settings of the "Kyrie" and "Gloria in excelsis," and the idea of grouping the five sections together as the Ordinary came about only as a gradually arising standardization which, we may observe, is a familiar consequence of the extreme clericalization of the liturgy during the same period.

Just as the celebration of the Mass became very much the domain of the priest, so also, for a sung Mass, the musical element became the domain of the choir, and along with that the settings of the Ordinary became increasingly complicated and beyond the capacity of the assembly to perform. In this evolution, of course, the laity were reduced to being observers and listeners, left at best with their private devotions and a piety of vision which focused on the elevation of the sacred elements. This is not said as a denunciation of the medieval liturgical model. We must recognize that it was very much a part of the culture in which it developed. But for us today, we are, I think, obliged to ask if this standardization of the texts known as the Ordinary of the Mass should be seen as a dimension of that highly clerical model and thus be scrutinized in the context of our rediscovery of the eucharistic liturgy as an action of the entire assembly under the pastoral leadership of the ordained.

What I would hope for in future revision is that the inherited model would remain as one option among a range of structural models for the celebration of the Eucharist. For many, of course, it would remain the preferred model, but for others, under the imperatives of the particularities of culture and place, of resources and particular gifts, I can well imagine a model in which a fundamental structure including a rite of gathering, a liturgy of the word, intercessions, a liturgy of the table, and a rite of dismissal might be allowed to include musical elements which correspond to the role they play in a particular part of the rite, but which would not necessarily be based upon the familiar texts of the Ordinary. It is certainly easy to conceive of a hymn or song as part of a gathering rite which would fulfil the purpose of the "Gloria in excelsis" but which would neither require the use of that text nor lead to the trivialization or mere recitation of that text. It will be immediately obvious that two sections of the traditional Ordinary would raise serious concern as to whether alternative forms might be appropriate. These are the "Credo" and the "Sanctus." Since the text of the "Sanctus" had a place in the eucharistic prayer from early, if not the very earliest, times, it is hard to imagine that an appropriate surrogate could be found to replace it within its usual framework. Yet it is certainly possible to allow that a new eucharistic prayer might be created utilizing images with which the traditional form of the "Sanctus" might not find an appropriate role and with which other musical elements, such as sung acclamations by the people, might be more fitting.[7]

The "Credo," given its own particular history and its late incorporation into the Western eucharistic rite, raises the very different question as to whether it belongs in the eucharistic rite as a normative element, which is certainly implied by its incorporation in the Ordinary and its elimination from the *missa brevis* model. The Nicene Creed first appeared in the Western rite only a few centuries prior to the standardization of the Ordinary, and it is perhaps likely that its inclusion with the other elements may well have contributed to an increased frequency in its use, especially when the Mass was sung. When the eucharistic prayer fulfills its proper role as a proclamation of faith, then the need for the "Credo" to be included on a regular basis in the celebration is greatly reduced.[8]

This second point has particular significance with regard to the type of music which would be used in liturgical celebrations. The romanticization of things medieval in the church of the nineteenth century led to the idealization of specific styles of architecture and design, and certainly of liturgical music as being in a preeminent way the church's norm. In the latter decades of the twentieth century we have seen that narrowing of the tradition giving way to the inclusion of artistic elements which are expressive of contemporary culture. But there has remained a kind of uncritical nostalgia for a period when there was greater standardization and stability. That standardization and comparative fixity is suggested even in the usual designation of the five sections as "the Ordinary," thus implying its primacy within the structure of the Western rite. When we come to see the local community and its culture as constitutive of the liturgical model of that community, we are, of course, opening the door to an extraordinary diversity within the life of the church as a whole. For some religious temperaments, this is difficult to accept, so it is not surprising when it is met with resistance. The former claim that the liturgy was the same no matter where one attended Mass in the world—and that was claimed not only by Roman Catholics but also by Anglicans as they exulted in the beauty of their "incomparable liturgy"—was never actually true in fact. For those who spent time in different cultures, it was obvious that the local culture always, to at least some degree, found expression within the celebration. What has changed since Vatican II is that the local culture is coming to be acknowledged as bearing within itself the capacity of expressing the signs of Christian faith, with the recognition that those signs will inevitably find different forms of expression in different cultures. If the *missa normativa* might be conceived not so much in terms of its authorized texts but rather in terms of its structural model, those places in the liturgy in which the Ordinary developed would seem likely to be the primary places where the local culture might be invited to find its own authentic voice.

Such a development would not mean the discarding of our inherited musical traditions, but it would place those traditions within a much wider spectrum of musical styles. Many years ago, the contemporary Italian composer Luigi Dallapiccola commented that the composer of today has unprecedented resources available when undertaking musical composition. It is, Dallapiccola said, like the task of an artist who has an enormous palette on which there is a great range of colors, and the challenge to the artist is to determine which colors and styles are appropriate to the work at hand. This, it seems to me, might serve as a metaphor for those who have responsibility for planning the liturgical celebrations of a community. The tradition upon which we draw need not be understood as a set piece determined in details through official directives. Rather, the whole tradition of Christian worship is our resource—and the gifts and cultural realities of each community are the counterpoint. Working together, these two elements will lead to liturgical models which are both faithful to the best of the tradition and at the same time reflective of the lives of the people gathered to pray.

Discography

For readers who would like to listen to some of the music which has been mentioned in this chapter, a brief list of recommendations follows:

Settings of Goethe's Text "Kennst du da Land?"

There is a recording of all of Beethoven's *lieder* by Hermann Prey and others in which this setting is included. The setting by Robert Schumann is found in a recording by Lorraine Hunt on which all of Mignon's songs are set by Schumann are included. Also, the version by Schumann may be found on a recording of Goethe *lieder* by Mozart, Schubert and Wolf, as well as Schumann, as sung by Dawn Upshaw. The setting by Hugo Wolf may be found in a number of recordings, but the finest performances in my opinion are those of Elizabeth Schwarzkopf, Arleen Auger, and Elly Ameling. Even with these recordings by three great artists one can find the differences of emotional intensity between one performer and another.

Recordings of the Haydn Missa Brevis

I can particularly recommend the recording by the Wiener Akademie. As an interesting contrast, you might also listen to Haydn's "Mass of St. Cecelia" or the "Lord Nelson Mass," which are full-blown settings of considerable length. As beautiful as these works are, they do give us some understanding of the demand for abbreviated settings.

Notes

1. James Empereur, "Is Liturgy an Art Form?", *Liturgical Ministry* 5 (Summer, 1996): 97–107.

2. Ibid. 104–107. Empereur refers to a doctoral dissertation of Mons A. Teig in demonstrating the appropriateness of applying Gadamer's views to the question at hand.

3. Ibid. 107.

4. Willi Schuh, *Goethe-Vertonungen* (Zurich: Artemis-Verlag), 44, no. 381.

5. A list of recordings of works mentioned in this chapter are listed at the end of this chapter. Readers may find it helpful to listen to some of the works which have shaped the ideas suggested here.

6. See the discussion of this question in *Music in the Middle Ages* by Gustave Reese (New York: Norton, 1940), 183.

7. A thorough examination of the place of the "Sanctus" in the eucharistic prayer may be found in *The Sanctus in the Eucharistic Prayer* by Bryan D. Spinks (Cambridge: Cambridge University Press, 1991).

8. For a fuller discussion of this issue, please see my essay, "Proclamation of Faith in the Eucharist,"*Time and Community*, ed. J. Neil Alexander (Washington, D.C.: Pastoral Press, 1990): 279–290.

LOUIS WEIL is professor of liturgics at Church Divinity School of the Pacific and chairs the doctoral faculty in liturgical studies at the Graduate Theological Union. He is author of *Sacraments and Liturgy* and *Gathered to Pray* and co-author of *Liturgy for Living*.

The Christian Worshiping Community and the Confucian Art of "Li"

Timothy D. Hoare

During the 1997 Christmas season I saw a television commercial in which two parents are attempting to assemble a bicycle for their daughter on Christmas Eve. After searching desperately for the instruction sheet, they conclude that it is missing from the box. Completely unarmed and helpless in the face of an ominous array of parts on the floor, they resign themselves to defeat. The daughter, however, has been eavesdropping on this drama from upstairs. She quickly runs into her bedroom, brings her computer online, locates the website for this particular bicycle manufacturer, and prints out a copy of the missing instruction sheet. Returning to the stairway landing, she quietly flings it over the railing. It comes to rest in the middle of the living room floor where her parents "discover" it with a sigh of relief. This was a clever and well-done piece of advertising (for computers, not for bicycles). And while I would agree that it is probably not advisable to attempt to assemble a bicycle without the guidance of step-by-step instructions, it occurs to me that this scenario is also a subtle affirmation of an overall methodology that has largely shaped our posttechnological consciousness: linearity. From as early as kindergarten, are we not taught the value of *lines* as indicators of rationalism, organization, and control? People must stand in a line. Desks are placed in a line. We learn to write on lines, to color within lines. The shortest distance between two points is a line. And in no time at all we learn to apply this linear methodology to more abstract agenda in time and space:

- ⇝ And then what happened? (stories, jokes, experiences, history)
- ⇝ What happens next? (ritual, ceremony)
- ⇝ What is the next step? (instructions, directions, recipes, education)
- ⇝ What will happen if I do this? (ethics and morality)
- ⇝ What should happen if this happens first? (scientific method)
- ⇝ What do I want to happen? (magic, supplication, manipulation)

In such ways as these, our consciousness is governed by the linear relationship of cause and effect, always focused one step ahead of, or one step behind, each act we perform. In other words, the very integrity or worth of many of our human activities is measured by how well they fulfill a future goal or respond to a previous condition. We play games in order to win them. We undertake an education in order to graduate in order to get a good job. We work in order to have money in order to have leisure. The list could go on indefinitely.

In the same manner, it seems to me that ritual activity is usually performed in accordance with this linear consciousness, either as a means of effecting a desirable end, averting an undesirable condition, or as a mechanical protocol that is mindless and yet somehow important to the given context. This is especially true in the case of Christian worship in the Reformed tradition. The very appellation, "Order of Worship" suggests a linear progression of events that is intended to achieve a certain end. Over a period of five hundred years, has the Reformed directive to "do all things decently and in order" reduced the liturgy to a quantitative step-by-step instruction sheet for assembling bicycles?

As a Presbyterian minister, I indeed value many qualities of my Reformed heritage. At the same time, however, I recognize that one of the greatest sins of Protestantism historically has been its iconoclastic distrust of the sensuous and, in turn, its traditionally shallow understanding of the transcendent power of the symbolic in ritual and worship. While reform was indeed a necessary response to the abuse of icon, image, and ecclesial authority, I question the direction in which that response has taken us. But I do not fault the Reformers themselves as much as I suspect the tradition's misappropriation of their agenda. As Margaret Miles has pointed out in her work on the history of Christian imagery,[1] written history, itself a product of linear consciousness, will tend to define and shape the destiny of a theological tradition by focusing, for example, on what John Calvin said here or Ulbrecht Zwingli said there as being indicative of "how it was" throughout Northern European Christendom. So much so, in fact, that Calvin is remembered only for such things as referring to the human mind as "a constantly working idol factory," while it is rarely if ever mentioned that Zwingli was a fine musician who loved good church music. When a statement such as Calvin's took root in the Reformed tradition as something akin to Scripture, it effectively denied the fact that human consciousness and imagination function metaphorically and that metaphorical or symbolic thinking is dependent upon a certain degree of sensuous reality. I find it hard to believe that the likes of Calvin and Zwingli would not acknowledge and accept this as so. In any case, in our ensuing introspection and preoccupation with the linearity of the written text, whether scriptural, liturgical, or historical, the non-linear, symbolic power of art and ritual has been regarded as something of a distraction and even today survives in many Protestant congregations as a kind of novel curiosity that we may invite into the sanctuary now and again to keep attendance up.

While I regard myself as a generalist in religious studies, I am an Asianist at heart. My previous work[2] dealt with the aesthetic and religious dimensions of the classical masked theater of Thailand as an ideal model of ritual performance with which to address this same question in the performance of Christian worship. I have drawn particularly on Susanne Langer's aesthetic theory of symbol[3] and Paul Tillich's theology of art.[4] Both Langer and Tillich were concerned with how we tend to fall prey to linearity, in that we mistakenly believe that symbolic expressions of artistic and religious significance must somehow point toward, indicate, or "mean" something beyond their own embodiments. In short, we reduce the qualitative power of the symbolic to the merely quantitative function of signification. In my introductory religion classes, I often use my wedding ring as an example because it illustrates both capacities. On the discursive level, my ring is a quantitative sign which simply means that I am a married man. Like a stop sign means "stop here and now," the ring directly indicates the marital state of the wearer. On the nondiscursive level, however, it is a qualitative symbol that, in relation to my experience and to that of my Thai wife, embodies the innumerable feelings and emotions of a marriage—the laughter and tears, the comedy and tragedy, the intercultural and bilingual joys, and occasional mix-ups that I could never begin to articulate because they dwell within the ineffable realm of the absolute.

So also, both art and ritual performance are necessarily composed of certain quantities (for example, color, mass, line, movement, time, space, etcetera), but what they express in relation to one another is a quality that is beyond the sum of the parts. The Thai classical masked theater, for example, is not composed of masks and movements that merely indicate or describe; rather, *in relation*, mask and movement embody and express the very core of the Thai identity as a quality of aesthetic, cultural and, in the broad sense of the term, religious significance. When they are at their best, art and ritual are not about absolute quantities in and of themselves but about the discerning of the absolute within the relational qualities that are created among them. In transcending the quantitative, they transcend linearity. In aesthetic theory and our perception of the visual and the performative arts, this is what the expression "form (quantity) and content (quality)" is all about. The form is a compilation of elements whose interrelationship creates a content that is discernible within, but not separable from, the form. Content is like an illusion, an apparency, whose presence is felt.

Inasmuch as I am a proponent of the fine arts in Christian worship, it is yet my contention that Christian worship will not be a vital context *for* the arts until we can recover and experience Christian worship itself *as* an art. As both clergy and laity alike, we need to explore more fully our overall sensibility of Christian worship as a medium of ritual performance that transcends linearity and whose integrity dwells in the existential event of its own enactment. But what is the content that is generated in and through the elements that form the experience of worship? What is created or made apparent in the enactment

that was not there before? The answer is, I believe, found in the relational nature of Christian worship itself.

After having spent some time teaching in the field of comparative studies in religion and fine arts, I have come across an additional aesthetic approach, also of Asian origin, that has proved helpful in shedding some light on this question. It is found within the Chinese tradition of Confucianism.

Regarded as the supreme editor of Chinese culture, Kung Fu Tze or Confucius (551–479 BCE), envisioned a social order whose integrity and well-being are grounded in a consciously cultivated awareness of ethical conduct, compassion, justice, and education as fundamental to the development of the relational human being. At first glance, such virtuous ideas may appear to be so abstract as to be almost trite. Indeed, a cursory reading of the *Analects* seems only to support such an evaluation. On one level, it can be said that the more abstractly the virtue is expressed, the more universal is its application to the life experience of any given person for his or her contemplation. But in order to appreciate fully the profound influence of Confucian humanism on Chinese culture, one must also understand the social context to which he responded.

Confucius lived during a time when social cohesion in China had deteriorated into anarchy. Following the collapse of the highly cultured Zhou Dynasty in the eighth century BCE, rival states of the fragmented confederation were left to their own devices. Traditionally held codes of chivalry and honor gave way to unrestrained brutality and an utter disregard for the basic human rights of conquered peoples. Genocide of entire populations was not unheard of. Then, as now, the question for Confucius was this: What, if anything, can prevent us from destroying one another? What is the "glue" that holds society together?

At the most fundamental level of human relation, he surmised, it is spontaneous tradition, that is, the customary behavior that simply evolves and takes shape over time through trial and error. No one sits down and determines tradition; it happens of its own accord and is transmitted through the culture. Whether we abide by it or not, most of us simply "know," for example, what sort of attire or behavior is appropriate for a given context. At the same time, however, few if any of us would be able to articulate clearly when and how we learned these things, except perhaps to say, "That is how I was brought up." There is no conscious effort at socialization on this level and yet it happens. Generally speaking, the expectations and assumptions of the corporate whole are so strong that they are accepted and internalized without question.

And yet, in every age and in every culture, there inevitably arises a transitional crisis in which the assumptions of the community or tribe are forced to give way to a new plane of awareness: that of the individual. This is precisely what occurred after the fall of the Zhou Dynasty. Says Huston Smith:

> China had reached a new point in its
> social evolution, a point marked
> by the emergence of large numbers
> of individuals in the full sense of that
> word. Self-conscious rather than
> group-conscious, these individuals
> had ceased to think of themselves
> primarily in the first person plural
> and were thinking of the first person
> singular. Reason was replacing social
> conventions, and self-interest
> outdistancing the expectations
> of the group. The fact that others
> were behaving in a given way or that
> their ancestors had done so from time
> immemorial could no longer be relied
> on as sufficient reason for individuals
> to follow suit. Proposals for action
> had now to face peoples' question,
> "What's in it for me?"[5]

Needless to say, how you handle such a crisis depends on where your loyalties dwell. In the West, for example, we embrace individualism in an almost cultic manner. The distinction between, say, a masked crimefighter and a masked criminal is one of name only: They are both above the law and therefore celebrated. In any case, Confucius, while perceiving that spontaneous tradition was no longer a reliable assumption, continued to focus on the principles of tradition as the primary shapers of socialization and values. But apparently here to stay, how could individualism be recognized and yet remain somehow continuous with the ancient models of graceful, ethical behavior? The only alternative was that the perception of tradition must shift from an unconscious to a conscious mode. Confucius referred to it as *deliberate* tradition: an ethical awareness of, and respect for, each other that is reinforced through conscious effort. Again, it is all too easy to reduce this to a triviality. But the point is not simply that one should work hard at being graceful and ethical in relation to others. The significance of deliberate tradition is found in what it suggests about the nature of the self in the context of relation. Self and other become so intimately bound to one another and consciously present to one another that the act of relation in itself becomes the medium from which the self is constructed. This is what the Confucian art of *Li* is about.

I refer to *Li* as an "art." *Li* is not an art in the strict sense of the word. But I apply the term "artistic" (and "religious," for that matter) in the same sense that I apply the term "symbolic:" any object, enactment, or experience that transcends the time and space of the elements of which it is comprised has artistic, religious, and symbolic import. Explicitly, art and religion are symbolic forms. Implicitly, all symbolic forms have artistic and religious import.

Li is a most interesting concept in Confucian thought because it unites what were once two distinctive ideas. Prior to Confucius, the conventional meaning of the term *Li* was equivalent to "sacred ritual," usually in reference to rituals of sacrifice in service to spiritual beings or ancestors. This would certainly be a term with which Confucius' contemporaries would be familiar. What Confucius did with this was quite remarkable: He appropriated the language and imagery of *Li* as metaphors for talking about the ancient traditions and conventions of graceful, ethical behavior in human relationships. In so doing, he presents human relation itself as a ritual act. By way of comparison, consider the Johannine appropriation of the divine *Logos*. Already a widely understood philosophical concept throughout Hellenistic culture, it served as a profound metaphor for the communication of the salvific act of God in the person of Jesus Christ.

Let us now examine *Li* in greater detail. What does it mean to approach ritual enactment consciously? Primarily, it means that the enactment must "take place;" one has "to be there." There is life and vitality in ritual performance when the individuals are wholly present to its enactment.

If I am not present at the sacrifice, it is as though there were no sacrifice.[6]

Confucius went into the great national shrine and asked about everything. Someone remarked, "Who says that old man knows the classical rites? When he goes to the great shrine, he asks about everything." Hearing this, Confucius said, "This is part of the ritual."[7]

The failure of *Li*, or more accurately, your failure to act according to *Li*, may be attributed to at least three limitations that are symptomatic of linearity: (a) the enactment may be performed awkwardly for lack of familiarity with it; (b) the performance may be so slick as to be utterly mindless; and (c) it may be carried out solely for the sake of efficaciousness. In all three of these scenarios, the participant is not a participant at all but a bystander, because he or she is not consciously present. Confucius gives new meaning to the oft-heard quip, "I guess you had to be there."

Once this spirit of ritual presentness is understood, it must be applied to the more mundane experiences of human relation. Consider, for example, all that is involved in an act so seemingly simple as a handshake:

> I see you on the street; I smile,
> walk toward you, put out my hand
> to shake yours. And behold—without
> any command, stratagem, force,
> special trick, or tools, without any effort
> on my part to make you do so,
> you spontaneously turn toward me,
> return my smile, raise your hand
> toward mine. We shake hands—not
> by my pulling your hand up and
> down or your pulling mine but
> by spontaneous and perfect cooperative
> action. Normally we do not notice
> the subtlety and amazing complexity
> of this coordinated "ritual" act.
> This subtlety and complexity become
> very evident, however, if one has had
> to earn the ceremony only from a book

of instructions, or if one is a foreigner from a nonhandshaking culture.[8]

Strangely, the ritual import of this act and others like it is often made known to us through our ineptness. We have all experienced logistically awkward situations in which we have been carrying, say, a large box and, rather than forgoing the act altogether, have felt that we had no choice but to extend the wrong hand in a clumsily improvised attempt at propriety. I have been in similarly awkward positions in Thailand where handshaking is rarely practiced. Thais greet one another with a *wai*. With a slightly forward inclination of the head, they bring the open palms together in a prayerlike position in front of the upper body. The subtleties include such criteria as who initiates the gesture, the position of the hands at any number of elevations between the sternum and the forehead (depending on the status of the recipient), how long the position is sustained, and even how rigidly the fingers and palms are pressed together. If the hands are the least bit encumbered, the *wai* becomes a formidable challenge. Just as the Westerner can imply and infer myriad messages from the tactile quality of a handshake, so also can the Thai from the visual quality of a *wai*. The forms are mundane; the content is sacred.

> These complex but familiar gestures
> are characteristic of human
> relationships at their most human;
> we are least like anything else in the
> world when we do not treat each other
> as physical objects, as animals or even
> as subhuman creatures to be driven,
> threatened, forced, maneuvered.
> Looking at these "ceremonies"
> through the image of *Li*, we realize
> that explicitly sacred rite can be seen
> as an emphatic, intensified and sharply
> elaborated extension of everyday
> *civilized* intercourse.[9]

What Confucius is ultimately saying is that *Li* transcends linearity. When it is at its best, human relation is never self-serving, exploitative, or manipulative. Infused with the spirit of *Li*, human relation fulfills its end in the irreducible, existential event of its own enactment. Confucius makes a similar point concerning the efficiency of language in relation to thought and act. This is the doctrine of *Cheng Ming*, or the "rectification of terms":

> Tsze-lu said, "The ruler of Wei
> has been waiting for you, in order
> with you to administer the government.
> What will you consider the first thing
> to be done?" The Master replied,
> "What is necessary is to rectify names
> ... If terms be not correct, language
> is not in accordance with the truth
> of things. If language is not in
> accordance with the truth of things,
> affairs cannot be carried out to success.
> Therefore, a superior [person]
> considers it necessary that the
> names [one] uses may be spoken
> appropriately, and also that what
> [one] speaks may be carried out
> appropriately."[10]

In the naming of titles, the making of requests, the giving of descriptions, and so forth, your use of language should be so efficient and semantically precise that thought/intention, utterance, and fulfillment/enactment are perceived by all concerned as virtually one in the same thing. Ritual word becomes ritual act. If I speak my words according to *Li*, there should be no occasion for my hearer to say to himself or herself, "Just what did he mean by that?" The underlying premise, of course, is that I, as a practitioner of *Li*, would never utilize my language in an "artful" manner, that is, as a tool of deception.

Before placing a template of the Christian worshiping community over our analysis of *Li*, we should touch briefly upon some basic theological presuppositions of the Judeo-Christian tradition that reflect a strong affinity to this Confucian ideal. Consider the Confucian relationship between language and act (*Cheng Ming*), as just described. It is a fundamental premise of biblical theology that in Israel's experience of YHWH, divine word and divine act are in a sense the same thing (cf. the Hebrew *debar* and the Greek *logos*). As the priestly writer repeatedly declares in the Genesis creation account, "And God said ... and it was so." This is by no means a linear statement of cause and effect. The *word* of God is in itself the very act or fulfillment of divine will. The *word* of God is the instance of divine self-disclosure. As such, it becomes the theological basis for the unity of form and content on which the entire Christian faith is based: the incarnation in Jesus Christ.

As the Council of Nicaea struggled so tediously to articulate in 325, Jesus Christ is fully human and yet of the same substance as God. On the linear plane of thinking, this is an ambiguity that the Western sensibility, in the twenty first century as well as the fourth, is tempted to resolve into binary closure (for example, half God/half mortal, God hidden in a mortal shell, and so forth). But to do so would be to reduce Jesus to the level of a semi-divine "god-man," often a politically-conferred status with which the ancient Hellenistic world had long been familiar via victorious athletes, military leaders, and the like. The incarnation, however, is a more complex symbolic expression in which the totality of God—not a half of God—is disclosed to the world through the finitude—but also the totality—of humankind. And while we generally restrict the significance of this idea to the person and identity of Jesus Christ alone, was this not the original covenantal intention for God's people as a whole? As theologian Aiden Nichols suggests, the significance of the incarnation is grounded in a much older and more broadly applied scriptural metaphor of the priestly creation account, that is, humankind created "in the image of God" (Gn 1:26–27):

> Images are conspicuous by their
> absence in the normative form
> of the religion of Yahweh, God of Israel.
> Since God may not be directly imaged
> in the cult there are no obvious
> candidates for the title "image of God"
> Yahweh can in some sense be seen
> in Israel, by means of the "form"
> of the existence of [Yahweh's] servants
> the prophets .... Both of these facets
> lie present in the implicit structure
> of the Priestly work. It outlines a cult
> where Yahweh is nowhere iconically
> represented, and it teaches
> the imagehood of God in [humankind]

while consistently avoiding
anthropomorphic language
about God.[11]

Just as *Li* calls upon the human community to be the multi-faceted vessel of ancient traditions and conventions of graceful, ethical behavior, so also YHWH's people, individually and collectively, are intended to "image" God, to be channels of grace, in their relationships to one another:

> The image of Holy Rite as a metaphor
> for human existence brings foremost
> to our attention the dimension of the
> holy in [human] existence .... Rite
> brings out forcefully not only the
> harmony and beauty of social forms,
> the inherent and ultimate dignity
> of human intercourse; it brings out
> also the moral perfection implicit
> in achieving one's ends by dealing
> with others as beings of equal dignity
> .... It is this beautiful and dignified,
> shared and open participation with
> others who are ultimately like oneself
> that [human beings] realize
> [themselves]. Thus perfect [human
> community]—the Confucian analogue
> to Christian [community]—becomes
> an inextricable part, the chief aspect,
> of Divine worship—again an analogy
> with the central law taught by Jesus.[12]

The central law taught by Jesus? Love God and love your neighbor.[13] Essentially, Jesus is telling his inquirers that the integrity of one depends upon the other. One is by necessity an inextricable quality of the other. Just as Confucius recovered ancient tradition and applied it within new relational contexts, so also Jesus reaffirmed that which has been so all along and yet has been forgotten or compromised. Love of God and neighbor: Has this not been the message of the Torah from the beginning? As the first-century CE Pharisaic leader Hillel is said to have expressed it, "All the rest is commentary."[14]

It is therefore ironic that while we articulate our Christian faith in and through the incarnation, we often overlook this incarnational character that is intended to be implicit in the performance of Christian worship. When we approach worship as a mere compilation of absolute quantities, that is, a linear arrangement of steps, texts, hymns, movements, persons, and objects to be utilized and carried out in a particular place, in a particular order, and for a particular end, we fail to discern the relational qualities that are "incarnated" among them. The Gospel of Matthew is not just being sentimental when it records Jesus as declaring, "For where two or three are gathered in my name, there am I in the midst of them."[15] To put it another way, we do not gather in the house of God; rather, "Christians and Jews, scattered peoples, with only themselves as temples, gather to house God's presence."[16]

But if this incarnational quality is central to both Judaic Law and Christian worship, let us make no mistake about what Jesus is suggesting about the nature of this gathering. Within the context of relation—the "house" of God's presence—Jesus reveals grace, dignity, and personhood in those who have little else:

> A man once gave a great banquet,
> and he invited many, and at the time
> for the banquet he sent his servant
> to say to those who had been invited,
> "Come; for all is now ready." But they
> all alike began to make excuses ....
> Then the householder said in anger
> to his servant, "Go quickly to the
> streets and the lanes of the city, and
> bring in the poor and maimed and blind
> and lame." And the servant said,
> "Sir, what you commanded has been
> done, and still there is room." And the
> master said to the servant, "Go out
> to the highways and hedges and compel
> people to come in, that my house may
> be filled"[17]

In Jesus' ministry, the table that Jesus shares with the downtrodden and the dispossessed becomes a primary context for revelatory disclosure of the kingdom. The Lukan parable presents Jesus' table as an overarching metaphor that is intended to inform and shape the relational quality of the worshiping community itself.

Did Confucius intend for *Li* to be understood as an expression of this same egalitarian spirit? For all the attention given to the sacramental quality of relation, is it possible that the proper practice of *Li* remains contingent upon each participant "knowing his or her place" within the socio-political strata? In a sense we may say that this is so, but not in the disenfranchising manner in which we are accustomed to interpreting such a statement. As a basis of *Cheng Ming*, (the rectification of terms), Confucius identified "the five constant relationships" as husband and wife, parent and child, older and younger siblings, older and younger friends, ruler and subject (the last from which I would speculate we could further infer employer and employee/teacher and student). When they are at their best, these relationships are not grounded in an arrogant presumption of power of one over another but in the mutual responsibility and respect of one for another. The loyalty of a man or woman to his or her partner, of a child to a parent, of one sibling to another, of one friend to another, of a subject to a ruler is only as strong as the desire and willingness of each party to lift up and preserve the dignity and the personhood of the other, regardless of who, if anyone, holds the position of temporal authority. This is no less so in the Christian worshiping community. Our pastoral authority is only as valid as our self-identity as a servant of the congregation. Our worshipful relationship to God is only as valid as our ethical relationship to others, both within and without the congregation. The integrity of the sacramental object and/or action is only as valid as our relational consciousness of each other as we corporately partake.

In the case of both Confucian *Li* and Christian worship, perhaps this is at best an elusive vision of what ought to be, what occasionally is, and yet usually isn't. As such, the difference between this relational ideal and its linear corruption, that is, liturgies, sacraments, and persons reduced to instrumental means to an end, is as minute and yet as vital as the slightest shift of an airfoil that can send a plane into the heavens or into a nosedive. The optimum path or trajectory is not so much something seen as it is something felt. In a similar manner, it is a basic truth of religion and art that, even if only for the most fleeting of moments, you experience the qualitative feeling of being simultaneously freed and challenged by the power of grace. Indeed, the freedom of grace gives us hope, but only insofar as the challenge of grace keeps us honest. When Confucian *Li* and Christian worship embrace and celebrate the creative tension of both paths, the tension itself is a channel of revelation. I am reminded of political theorist Jean-Jacques Rousseau; while known primarily for his writings on the delicate balance of individual freedom with responsibility to the sovereign state, Rousseau's words nevertheless ring true in the case of our tendency to resist vulnerability to the simultaneous freedom and challenge of grace: If we are to understand that the self as a fully developed individual is sculpted from the medium of our ethical responsibility to each other, sometimes we must be "forced to be free."[18] And is it not strange that the single greatest obstacle to this liberating challenge of grace is not an atheistic denial of God, nor a misanthropic denial of others, but a subjective hatred of self?

In his 1996 PBS series, *The Wisdom of Faith* religious historian Huston Smith shared a memory with Bill Moyers from his early childhood in China that reflects the very point that Christian worship and Confucian *Li* are both making. He described the Chinese primary school primers from which he learned to read and compared them to those from which Western children have been taught, that is, the stories of "Dick and Jane," et al. The Dick and Jane stories are primarily concerned with the development of the linear awareness of time and space as objective perceptions that tend to distinguish and separate one person, place, or thing from another. In stark contrast, the Chinese primers focused on the immediate and subjective relationships between persons, places, and things. While Dick and Jane might observe, "See Spot run. Run, run, run!" the Chinese would declare, "This is my family's dog. We love our dog."[19] The existential immediacy of relation is gracefully lifted up as holiness.

When I was in elementary school in Kansas City, my class went on a museum tour of Asian art during which I heard an old Chinese story that has remained with me for some thirty-five years. A boy and his father are carrying the boy's grandfather up to the top of a mountain on a wooden stretcher. He is old and crippled and they are going to leave him up there to die. As soon as they arrive, the boy tilts his grandfather off the stretcher onto the rocky ground, puts the stretcher under his arm, and begins to make his way back down the mountain. The boy's father stares at him in disbelief and says, "Why did you do that? Can't your grandfather at least have something to lay his head upon during these, the last days of his life?" The boy answered, "But Father, we'll need this stretcher when my son and I bring you up here."

With that, the boy and his father brought the grandfather back home to live his final days in dignity with his family.

As a worshiping community, we are at our qualitative best when we discern that the sanctuary of God is not our dwelling place. Rather, we, in our gathering and in our relationships with each other, are God's dwelling place.

Notes

1. M. Miles, *Image As Insight* (Boston: Beacon Press, 1985).

2. T. Hoare, *Pulling the Siamese Dragon* (Lanham, Md.: University Press of America, 1997).

3. S. Langer, *Feeling and Form* (New York: Charles Scribner's Sons, 1953).

4. P. Tillich, *On Art and Architecture*, Jane and John Dillenberger, eds. (New York: Crossroads, 1987).

5. H. Smith, *The World's Religions* (San Francisco: Harper Collins, 1991), 162–163.

6. *Analects* III: 12.

7. *Analects* III: 15.

8. H. Fingarette, *Confucius—The Secular as Sacred* (New York: Harper and Row, 1972), 9.

9. Ibid. 11.

10. *Analects* XIII: 3.

11. A. Nichols, *The Art of God Incarnate* (New York: Paulist Press, 1980), 13–14.

12. Fingarette 16.

13. cf. Mt 22:35–40.

14. Quoted in S. Harris, *Understanding the Bible* (Mountain View, Calif.: Mayfield, 1997), 291.

15. Mt 18:20 RSV.

16. J. Burkhart, *Worship* (Philadelphia: Westminster, 1980), 38.

17. Lk 14:16–18, 21–23 RSV.

18. Jean-Jacques Rousseau, "The Social Contract," Book I, Chapter 7.

19. Contemporary Thai primary school primers tend to emphasize these same subjective relationships.

TIMOTHY D. HOARE is assistant professor of humanities and religion at Johnson County Community College in Overland Park, Kansas, and an ordained Presbyterian minister. His publications include *Pulling the Siamese Dragon: Performance As a Theological Agenda for Christian Ritual Praxis* and *I Am, I Am Not, I Am Not Not: The Mask As Metaphor in the Arts and Humanities*.

The Role of the Arts in Worship

Joan Carter

When religious imagination
is the dominant force in society,
art is scarcely separable from it ...
indifference to art is the most serious
sign of decay in any institution.[1]

Art has always had a major role to play in giving life and meaning to faith communities everywhere. Without the arts, religious experience can become caught up in a form of literalism that makes no allowance for the depth dimension in religious practice. But when art is incorporated into the worship and spiritual practices of a community, it evokes an experience of the sacred that is beyond rational thought. Art discloses a deeper level of meaning than that normally called forth by other modes of language. It has the power to do this because art is symbolic in nature. An important key to understanding how visual art can function in a spiritual context then, lies in an understanding of the nature of symbols.

Paul Tillich describes the nature of symbols by identifying six common characteristics:

1. symbols point beyond themselves to an absent reality
2. symbols participate in the reality to which they point
3. symbols open up levels of that reality which would otherwise remain closed
4. symbols unlock dimensions and elements of one's soul which correspond to the dimensions and elements of reality
5. symbols cannot be produced intentionally
6. symbols grow and they die.[2]

The first two characteristics are commonly referred to in any discussion of symbols. The first identifies the one element that symbols have in common with signs, and the second discloses what sets them apart from signs. Arbitrarily chosen, a sign functions on the surface pointing to an absent reality. It is the nature of a symbol to penetrate the surface and to make accessible an otherwise absent reality.

The third and fourth characteristics are not easy to explain in print. They are easier to understand at the level of experience in which one comes to "know" on an intuitive level that which is difficult to articulate on an intellectual level. These two characteristics, functioning together, give a symbol its transforming potential. But while a symbol opens up new levels of reality, those levels are only accessible when there has been a corresponding unlocking of the dimensions and elements of the soul that correspond to the dimensions and elements of those realities.

The two final characteristics set out by Tillich are also inter-related. The sixth, and final characteristic, that symbols follow a natural pathway of birth, maturation and death, is a consequence of the fifth, that symbols cannot be invented or arbitrarily chosen. They come into being when the time and the situation are right for them to emerge, and they die when they lose their force. But, as Tillich cautions, "symbols do not grow because people are longing for them, and they do not die because of scientific or practical criticism. They die because they can no longer produce a response in the group where they originally found expression."[3]

A grave danger is posed when symbols that are no longer efficacious are allowed to remain in force. When symbols no longer "symbolize," they can lead to a literalistic world view in which their surface or literal meaning becomes mistaken for the reality itself.

This crisis in meaning is attested to by Jake Empereur: "In moving away from the identifying and comforting symbols of the past, we have found ourselves no longer able to make use of the old, but have not been able to integrate the new. There is even some question whether these new symbols exist."[4] Based upon the growing unrest that is surfacing in many spiritual communities today, it seems safe to say that all of the new symbols needed to connect the worshiper with the sacred are not only not yet in place; they may only now be entering the gestation period.

It is important to recognize, however, that failing symbols provide us with a creative potential as well as a dark side. Symbols that have lost their force as beliefs can indeed be replaced by new symbols. However, what is needed are not symbols whose references are direct and specific; what is needed are symbols that are so elemental that they can move beyond subjectivity and into the depth dimension beyond all surface concerns; what is needed are symbols so elemental that they move beyond doctrine and a set of specific beliefs.[5]

It is on the level of elemental symbols that the arts can make their greatest contribution. They invite those who are willing to enter the symbol's realm into an encounter with reality that is not restricted to an intellectual assent of a particular dogma or creed. The result of this kind of encounter, because it is deeply experiential, is transforming. Caught up in the symbol's power to transform, the individual experiences a new ground of being that affects every area of his or her life. To open the way to that kind of transforming encounter is the task and calling of a spiritual community as it gathers in worship to re-enact the Christian myth in all of its richness.

In many ways, worship is like a game—a game with sacred space and sacred time as important constructs. It is a valuable game in which the worshiping community sets out to rehearse and practice, work and act, and then play its way into the "Kingdom of God." Human beings begin in early childhood the process of rehearsing their way into new states of being for as Tom Driver, former Professor of Theology and Culture at Union Seminary, reminds us, "the necessity to act or rehearse one's way into a new state of being seems to be imperative for our entire species ... the being of humanity is a becoming. We become what we learn by doing."[6] In other words, we become what we experience through a form of playing it out, by opening ourselves to experiment or as Driver says, "to produce and reproduce, invent and repeat, try things this way and that until a response, either from oneself or from outside, gives satisfaction.[7]

One of the impediments to this kind of ritual exploration comes about in part because the possibilities that reside in "kingdom living" are so far removed from the realities which surround us. Each of us lives in a world of practical everyday realities—one that often results in a pre-occupation that takes extraordinary means to break through. When allowed to function as symbols, the arts have the power to disengage those lost in self absorption. The arts do not guide an observer to something tangible and practical; they invite the setting aside of the everyday world and its concerns in favor of a world of possibility and newness. In Empereur's words, "They provide us with a window on reality ... an alternate world which we can enter to find there the meaning of our usual ordinary world."[8] They do this because in their role as symbols, the arts create a detachment from actuality—an otherness that Langer labels as "virtual reality," a reality that is for perception only. It is this aloofness from reality— a kind of psychical distancing—that gives the symbol its transparent nature inviting contemplation and an entertaining of alternate ways of being in the world.

Driver reminds us of ritual's role in this symbolizing process: "To ritualize," he says, "is to make or utilize a pathway through what would otherwise be uncharted territory."[9] But there is also an inherent danger in ritual action. When any given act of ritualizing becomes so familiar that its action becomes rote, it ceases to serve as a pathway and becomes merely a shelter. Its symbolic power to open up multiple, ever deepening layers of meaning becomes trapped in proscribed rules and traditions that no longer have meaning for the individual engaged in its action. The question for us then becomes, are we sensitive enough to leave in place those that still serve as guides, courageous enough to open to new forms those that have become only shelters for the status quo and wise enough to know the difference? Driver encourages the attempt when he says:

> Ours is an age that needs both the marking of known ways that are worthy of repetition and the groping for new ways in situations with scant precedent. Humanity's ritual traditions are rich but they were not devised to deal with the split atom, nor space flight, nor the hole in the ozone layer. Neither were most of them fashioned to uphold sexual, racial, cultural, and social-class equality ... never-the-less, rituals have

> a kind of 'ideal' character. They tidy up what is messy in ordinary life. They celebrate not the quotidian actual but the once-upon-a-time or the one-day-some- day potential. In the ritual mode ... tomorrow is another day.[10]

To enter into that tomorrow requires new ways and forms. Ways that can empower us to entertain new visions for the future; worship forms and ritual actions that will make it possible for us to suspend—even momentarily—our disbelief; forms that will free us to dwell in the imagination where we can experience possibility and freedom. All forms of imaginative constructions whether they be works of visual art, drama, music, rituals, story telling, poetry or dreams have the power to lead us into a new world of possibility. They invite us into the "world building" realm of our imaginations.

What is the imagination that it can be such a powerful vehicle? Imagination is a God-given faculty for gathering isolated fragments of information and integrating them in ways that allow new realities and meanings to emerge. The imagination is an incredible tool for transformation. It supports the creation of the sacred space and sacred time of religious rituals, the kind of space and time that are themselves imaginative constructions or as Victor Turner called them, "rules of the game." And, as with any game, the rules are critical to the playing.

Campbell touched our hunger and our thirst when he wrote:

> The spirit of the festival, the holiday, the holy day of the religious ceremonial, requires that the normal attitude toward the cares of the world should have been temporarily set aside in favor of a particular mood of 'dressing up.' For the whole purpose of entering a sanctuary or participating in a festival is that one should be overtaken by the state known in India as 'the other mind' ... where one is 'beside oneself,' spellbound, set apart from one's logic of self-possession and overpowered

by the force of a logic of indissociation, where A is B and C also is B.[11]

It is into this 'other mind' state and its fruits that the arts along with ritual action can and should lead us.

To have the power to transform, the enactment of the Christian myth must move into the realm of our experience for it is on the level of experience that the kind of meaning that grows out of our encounter with the symbolic power of the arts takes roots. Stephen Larsen says this kind of experiential meaning does not show itself to the critical scientist, nor to those stuck in logical, analytical modes of secondary meaning. "It simply presents itself to the receptive consciousness, and we can only truly know it in that moment of experiential impact. This, then is the moment of meaning that takes us beyond ourselves."[12]

It is possible to store old wine in old skins, but new wine, young and effervescent, bubbling full of life and possibility needs new skins ... skins capable of allowing that effervescent quality to do its work.

Is it possible that the time-worn symbol of the mask, efficacious in so many ways throughout the history of humankind, can now serve us in the Christian community as a symbolic vehicle into another world? As the Shaman was led by the mask into worlds that he or she experienced as outside of this reality, can the mask be made to work in an analogous way for both the Christian mystic who seeks the spirit of Christ in an inner world and for the everyday Christian who can only approach the Kingdom of God as a world created by and in the imagination; a make believe world that holds the promise of coming to reality in its performance or acting out?

For those who feel concern over the notion of performance or acting out in worship, it is important to draw a distinction between theatrical performance—which at times can be experienced as sacred—and performance in the ritual mode which carries with it an efficacy that has been recognized in all cultures and arenas of life. It has been said that one who has been given a vision is not able to use the power of it until after he or she has performed the vision on earth for the people to see[13] and that human beings are by nature actors, who cannot become something until first they have pretended to be it.[14]

There is an immensely important sense, in which "who we are," waits upon who we say we are. When we perform ourselves, we do not simply express what we already are; we perform our becoming, and become our performing. As Tom Driver says, "there is fate in this, and freedom, too, and something of mystery."[15] The mystery and efficacy of becoming our performing is therefore unbelievably powerful.

In ritual performance, we act out a what-if possibility and in the acting out, it has the potential to become a reality in our lives. If we in the worshiping community can somehow manifest a love for one another that transcends judgment and conditionality, a love that seeks to copy God's graceful act toward us, then maybe, just maybe, that same act can become a part of the way in which we live our daily lives.

This notion of ritual performance is closely connected to drama for drama, like ritual, moves toward something beyond. It deals with commitments and consequences by creating a perpetual present moment ... one that springs from the past while at the same time is filled with its own future ... a virtual future.[16]

Drama concerns itself with hard issues such as death, injustice, betrayal, and exile. The challenge for the playwright, the director and the actors is in finding ways that enable the viewer to get close enough to them and yet stay far enough away from them to carry through on the removal from the exigencies of the everyday world that the entertaining of possibility requires. Many have given expression to the notion of distancing as a necessary requirement. Philosophist Susanne Langer talks about psychical distancing; psychologist T. J. Scheff about under distancing and over distancing. Numerous others have developed theories regarding the aesthetic distance.

Edward Bullough defines psychical distance as that which is "obtained by separating the object and its appeal from one's own self, by putting it out of gear with practical needs and ends." He extends his statement by adding, "but, [that] does not mean that the relation between the self and the object is broken to the extent of becoming 'impersonal' ... on the contrary it describes a personal relation ... of a peculiar character. This relation of a peculiar character is ... our natural relation to a symbol that embodies an idea and presents it for our contemplation, not for practical action but cleared of the practical, concrete nature of its appeal. It is for the sake of this removal that art deals in illusions, which, because of practical concrete nature are readily distanced as symbolic forms."[17]

Langer seeks to make it clear that the kind of illusion that art creates has nothing to do with delusion, nor does it have anything to do with self-deception or pretense. While delusion aims at the greatest possible nearness, illusion permits and even celebrates the distancing that gives rise to and empowers symbolic action.[18]

The confirmation that art can serve as a distancing symbol comes from many disciplines. Among them, art historian Kenneth Clark, notes that "art, above all other forms of human activity, has the potential for creating a balance between intense participation and absolute detachment."[19] A work of art is more than its objective form. In Langer's terms, it is "a glass and a transparency ... a symbol."[20]

But this transparency is what is obscured when in imitative art, our interest is distracted by the meanings of the objects being imitated; then the art work takes on literal rather than symbolic or metaphorical significance.[21]

Playwright Kenneth Macgowan in an article titled, "The Content of the Future," applauds what he sees as this same kind of movement away from realism and toward symbolic representation in the theater in this century. The movement from imitative to symbolic art restores transparency in both its visual and its dramatic forms. Creating a powerful synthesis, this new symbolic theater draws upon the ancient theater of ritual, pageant, masque, commedia dell'-arte, and masks for its form, imbuing that form with relevance by taking its content from this century. "It will," he said, "attempt to transfer to dramatic art the illumination of those deep and vigorous and eternal processes of the human soul."[22]

In this kind of symbolic theater, experiments with masks have yielded some exciting results. Through their use, Macgowan was able to successfully create a "group-being," that is a group of actors who, in place of and consequently more than an individual, could speak for all of humankind. To attempt to speak for all of humankind seems presumptuous, but the concept is a viable one. Macgowan believed

that the group-being, rooted in the traditional antique drama yet voicing the modern unconscious, provided a viable solution to the problem of how to dramatize the content of the future.

In a similar attempt to transcend the limits of individual action, T.S. Eliot and his director, E. Martin Browne, in Eliot's play *The Rock* were able, through the use of half-masks and stiff robes, to pose a group of impersonal, abstract figures, as representatives of the church. They designated this group as "the chorus."[23] The masks worked better than Eliot and Browne had hoped. They found that through the mechanism of the chorus both a spiritual community and a social one could be addressed.[24] Drama critics reviewing the play verified the success of their method.

As a result of his experiments, Macgowan recommends the mask as a tool of the theater of tomorrow because, "as inanimate devices animated by art, they capture the necessary mystic quality ... one can conceive," he says, "of a drama of group-beings in which great individuals, round whom these groups coalesce, could be fitly presented only under the impersonal and eternal aspect of the mask."[25]

Not all of the theater models appropriate for our consideration are Western models. Many of the Noh theater plays of Japan with their striking masks focus on spiritual, metaphysical, and moral problems. Like images in a mirror, the Noh masks are experienced as symbols of these emotional and moral states. For example, the Noh masks of demons are intended to represent human passions. In a revealing "pre-ritual" ritual, the Noh actor before donning his mask, first sits before that mask for sometimes an hour or longer, silently contemplating its spirit and meaning. Then, and only then, he places the mask upon his face. He then continues to study his masked face in the mirror until he himself becomes its reflection. To put the mask on and take his place on stage without this ritual would be unthinkable.[26]

The Noh Theatre has directly or indirectly influenced many of this century's dramatists and playwrights. Among them is William Butler Yeats whose experiments with masks can provide valuable insight for any exploration and experimentation in religious ritual drama. For his work Yeats chose a Noh type of mask. He had some specific reasons for doing this.

First, he believed the Noh mask helped focus attention on both the actor's voice and the content of his words. Second, the mask as an artificial and symbolic presence could keep the audience at an optimal distance. Yeats asserts that "all imaginative art remains at a distance."[27] Third, and Smith believes for Yeats the most important, the Noh mask elevated the actor, releasing him from a merely human realm.

Bringing his discoveries from the Noh tradition to bear upon his work with Gaelic folk tales, Yeats attempted to create an Irish theatrical tradition. In a letter to his friend T. Sturge Moore, Yeats expressed his yearning: "I hope to have attained the distance from life which can make credible strange events, and elaborate words."[28] The mask, he believed, was essential to producing that required distance from life. The mask, as an unalterable sculptured image, could focus the audience's attention and resisting individual emotional response could fix in place a universal dramatic conflict.[29]

In speaking about Yeats' play *Calvary,* Smith says: "The masks of all the characters remove them from their mere humanity, making them symbols, not men. Signaling [the characters] isolation from each other, [the masks] stress the theological and philosophical meaning of the play ... Aside from the general effects of the masking, each character's unique role is suggested by his mask. Christ's mask, the emblem of his isolation and loneliness, indicates his double nature: he is at once man and god .... The stasis of the mask underscores Judas's stony indifference and Lazarus' deathly hue. The soldiers, fixed in their indifference, are also beyond Christ's help."[30]

Smith claims that when the masked actor is removed to a spiritual state, so too is the audience. That's a difficult claim to confirm or even to measure but what a wonderful thing it would be. There must, however, be times when that kind of natural and sequential entry into a spiritual state occurs. Proponents of the use of masks in ritual drama believe that it is the mask that effects the possibility of that transformation. They assert that the mask which "protects the audience by advertising the unreality and checking the illusion of passion before it becomes too moving"[31] allows the audience to become vulnerable enough to make that transition into a spiritual state.

Over and over, the statements of dramatists, directors, actors, critics, philosophers, psychologists, and art historians claim that the single most important criteria necessary for opening the door to transformation is the presence of the kind of distancing from reality that variously gets described as psychical, aesthetic, and optimal. It is this kind of distancing that lets us step back far enough from our anxious involvement to entertain new possibilities.

These same voices stand together in their faith in the ability of the mask to help effect that element of distance. I join them in believing that the mask can allow, even create moments full of mystery in which we are quite literally beside ourselves. Masks, taken seriously as metaphors/symbols/vehicles of transformation can begin the yawning, stretching process that stirs imaginations from their slumber, exciting them into the dancing movements of full engagement.

> The distant being, perceptible only far off, flows into our presence through the mask. — Kerenyi

Notes

1. Susanne K. Langer, *Feeling and Form* (New York: Charles Scribner's Sons, 1953), 403.

2. Paul Tillich, *Dynamics of Faith* (New York: Harper and Row, 1957), 41–43.

3. Ibid.

4. Jake Empereur, *Exploring the Sacred* (Washington D.C.: The Pastoral Press, 1987), 21.

5. Ira Progroff, *The Symbolic and the Real* (New York: McGraw-Hill Book Company, 1963), 176 ff.

6. Tom F. Driver, *The Magic of Ritual* (New York: Harper Collins, 1991), 16.

7. Ibid.

8. Jake Empereur, *Is Liturgy an Art Form?* (an unpublished essay, April 1996), 16.

9. Driver 16–17.

10. Ibid. 58.

11. Joseph Campbell, "The Historical Development of Mythology," in Murray, *Myth and Mythmaking*, 40 as quoted in Stephen Laarsen, *The Shaman's Doorway* (New York: Harper & Row, 1976; Station Hill Press, 1988), 32.

12. Stephen Larsen, *The Shaman's Doorway* (New York: Harper & Row, 1976; Station Hill Press, 1988), 31.

13. Black Elk, Oglala Sioux Shaman.

14. Attributed to W. H. Auden.

15. Driver 17.

16. Langer 307.

17. Edward Bullough, "Psychical Distance as a Factor In Art and An Aesthetic Principal," *British Journal of Psychology* (June 1912).

18. Langer XI.

19. Kenneth Clark, *The Nude*, Bollingen Series XXXV-2 (Princeton: Princeton University Press, 1956), 130.

20. Langer 58.

21. Ibid.

22. Kenneth Macgowan, "The Content of the Future," in *The Theatre of Tomorrow* (New York: Boni & Liveright, 1921), 248, quoted in Susan Harris Smith, *Masks in Modern Drama* 65.

23. E. Martin Browne, *The Making of T. S. Eliot's Plays* (Cambridge: Cambridge University Press, 1969), 20, quoted in Susan Harris Smith, *Masks in Modern Drama* 61.

24. Susan Harris Smith, *Masks in Modern Drama* (Berkeley: University of California Press, 1984), 51.

25. Kenneth Macgowan, *Theater of Tomorrow* 275, quoted in Susan Harris Smith, *Masks in Modern Drama*.

26. *No: The Classical Theatre of Japan* (Tokyo: Kodansha International, 1966), 19, quoted in Susan Harris Smith, *Masks in Modern Drama*.

27. W. B. Yeats, *Certain Noble Plays of Japan* as quoted in Susan Harris Smith, *Masks in Modern Drama* 55.

28. Ibid.

29. Harris Smith 56.

30. Ibid. 59.

31. *Clowns and Pantomimes* (New York: Houghton Mifflin, 1925), 28, as quoted in Susan Harris Smith, *Masks in Modern Drama*.

JOAN CARTER is president and professor of visual and dramatic arts in worship at the Center for the Arts, Religion, and Education of the Graduate Theological Union. She is author of *The Influence of Medieval Liturgical Drama on Giotto's Frescoes in the Arena Chapel in Padua, Italy*.

Anselm Kiefer's Covenant with the Land

Sacramental Art

Xavier John Seubert, OFM

In his discussion of genius in *The Critique of Judgment*, Kant states that the artist transforms nature by moving it beyond itself.[1] One cannot have art without a connection to nature. But one cannot truly understand or appreciate nature without art. Kant articulates here the dynamics of a relationship between human being and nature. It is an essential connection, which is transformative of both. The artist is the one who stands between the two, articulates, and furthers the relationship—wherever it might be on the gamut between transformative inter-relation and destructive rupture. Anselm Kiefer, like few contemporary artists, fulfills Kant's criteria for the artist-genius.[2]

To painterly articulate is to create the otherwise non-existent space within which the force of the connecting or distancing between human being and nature is newly embodied and intensely let be. This intensity of being otherwise does not exist, but is only dormant or stuck at a certain level outside the painting. It is not simply nature, which is articulated. It is how human being and nature are or are not living toward each other and because of each other—each constantly conditioning the other's quality of existence. The artist articulates both the condition of the relationship and the necessary and otherwise non-existent space for its advance or decline.

In this respect Kiefer's art is sacramental. For something to be sacramental it must give contour or expressive embodiment to a relationship of human being and a movement of Godlife which approaches to give us healing and salvific delight. Where the power and presence of this relationship mingles with, appropriates, and is accommodated to the shaping capacity of some stuff of our human world, and is permitted there a placing or an announcement of itself, the process of sacramentality is functioning. I believe Kiefer has intuited the power of the covenant, which is described as being forged by the God of the Book of Genesis between human being and creation. This covenant is a necessary and life-giving connection for us, which we have variously forgotten, denied, and ravaged. In his art Kiefer gathers the stuff—the consequences[3]—of our forgetfulness and shapes there a placing for what has become the almost unrecognizable covenanted relationship, which he so keenly intuits. I propose in the course of this chapter to highlight this sacramental dimension of Kiefer's art.[4]

In his own artistic articulation, Anselm Kiefer does not rate highly natural science's ability to solve the breakdown of meaning in the human world.[5] He looks to the narratives of religion and to archetypal myths to provide instruction in the energies and dynamics whose spiritual or non-calculable power transgresses the necessary limits of the scientific method. How can the intuitions of these narratives and myths be opened and combined with the shattered meaning of our own world—and in such a way that this world is advanced beyond the dead end of impending despair?

The landscapes of Anselm Kiefer portray the cost of the illusions of unrestrained human arrogance and technological abandon. But they also portray in the same scene seemingly mystical powers of the cosmos in redressing the damage caused by those illusions and in advancing us beyond the ravaging shallowness of our various ideologies. The landscapes are redemptive in how they forge and re-forge a covenant between human being and the earth—and in such a way that we are delivered from ourselves.

Born in 1945 in a devastated Germany, Kiefer inherited a national soul whose world of meaning had collapsed and whose legendary and regenerative connection to nature[6] had all but been severed by war. Kiefer enters the devastation of this soul and wanders through all the rooms, which have housed it through many centuries: the great German legends and myths,[7] the poets, the philosophers, the musicians, the warrior aristocracy. Many of these rooms have been destroyed or have been compromised by how they were used or misused by the megalomania of Hitler and his tribe. Shards of a once glorious past, humiliated by its chronological and spiritual culmination in Nazism, are carefully held—sometimes cherished—by Kiefer until they give him access to a sense of what had shaped and birthed the now devastated soul of his people.[8]

We sense his asking the question: "To what should we have entrusted ourselves? Is there something which could have saved us from the path we had taken?" An answer that emerges in a number of his paintings is: the land. The way the land has access to and embodies the nurturing life of the cosmos will be redemptive for Germany and for the rest of us.

I believe that Kiefer has reconstructed the covenant between human being and the land. He has not simply depicted it or given instruction about it. Rather, he has woven the fact of human self-destruction and the redemptive connection to the land into each other to create a space which is hospitable to regenerative covenantal dynamics. This, as I mentioned before, finally allows his art to be sacramental. But this is something which becomes clear in the examination of his paintings. The three I will examine are: *Nigredo*, *Winterlandschaft* ("Winter Landscape") and *Milchstrasse* ("Milky Way").[9]

Anselm Kiefer's *Nigredo* is reminiscent in size and function of certain abstract expressionist paintings in which the viewer is drawn into a canyon-like vortex of shape and color. The *Nigredo* is 130" by 218.5". When you walk through the standard sized doorway into the small gallery of the Philadelphia Museum of Art, in which the *Nigredo* hangs, you are disarmed by the heroic size of the painting and are swept into the patterns of the mythical landscape.

The painting is composed of oil paint, acrylic, emulsion, shellac, and straw and, in a sense, transgresses the division between painting and sculpture. Underneath the painting is a photograph whose re-working, or being painted over, or destruction signals the meaning of the piece: Transformation based in the destruction of previous form. *Nigredo* is a stage of the medieval alchemical process of transforming base material into gold. The *nigredo* stage occurs when everything is turned black, through burning, for instance. The previous form of something is dissolved and is capable of combining with other similarly dissolved or formless realities. The transformation and, hence, redemption of a reality lies in its transcendent ability to combine and be one with something else. The tortured destruction and symbolic death of an element's form—its *nigredo*—must occur one way or another, if it is to survive. The *nigredo* death is the necessary threshold to the next and, hoped for, qualitatively higher level of existence.

This alchemical vision provides Kiefer with the motivation and the pattern for continuing meaningful existence in the place in which European civilization had self-destructed in the abandoning of its moral heritage. Germany had become the *nigredo* of Europe. It seems that for Kiefer the only hope is to resist what would be the dead end of life in the ceaseless and immobilizing lamentation in the face of unimaginable horror. He accepts as a fact that the civilizing forms of European culture had been dissolved into a hellish blackness, to which alchemy instructs everything must in any case be reduced, if it is to be redeemed in necessary recombination. The devastation which Germany and the entire Western civilization experienced becomes one moment in the alchemical process, which Kiefer's landscapes continue.

The central part of the painting is controlled by a vanishing point in the upper left hand section. Ploughed rows of post-harvest stubble in white, black, brown, and red-brown move toward the vanishing point.[10] They funnel rows of material similar to what is in the foreground of the painting.

The foreground is a seemingly static space which allows the viewer access into the painting. There is a series of blackened, oddly rectangular shapes, which seemed to have been burned and collaged onto the surface. Below and around them are white, brown, reddish brown, black, and burned chunks of paint resembling the pressed down layer of a fossilizing field.[11] What seemed static all of a sudden seems to be a primordial emergence or oozing to the surface. The blackened collaged pieces seem like boulders churned up to earth's surface and waiting to be cracked open.

Underneath these boulders is a photograph of a train moving across the landscape. One thinks of the train as an ultimate instrument of technology symbolizing unstoppable movement and disregard for the landscape through which it cuts. It was also the means of transport which made realizable the near destruction of the European Jewish community. The

trains have reverted to boulders to which the earth has given birth. Or are they meteorites which have fallen from the heavens? In either case they symbolize spiritual and cosmic power which is regenerative for the one who understands their nature and how to gain access to them.[12] The trains have been reduced, destroyed, dissolved. But even this situation is redemptive if one knows how to combine their burned formlessness with more primordial energies. It is the ritualizing of redemptive combination which Kiefer's painting performs.[13]

Beyond the horizon in the upper level of the painting is the sky which is a grey-white wash over strewn straw. It is as if a liquefied lead is dripping from the heavens and into the earth. The becoming lead of elements is also an alchemical stage in the process of transformation into gold—as is the burning of straw. One feels the whole canvas writhing in an alchemical birth. It is a landscape of winter and devastation. The canvas heaves in a blackened expectation which is relieved in the browns and greys of the upper left hand corner as it turns into a type of heavy gold.

Devastation has been combined with cosmic elements as forces of regeneration and redemption. The artist becomes the alchemist who understands how to ritualize the salvific combining through the contours of his landscape.

This process is comparable to that of the maker of icons. This person through spiritual discipline and asceticism becomes involved in the spirit and presence of that which he or she will paint. The icon becomes the physical contouring of access to that to which the icon maker is connected; it is the bodily performance of that connection. This is why the icon is believed to be the real presence of the one who is depicted. The icon performs the liturgical function of connecting the viewer with the presence at the root of the icon. When the viewer is drawn into the icon, she herself becomes contoured by the icon's patterns which makes of her life an access to the presence which literally inspired the icon's formation.

Kiefer is performing a similar function. In alchemy it was thought that every physical reality desired perfection and this consisted in the transformation into gold. Everything had this possibility and it was simply a matter of time—of the length of the maturation process—before this occurred. Ore, base metals would lie in the womb of the earth with its transformative powers and would become gold. The alchemist was one who so understood the process of transformation that he could accelerate it. The root intuition is that the cosmic, the divine, and the human are intended to combine for the redemption or resurrection of the earth and humanity. The alchemist understood the patterns of combination and facilitated them.

It is this that Kiefer performs in the *Nigredo*. Like the icon-maker he has intuited salvific combinations and has performed them in the painting. In this sense *Nigredo* becomes an icon of redemption— a religious painting in its most significant sense. When the viewer allows himself to enter the painting and its patterns he is himself so contoured by his connection that he becomes an access to the salvific combining out of which the painting was originally performed. It is a liturgical function that has occurred.

For Kiefer, the land with its own regenerative womblike powers and its ability, like a ploughed field, to absorb all the cosmic resources that rain and shine down upon it—this becomes the place where human being choking on the "black milk"[14] of its own self-destruction recombines toward redemption and resurrection.[15] These latter are terms for survival and transformation into what is unexpectedly beyond ourselves.

In the second of the paintings, *Winterlandshaft* ("Winter Landscape") of 1979,[16] Kiefer depicts an area of land covered with snow. The blanketing only allows isolated clumps of dirt to appear in helter-skelter fashion. There are no ploughed rows ushering the viewer ineluctably into the horizon, as in the *Nigredo*. One feels immobilized. The path which cuts diagonally through the lower left hand corner begins off the painting and quickly exits from it. It comes from nowhere and goes nowhere. The scarcity of trees and the rocklike mountain range in the distance add a note of sterility to the scene. Floating in the sky above this wintry death is a severed head, which at one and the same time stains and waters the landscape with its blood. The staining and watering qualities are made more intense through the medium of water colors.

It is the nature of the earth to give life. Even where it is mutilated by human projects, the indefatigable urge to nourish continues. The decapitated personi-

fication of the land or nature pours its life into the body ravaged by human history. But its position in the sky signals its transcendent and trans-historical quality. We once again experience the death that is the essence of the alchemical *nigredo*. But Kiefer sees in the cycles of the land recombining and redemptive resurrection.[17] Human being must be able to connect with cosmic and heavenly powers at the pivot point of the land if it is not only to survive but also flourish. It is precisely this pivot point and the viewer's access to it which Kiefer creates in these paintings. If sacramentality is considered the organization of an embodiment which allows the emergence of saving presence and participation in it, then Kiefer's landscapes are eminently sacramental.

The last painting to consider is *Milchstrasse* ("Milky Way") in the collection of The Albright-Knox Art Gallery in Buffalo, New York. This piece, which is also heroic in size, immediately involves you in a paradox. The Milky Way, which is a galaxy of stars, is the name written in a deep gash in the landscape from which a luminous white liquid seems to be pouring. The Milky Way is embedded in or pours forth from the scarred earth. The gash is like the slashing open of the tortured and charred flesh of something which reveals its life's liquid.

Cleaving the earth was associated with the copulation of the earth goddess and the thunder god, who penetrated the earth with lightning. Here you have the penetration and fertilization of the earth by the heavens. Swords and axes made from the ore of meteorites were considered symbols and instruments of the regenerative and heavenly cleaving. Kiefer appropriates this theme in the painting "Nothung," which is the name of Wotan's sword, and "My Father Promised Me a Sword."[18] But in the "Tree With Palette"[19] a metal palette is embedded in the tree trunk. The palette cleaves and cleaves to the trunk as have other mythological instruments of regenerative opening in the past. The painter is the one who will accomplish the redemption formerly ascribed to gods and heroes. *Milchstrasse* is one of Kiefer's most complex performances of redemptive opening and combining.

The slash and cleaving have to do with fertilization (the iron plow opening up the earth, for instance) and birth—the opening up of the inner life of the womb in which the life of the earth gestates.

The cleaving—whether done by the warrior-hero, the alchemist, or the painter—opens the redemptive resources. It is at this point that Kiefer's performance becomes incredibly complex. In the *Milchstrasse* a milky white substance pours from the slash. White indicates a stage of alchemical transformation beyond *nigredo*. But it is also like mother's milk—Mother Earth nourishing its life even within death and destruction. What is curious here is that the milk is pouring down out of the slash. There is an overflow of the white on the underside of the slash, but not the upper. This causes a change in perspective. It is all of a sudden as if you are looking up instead of into the distance. Is it the earth we are looking at or is it a great tree reaching up to the heavens over us?

At a time when I was frequently viewing this painting, I was out jogging and a great trunked tree caught my eye. The way the bark had grown and hardened and was patterned in rows moving up and down the tree looked exactly like the ploughed scarred earth in the Kiefer painting. The vanishing point in the painting is raised in such a way that you don't know whether you are looking into the distance or straight up. Is Kiefer combining both things in the one image—the earth and the great tree? And is he indicating how they are inseparably connected and are resources of life for each other?[20]

Another motif that runs through Kiefer's work is the Edda myth of the Yggdrasil Tree.

> One of the most widely disseminated
> motifs in mythology and religious
> iconography is that of the sacred tree
> as both *imago mundi* and *axis mundi*.
> There seems no way to reconstruct
> with certainty the process whereby
> the tree came to represent both
> the cosmos as a whole and it (*sic*)
> cardinal axis, joining the three domains
> (heaven, earth, and underworld)
> together and making communication
> among them possible.[21]

Ancient peoples created sacred spaces out of stone, water, and trees. They organized the patterns of the macrocosm into a microcosmic landscape. By participating in its patterns they created in them-selves a correspondence to the ways in which the levels of life of the cosmos combine and flourish. This is similar to the ritual of the icon and the liturgies of religion's sacraments. It is this most ancient tradition which Kiefer not only preserves but performs in such a way that the sympathetic viewer develops a correspondence to the cosmos' combining and a hospitality to the energies in the world around us.

At the top of *Milchstrasse* is a burned horizon worked with gold and lead—with light and materiality. It is as if rivers of milk are pouring down along the field crevices. One thinks of the biblical promised land flowing with milk and honey or the great axial cosmic tree drawing together all the elements of the cosmos to create a place of flourishing for the earth and for human being.

The optimism, however, is tempered by an ambiguity that runs through Kiefer's work. Affixed to the canvas above the slash is a funnel with the word *Alkahest* written on it. *Alkahest* in the alchemical understanding is a type of universal solvent which reduced elements to a formlessness which further made them susceptible to recombining with other energies and elements toward a more noble reconfiguration. The dissolution, recombining, and perfection are given names such as *passio, mortarium, resurrectio* associating them with the passion, death, and resurrection of Jesus Christ.[22] What Kiefer has done is to physically distill and newly contour a way of engaging the regenerative forces of the cosmos—which pattern is utterly marginalized in the predominantly natural scientific and technological appropriation of reality. He has tried to restore the connection to the land that had from ancient times been thought salvific for human being.

But I mentioned ambiguity before. The funnel which represents the flowing of the cosmos into the earth (the Milky Way is embedded in the ground/tree) also looks like the nose of a plane that has crashed. The strands of metal attached to the funnel—and which connected earth to heaven in the painting "Order of Angels"[23]—seem like they have become detached and no longer function according to plan or nature. One thinks of Icarus falling to the earth, or the planes of the *Luftwaffe* or Allied Forces crashing into the sacred German forests—or bombing them. This is also a cleaving, but a vastly destructive one. However, the way in which the artist connects what is destroyed with cosmic life urges resurrection and transformation. Kiefer seems to be saying that whether the cleaving is done by good or by evil, the opening of the charred crust of the earth is necessary in order to begin a process of transformation.

Again, the painting has become an icon in the strict sense of the word. Kiefer has created the structures of connection for redemptive regeneration. The viewer, in entering the painting, assimilates these structures and bodily becomes in her own life a means to that end. In doing the *opus* (the alchemical process), the alchemist experiences transformation in himself which parallels the transformation of the materials with which he is working. What is the basis of this *sympatheia*? Is it that all existence is interconnected and, hence, vulnerable to the processes that are at work in something other? Are we actually so porous that where we direct our lives in openness toward something, its dynamics of life can take place within us? This, it seems to me, is at the basis of sacramentality and is foundational to the making of the icon. Kiefer presents us with an icon of the land in transformation from humanly inflicted death to resurrection in which those attentive to his construction can participate in and absorb those dynamics within themselves.[24]

Let's conclude by considering Kiefer's project in terms of another metaphor—the covenantal understanding of land in the Hebrew scriptures.[25] This has been developed in various writings by the scripture scholar, Walter Brueggemann.[26] In his exegesis of the second creation story in Genesis 2:4–24,[27] he exposes some ordinarily missed cues in the text. Adam's statement: "This one at last is bone of my bone and flesh of my flesh!" is not some primordial nuptial formula. "Bone" was a symbol of strength; "flesh" was a symbol of weakness. Each term describes the whole human being from a certain point of view. The formula is used in various situations in the Scriptures to describe the commitment to each other of covenant partners. It meant that the partners would support each other in times of power and success and in times of utter weakness and failure. No situation would ever occur in which they would not be there for each other. Adam and Eve in this reading are equal covenantal partners. The surprising element, however, is that a purpose of the covenant is to cultivate the connection with the land and to aid each other in caring for it: "The Lord God took the man and put him in the garden of Eden to till it and look after it" (Gn 2:15). On one level the *land* is the object of the covenant![28] Why is that?

In the first part of the Genesis 2 narrative we hear of the creation of the world. Everything comes to be by the power of God—it is of God's life. It is from the dust of the land that the man is formed. But there is an interesting play on words here: human being is *adam* and dust from the ground is *adama*. There is an essential relationship between the man and the ground from which he is formed.[29] In being formed from the dust human being is already connected to Godlife. This is where he is rooted. It is from out of this that he "takes place" at all. The man becomes a living creature when God breathes life into him. But this needs a place to happen and that place is formed out of the ground. Both the foundational dust and the divine breath are gifts.

Gifting and receiving are the irreplaceable and inviolable dynamics of human life. These are opposed to a willful disposition which only recognizes its own projects. Wherever human beings engage in this latter stance they become rootless—they cut themselves off from the way in which they are essentially connected to the dust of the ground—they cut themselves off from the essential place for the gifting and receiving of Godlife.

The land as the object of the initial covenanting is where connections are preserved or lost.[30] And where human beings become exiled in rootlessness, there is no place for Yahweh to breathe life into them. They cannot be found because they have removed themselves from the possibility of place. Their existence is essentially threatened. This is very similar to Kiefer's *nigredo* stage. Only where the human projects of disposition, which are inattentive to the land in the ways in which it is the pivot of giving and receiving, are exhausted and completely fail can the covenantal recombining with land and Godlife begin again. Only here can the exiles be found and recalled to a place of flourishing.

This is enchantingly related in the third chapter of Genesis in which God is walking in the garden at the time of the evening breeze and cannot find the man and the woman.[31] To be found is to have a foundation—to be so rooted in a place that life can emerge and show itself. God cannot find the man and the woman—they have ceased to be apparent because they no longer are founded in the connections that give life. In some sense they already are not!

In Genesis 2:17 the man is told that he may not eat of the tree of the knowledge of good and evil. Human life is completely a receiving of gift. There are boundaries within which that receiving is ordered and exclusively can be cultivated. Where these are ignored there can only be exile and death,[32] for then we have removed ourselves from the only place in which Godlife can engage us. Only where the willful disposition over land, God, and self is exhausted—is reduced to ash and dust—can Yahweh begin again to shape a place of engagement out of the nothingness that we have become.

Brueggemann follows this pattern through the history of the Jews and up to the death of Jesus Christ. Jesus' being raised up on the cross is the ultimate symbol of being ripped up from the foundations—from the connections to land and Godlife—which are our only possibility of coming to a stand and existing. His death is the absolute rootlessness in which the fullest possible life takes place. And in his rootlessness he is able to create places out of the lives of the little ones who have been reduced to nothing by the projects of the powerful. This is the process of recombination out of death which we call resurrection. It is a process which continues to this day and is choreographed in the landscape paintings of Anselm Kiefer. To be alive is a ritual of connecting and receiving. Kiefer performs this ritual and distills its gestures.

What Kiefer has recovered is not primarily the sense of the inexhaustible faithfulness of a covenantal God but how the land as an essential component of the primordial covenantal configuration will never refuse to give place of flourishing to the human being who is faithful to that covenant. If our lives don't take place somewhere, then we cannot be found—and we cannot find ourselves. Being rootless we do not have power or resources to create the spaces for binding and life-giving recombination. Where we receive the land as a gift, there we place ourselves at the pivot point at which the gifts of all life converge and are dispensed toward us for as long as we can be faithful to the land. This happens even when the only thing we have left and have become are the ashes and the dust of all our faithless projects.

This is Kiefer's discovery. And he has performed its dynamics in such a way that we can enter them and make them our own. He has ritually reconnected us to the land!

Notes

1. Immanuel Kant, "Critique of Judgment," in *Philosophical Writings*, Ernst Behler, ed. (New York: Continuum, 1993), 230–236).

2. The artist-genius in this sense is to be distinguished from the later Neo-Kantian understanding of the artist as utterly beyond boundary in the expression of self. The modern lionizing of the mad genius-artist stems from this period. In Kant's understanding the artist is the one who experiences the aesthetic idea in which a rational content is joined to and exceeded—exploded—by an imaginative intuition. This excess transgresses the current worldview and is in Heideggger's terms, for instance, an event of opening when performed as the work of art. Heidegger will oppose world to earth. "World" is the organization and articulated patterns of our daily and functional lives. "Earth" is the as yet and ultimately hidden dynamics and possibilities of reality which are never exhausted in articulation. In this sense, Anselm Kiefer's landscapes are an event of earth. See Martin Heidegger, "Der Ursprung des Kunstwerkes" in *Holzwege* (Frankfurt am Main: Klostermann, 1972), 7–68. See also Hans-Georg Gadamer, "The Truth of the Work of Art" in *Heidegger's Ways* (Albany: SUNY, 1994), 95–109; Michael E. Zimmerman, "Hoelderlin and the Saving Power of Art" in *Heidegger's Confrontation With Modernity: Technology, Politics, Art* (Bloomington: University of Indiana Press, 1990), 113–133.

3. John C. Gilmour provides a brilliant analysis of this aspect of Kiefer's art in his *Fire on the Earth: Anselm Kiefer and the Postmodern World* (Philadelphia: Temple University Press, 1990).

4. The liturgical quality of Kiefer's art is also considered in Danilo Eccher's *Kiefer: Stelle cadenti* (Bologna: Galleria d'Arte Moderna di Bologna, 1999).

5. Kiefer is highly influenced by Martin Heidegger, who articulated both the essential connection between human being and the cosmos and also the destructive path of industrial technology

for that connection. See for instance his "Die Frage nach der Technik" in *Vortraege und Aufsaetze* (Pfullingen: Neske, 1978), 9–40. For the English translation see *The Question of Technology and Other Essays*, William Lovitt, trans. and intro. (New York: Harper and Row, 1977), 3–35. See also Mark Rosenthal, *Anselm Kiefer* (Philadelphia: The Philadelphia Museum of Art, 1987), 26. For a thorough analysis of the influence of Heidegger on Kiefer and the parallels between the two, see Matthew Biro's *Anselm Kiefer and the Philosophy of Martin Heidegger* (Cambridge: University Press, 1998).

6. For a wonderfully erudite and delightfully critical overview of the history of this connection from Tacitus' *Germania* to Anselm Kiefer's woodcuts, see Simon Schama's "Der Holzweg: The Track Through the Woods" in *Landscape and Memory* (Toronto: Random House, 1995), 74–134. In the final quote of the chapter, however, Schama seems to represent the Enlightenment attitude that we should ultimately outgrow our myths. This in itself is a myth which can have as deleterious consequences as our century's horrendous misuse of myths, such as those based on the *Germania*. Kiefer is aware of both the deadliness and life potential of myths. He leads us down a *Holzweg* that clearly highlights the former, while attempting to retrieve the latter. If there is a "Kiefer-Syndrome," it would be this.

7. Kiefer, like Richard Wagner before him, finds fecund suggestions in the Scandinavian collection of myths known as the *Eddas*. Most memory of national myths of the Teutonic world were lost with the introduction of Christianity. It is only the Scandinavian poets and scholars who preserved the tales of the heroes and pagan gods. In this collection the primordial roots of Teutonic consciousness are preserved. See Robert Graves, intro., *New Laorusse Encyclopedia of Mythology* (New York: Hamlyn, 1981), 248. For an analysis of Kiefer's use of myth and history from a Jungian perspective see Rafael Lopez-Pedraza's *Anselm Kiefer: The Psychology of "After the Catastrophe"* (New York: George Braziller, 1996). "After the Catastrophe" in the title refers to an essay by Carl Jung in which he discusses the tragic fate of the psychological collective guilt, not only of Germany but of the whole of Europe in the aftermath of World War II and the Holocaust.

8. This journey is stunningly chronicled in the recent exhibition of the Metropolitan Museum of Art's 1995 acquisition of fifty-four works on paper by Anselm Kiefer ("Anselm Kiefer: Works on Paper: 1969-1993." December 15, 1998 through March 21, 1999). See Nan Rosenthal, *Anselm Kiefer: Works on Paper in The Metropolitan Museum of Art* (New York: Harry N. Abrams, Inc., 1998).

9. Prints of these paintings can be found in 1) Mark Rosenthal 128, for *Nigredo*; 2) Nan Rosenthal 25, for *Winterlandschaft*; and 3) Massimo Cacciari and Germano Celant,

Anselm Kiefer (Milan: Edizioni Charta, 1997), 268–269, for *Milchstrasse*.

10. White and red indicate stages of the alchemical process. "Transmutation, the *magnum opus* which culminated in the Philosopher's Stone, is achieved by causing matter to pass through four phases, named from the colours taken on by the ingredients: *melansis* (black), *leukosis* (white), *xanthosis* (yellow) and *iosis* (red). Black (the *nigredo* of medieval writers) symbolizes death. With innumerable variations, the four (or five) phases of the work (*nigredo, albedo, citrinitas, rubedo,* sometimes *vividitas,* sometimes *cauda pavonis*) are retained throughout the whole history of Arabian Western alchemy." Mircea Eliade, *The Forge and the Crucible* (New York: Harper Torchbooks, 1971), 149.

11. Rosenthal 127.

12. Mircea Eliade, 8–9, 42, 148–149. Another possible allusion to the boulders is Wotan and the Yggdrasil tree is described by Simon Schama in his *Landscape and Memory* (84–85): "It seems possible that the grisly rite [*human sacrifice by hanging*] was a re-enactment of the self-sacrifice of the Teutonic god Wotan, who hanged himself on the boughs of the cosmic ash tree Yggdrasil (the Nordic symbol of the universe) for nine days and nights, in a ritual of death and resurrection. Waiting in vain for succor, Wotan saw beneath the great tree a vast pile of stone runes, which he succeeded in raising through the force of his supernatural will. Standing erect, the runes liberated Wotan from his arboreal ordeal and into a new, rejuvenated life of unprecedented power and strength."

13. An exhibit entitled "Anselm Kiefer: *Dein und mein Alter und das Alter der Welt* (Your Age and Mine and the Age of the World)" at the Gagosian Gallery in Manhattan (January 24– February 28, 1998) featured recent work of Anselm Kiefer. One of the paintings was called "Geviert" which means "The Fourfold" and refers to the four elements of which all reality is composed: Divinity, Mortality, Earth, the Heavens. This theme is borrowed from Martin Heidegger who treats of the fourfold in, among others, his essay, "Das Ding" ("The Thing") in *Vortraege und Aufsaetze* (Pfullingen: Neske, 1978), 157–175. When something is "just a thing" it is reduced to the common properties of every thing: the quantifiable, the being at hand, the properties manipulated by natural science. But when a thing is seen in its essence, it is experienced as a gathering of the fourfold in its own distinctive way. Kiefer's landscapes are a gathering of the fourfold in such a way that human being is redemptively connected to them beyond the limits of humanity's projects and static points of view. Kiefer is literally performing the essence of every work of art. The fourfold is constituent of all reality in both Aristotle and alchemy. In every reality the four elements must be able to bind with each other if

Kiefer, Anselm (German, b. 1945), *Nigredo*, 1984. Oil, acrylic, emulsion, shellac, and straw on photograph on canvas, with woodcut. 130" x 218 ½" . Philadelphia Museum of Art: Gift of the friends of the Philadelphia Museum of Art in celebration of their 20th anniversary. Accession #1985-5-1.

Kiefer, Anselm (1945-   ) *Winter Landscape*. Watercolor, gouache, and graphite pencil on paper. H. 16⅞ in. W. 14 in. (42.9 x 35.6 cm.) The Metropolitan Museum of Art, Denise and Andrew Saul Fund, 1995. (1995.14.5) Photograph © 1997 The Metropolitan Museum of Art

Kiefer, Anselm, German, born 1945, *die Milchstrasse* (*Milky Way*), 1985-86. Emulsion paint, oil, acrylic and shellac on canvas with applied wires and lead objects. 12 ½' x 18 ½'. Albright-Knox Art Gallery, Buffalo, New York. In celebration of the 125th anniversary of The Buffalo, Fine Arts Academy, General and Restricted Purchase Funds, 1988.

that reality is to survive and flourish. Kiefer ritualizes this binding.

14. Nothing perhaps has artistically crystallized the incomprehensible horror and evil of the death camps of World War II as does Paul Celan's poem, "Todesfuge" ("Death Fugue"). In the poem the Jews and the Germans are personified in the names of two women, respectively Sulamith and Margarete. Both these names appear in Kiefer paintings and both are objects of destruction, seemingly indicating that in the annihilation of the Jews something essentially German was destroyed. The "black milk," which in the poem the Jews are forced to drink as their constant daily fare, carries the sense of all that is intolerably demeaning unto death. For the full German text of Celan's poem see "Todesfuge" in *Paul Celan. Gedichte I* (Frankfurt am Main: Suhrkamp Verlag, 1975), 39–42. For the English translation see Michael Hamburger, *German Poetry, 1910-1975: An Anthology* (New York: Persea Books, 1977), 318–321. For an analysis of the *Sulamith-Margarete* paintings and theme in Kiefer see Rosenthal 95–119; Lopez-Pedraza 61–73; Nan Rosenthal 86–90; and Lisa Saltzman, *Anselm Kiefer and Art After Auschwitz* (Cambridge: University Press, 1999), 27–32.

15. Kiefer entitles certain paintings *Resumptio* and *Resurrexit* which connotes a parallel dynamic between what the artist is about and the resurrection of Christ. Eliade will further state: "That cosmic night was compared to death (darkness) as well as the regression *ad uterum* is something which emerges both from the history of religions and from the alchemical texts already quoted. Western alchemists integrated their symbolism into Christian theology. The 'death' of matter was sanctified by the death of Christ who assured its redemption" (157).

16. The *Winterlandschaft* is one of the works on paper by Kiefer purchased by the Metropolitan Museum of Art in 1995. See Nan Rosenthal 22–26.

17. Eliade 148–152.

18. Mark Rosenthal 25, 75.

19. Ibid. 71.

20. Kiefer is an admirer of the Baroque (see Rosenthal 74). I could not help wondering if he is here doing something similar to Giambattista Tiepolo's *Allegory of the Planets and Continents* (1752, oil on canvas) in the Metropolitan Museum of Art in New York City. This oil painting is the sketch for the ceiling fresco of *Apollo and the Four Continents*, 1752–53, in the Residenz in Wuerzburg, Germany. The illusion created in the Tiepolo painting is very similar to what Kiefer accomplishes in *Milchstrasse*: One is looking and is drawn straight into the painting. At the same time one is looking straight upwards! See Linda Wolk-Simon, "Domenico Tiepolo: Drawings, Prints, and Paintings in The Metropolitan Museum of Art," *The Metropolitan Museum of Art Bulletin* 54 (Winter 1996/97): 42. This reading of Kiefer is confirmed, I believe, by the red engineer/architect's aligning string which is screwed to the top center of the *Milchstrasse* and drops to the base. When one follows the string the movement into the horizon is abruptly lifted up into the top/bottom movement of the tree trunk.

21. Mircea Eliade, *The Encyclopedia of Religion* 15 (New York: Macmillan, 1987), 244.

22. The Christian alchemical tradition believed that it was the passion, death, and resurrection of Jesus Christ within history which enabled the alchemical transformation of all reality.

23. Mark Rosenthal 136.

24. Eliade 1971, 160–161.

25. This comparison is not unwarranted when one considers the distinctively Jewish covenantal themes in several of Kiefer's paintings: 1. *Durchzug durch das rote Meer* (Passage through the Red Sea); 2. *Auszug aus Aegypten*, 1984–85 (Departure from Egypt); 3. *Das Schlangenwunder* (The Miracle of the Serpents); 4. *Aaron*; 5. *Auszug aus Aegyten*, 1984 (Departure from Egypt); 6. *Das rote Meer*, 1984–85 (The Red Sea); 7. *Das Buch*, 1979–85 (The Book); 8. *Jerusalem*, 1986. See Rosenthal respectively: 1. i–xxxvi; 2. 122; 3. 123; 4. 124; 5. 125; 6. 126; 7. 134; 8. 144.

26. See especially Walter Brueggemann, *The Land: Place as Gift, Promise and Challenge in Biblical Faith* (Philadelphia: Fortress, 1977). For related discussions of this topic see Belden C. Lane, *Landscape of the Sacred: Geography and Narrative in American Spirituality* (New York: Paulist, 1988); Djelal Kadir, *Columbus and the Ends of the Earth: Europe's Prophetic Rhetoric as Conquering Ideology* (Berkeley: University of California Press, 1992); Marc Auge, *Non-Places: Introduction to an Anthropology of Supermodernity* (New York: Verso, 1995); and William Vitek and Wes Jackson, eds., *Rooted in the Land: Essays on Community and Place* (New Haven: Yale University Press, 1996).

27. Walter Brueggemann, "Of the Same Flesh and Bone (Gn 2,23a)," *Catholic Biblical Quarterly* 32 (1970): 532–543. For the broader context see his "Creation as Yahweh's Partner" in *Theology of the Old Testament: Testimony, Dispute, Advocacy* (Minneapolis: Fortress, 1997), 528–551.

28. Brueggemann 1970, 540, 542.

29. Gerhard von Rad, *Genesis: A Commentary* (Philadelphia: Westminster Press, 1961), 74–75.

30. Brueggemann (1977) masterfully follows this pattern through the course of Israel's history. He sees it focused and radically articulated in the "Elijah/Naboth/Jezebel/Ahab sequence" in chapter 21 of the First Book of Kings. See his chapter "'Because You Forgot Me,'" 90–106. For an extended development of willful disposition in biblical terms see his *The Prophetic Imagination* (Philadelphia: Fortress Press, 1978).

31. "Here is a glimmer of the older conception of Yahweh as owner of the park. Accordingly, the narrative clearly regards this tree garden as a *holy* region, enclosing God's presence and therefore guarded by cherubim(cf. at ch.3.24)." G. von Rad 75–76.

32. When we do our lives in such a way that it is a violation of the dynamics of the land, the land becomes polluted and can no longer sustain life. Even Yahweh is exiled from the land. Godlife cannot take place because human projects have taken place away. There is nothing to support life. For a stunning articulation of the exile of Yahweh in Ezekiel see Brueggemann 1977, 138.

XAVIER JOHN SEUBERT, OFM, is professor of systematic theology and director of graduate theology at St. Bonaventure University. He has published numerous articles on sacramentality, symbol, and art in such journals as *Worship, Cross Currents, New Theology Review*, and *The Heythrop Journal*.

Liturgical Dance

State of the Art

Carla De Sola

sked to imagine where sacred dance was going as we head into the new millennium, it seemed appropriate to reconsider some of the significant aspects of the field which I had recently documented for *Liturgical Ministry*. This review confirmed my belief in the ongoing value of liturgical dance and embodied spirituality as a powerful path for prayer, as a way for self and group healing, and a profound way to share, update, and integrate spiritual wisdom. Sacred dance is one of many spiritual ways that build a web of connection on a level interior to the internet—an internet of the Spirit. This is accomplished through sacred rituals involving liturgical dance which reaches out to all peoples and which draws upon the vast and diverse cultural traditions of the planet. A healthy heart is fed by blood flowing freely through the arteries: Sacred dance, flowing from many hearts into the life blood of the world, is a sacred path for the spirituality of peoples into the next millennium.

Introduction

If not for the liturgical movement and liturgical reforms of Vatican II, it is unlikely that we would be discussing the modern expression of liturgical dance today (particularly in the Roman Catholic Church) much less the state of the art. While the documents of Vatican II opened the way, the general worshiping public needs a deeper understanding of the spirituality and gifts of dance before it is accepted.

In this article I discuss beginning and local efforts in the post-Vatican II church, and draw upon my experiences as a modern day pioneer in the field, one who has been in touch with many dancers, students, and liturgies. Included are major resources for available training and authenticity in dance and practice. I touch on styles of expression emerging from grass-roots movements, folk, meditative practices, and fine art forms. Throughout, I am concerned with the quality of dance, keeping a flexibility of approach as I ponder the unexpected ways of the Spirit. This leads into a consideration of where we are now, including dance as a ministry, the gift of the arts, and what is coming to pass. Where is liturgical dance headed? What is its role in times of crisis and change? The chapter concludes with reflections on the spirituality of the sacred dancer, so integral to the development of a multi-faceted flowering of the field.

Liturgical Dance's Development Out of the Liturgical Renewal of Vatican II

The Vatican II documents, particularly *Sacrosanctum Concilium (The Constitution on the Sacred Liturgy)* reaffirmed the importance of the body and the active participation of the faithful in the liturgy. "To promote active participation, the people should be encouraged to take part by means of acclamations, responses, psalmody, antiphons, and songs as well as by actions, gestures, and bodily attitudes ..." (30). The door seemed open to reinclusion of the sacred art of dance, of which Hugo Rahner stated that in almost every age, sacral dance "has been woven around the austere core of the liturgy."[1]

In *Introducing Dance in Christian Worship*, Ronald Gagne, studying the research of the French Benedictine Dom Gougaud (who wrote at the beginning of the twentieth century on Christian liturgical dance), concludes that generally "the Church, without approving of (the dance) ... being grafted onto her liturgy, seemed to have *closed her eyes*."[2] That is to say, dance though present, was never *blessed* by the church in a consistent and public way. Implementation and progress have been very slow. It is ironic that the arts—whose gifts make our inner life visible, empowering our ability to see, hear, and feel, and to be touched by the presence of God—should be met by some with fear and closed eyes.

The documents and spirit of Vatican II opened the door to our discussion of the state of the art of liturgical dance. How much more might we be reporting if dance was to become a prime subject of theological and spiritual learning—even more so if encouraged, blessed, participated in, and proclaimed with joy. Benedictine monk Vincent Martin has promoted art workshops for two decades at St. Andrew's Priory in Valyermo, Calif. He notes that it is not a question of dance being "in the church" but of the well-being of the church. He further reflects that society is losing the sense of the sacred and the church's task is to bring the sacred into everyday life. In my opinion, by an extended sense of the sacrament, the church hallows all of life and makes what is sacred visible for all to see. Dance contributes to a sacramental way of viewing and understanding life. The liturgical dancer ideally holds together in his or her being, and in the community's consciousness, the unity of body, soul, and spirit, responding to the movement of the Spirit. The dancer lives the theology of incarnation and resurrection. It is interesting to note that *perichoreses*, a word used to describe the inner, intimate activity of the mystery of the Trinity, is so descriptive of dance. May the day come when one goes to church, to the sacred liturgy, and comes away proclaiming, "now the eyes of my eyes are opened ..." (e.e. cummings).

Beginning and Local Efforts

I experienced the beginning of liturgical dance through a *gesture*. It was on a fall day after Vatican II, and we, the faithful, were to try extending a "kiss of peace." I felt it would be a moment of portent, or turning point to be witnesses. So as not to miss the occasion, I bicycled to church in a strange town. Reaching toward, looking at, and touching a fellow worshiper felt daring, strange, yet very good. I felt in my whole being how important this step was. I saw the kiss of peace as an outward manifestation of one of many inner gestures of prayer. It seemed to me that if we could not make this step, there would be no hope for liturgical dance. The Roman Church, however, struggled for a long time before this step was generally accepted.

The following informal "stages" of liturgical dance development are predicated on my own experience and experimentation over the last twenty-five years (post-Vatican II). This includes meetings with many liturgical dance leaders, extensive teaching, workshops, and conferences. Recognizing these developmental steps guides me in directing the progress of many local groups in their own inclusion of dance in worship.

The first dances I created for the liturgy were processionals: entrance rites and recessionals, followed occasionally by circle dances when there was call for a special celebration.[3]

Experiments with gestural movement sequences for the Our Father were requested. These seemed unnecessary when people began simply joining hands, often across aisles, raising them at the conclusion of the prayer.

In the back of my mind a voice said: "Liturgical dance is a ministry, it is prophecy, it lifts people's spirits, it disturbs people." A decade later, after returning from a sacred dance festival in Avignon, France, I wrote: "The people representing the churches in France brought tremendous piety but little experience with experimentation. We have that experience and have developed a range of theory with Father Thomas Kane, CSP, a liturgist."[4]

A later stage saw the inclusion of "offertory" dances (presentation of the gifts, sometimes extended to be considered "table-setting" dances). There were also requests for congregational gestures to accompany the psalm refrain, while dancers or dance choirs were invited to interpret the verses. The Alleluia, before and after the Gospel proclamation, became a popular place for liturgical dance. Frequently, dance was requested to proclaim the readings. Meditation dances, sometimes based on the general theme of the day, were placed after communion.

I believe dance is being blessed by God. If this is so, I must ask "why?" One direction in thought might be to understand the role dance plays as a "tonic," a revitalizer of the spirit, especially needed at times of crisis or hope.

The breadth, life, and impact of the feast of St. Francis, popularly know as the Earth Mass or Miss Gaia, held annually at the Cathedral of St. John the Divine in New York City, deserves special note. Earth Mass dramatically focuses us on the fragile ecological balance in nature and our interdependence with all forms of life. This contributes to the fervor of performers and congregation. Herein dancers witness to the common sacredness of the human body and the body of the earth, with all her myriad creatures. It is a beautiful example of dancing, music, and all forms of creaturely life praising in harmony with the divine liturgy. Paul Winter's glorious saxophone, a tenor echoing the recorded wolf sounds, and the wild call of "brother wolf" are woven into the Kyrie. The dancers respond, hearing the cry, running down the aisles for the life of the wolves; in the Sanctus they dive and leap to the hosannas of the whales; in the Canticle to Brother Sun they burst forth from behind the altar like the sun, and, with the congregation lift their arms in praise, as if guided by the spirit of St. Francis. A great hush falls as a majestic elephant moves slowly down the aisle, the very strangeness of it all opening us into the mystery of the universe.

It is fitting, natural, and right that dance be an integral part of Earth Mass, for this is a celebration of the dance of life. Of coexistence in peace and fullness of being. Earth Mass is a living testimony to the human race's ability to live in harmony with all living things. It is a liturgical model for the people of the world as we enter the twenty-first century.

Training for Sacred Dancers

Training to become a liturgical dancer is ideally a two-fold process: The study of dance as an art form, which may include technical training in a variety of styles; and spiritual development, which may include theological, liturgical and biblical studies, together with spiritual practices. Workshops have been a large part of both the development of liturgical dancers and dissemination of liturgical dance in the United States. They continue to offer more opportunities for sharing and growth, technically, spiritually, and theologically. Requests for both workshops and dance leaders come from retreat centers, colleges, and religious orders, including monasteries and convents, as well as individual churches. To spread the cost of bringing in a trained dance choreographer/liturgist, clusters of churches often culminate in a community service in which dance is featured. It is encouraging to learn that occasionally dancers are sponsored by their churches with special funding and scholarships to attend these sessions.

The Sacred Dance Guild, founded in 1958, is an interfaith organization which holds regional and national conferences on all aspects of sacred dance. The annual festival draws between 100–200 participants from all over the country as well as internationally. Its present membership is more than six hundred people, organized in local chapters in almost every state.

As a participating seminary in the Graduate Theological Union in Berkeley, Calif., the Pacific School of Religion has offered courses and week-long workshops on sacred dance since 1976, under the guidance of Professor Doug Adams. Here and at other seminaries, Iliff in Denver and Union Theological Seminary in New York City, the field of sacred dance develops through the reflective study embedded within traditional studies required by master's and doctoral programs. In recent years, courses in sacred dance, under the auspices of the Graduate Theological Union, Center for the Arts, Religion and Education, and at the Pacific School of Religion, have included: Introduction to Liturgical Dance, Dancing Your Spiritual Journey, Dance of the Woman's Spirit, Dancing Seasons and Passages, Dance and the Art of Peace-making, Dance: Body Wisdom/Bible Wisdom, Sacred Dance and Healing, Dances as a Sacred Art Form, Dance and Liberation, and Dance in Modern Worship and Theology.[5] A program offering both technical training in a variety of dance styles, as well as spiritual and theological studies is being designed.[6]

Where Are We Now?

Within the last twenty-five years I have seen curves of interest, ups and downs, in dance as a significant part of worship. Yet seeds have been sown and taken root. I believe we are now seeing a flowering of opportunity, perhaps reflecting society's growing interest in spirituality and ways that integrate body and spirit. A nun recently remarked that, "Acceptance of dance is a reading of how the integration of body, mind, and spirit is in a community. It is indicative of the willingness and desire and readiness to move on." I feel we are on the verge of a renaissance, after a rather dormant period following the initial excitement of Vatican II. Sacred dance has even reached the internet, with notices of events spanning all denominations across the country too numerous to mention here. In Oakland or the East Bay Area alone, I discovered dance participation in six local churches, as well as active ministry in a

number of the colleges. At St. Gregory Nyssen Episcopal Church in San Francisco, Rector Richard Fabian has been leading and training people in folk style forms for two decades. A modern sanctuary is designed to facilitate dance. Fabian, writing in their publication *God's Friends*, notes: "Our simplest steps come from opposite world hemispheres. The Tripudium ... was universally known in Europe. From Africa comes High Life." In a recent story on liturgical dance in *Dance Magazine*, a survey reported 2,221 events over the past several years were described as dance performances in a worship setting.[7]

Though we have reviewed sacred dance from the foundational work of the Vatican II documents, it is in practice a highly ecumenical field, for sacred dancers pray and work together crossing denominational lines as easily as they leap. Thus, through networking, a sacred dance company may be formed consisting of dancers from different religious traditions, held together by geography, their love of sacred dance, and each other. The dancers are then positioned to serve a variety of churches in the area, and witness to the underlying communality of God's spirit.

Tempering the ecumenical approach of dancers, I currently discern a developing trend toward formation of a "ministry of sacred dance" from within a church. At Old Saint Mary's Cathedral in San Francisco, where Omega West Dance Company is now in its third year of residency, liturgical dance is regarded as a ministry, with a budget set aside for dance. This has given us an opportunity to create dances for Advent, Christmas, Epiphany, Lent, Palm Sunday, Good Friday, and Pentecost. The cathedral staff is interested in both the professional work of the company, and what is now beginning to be described as "pastoral dance," a term coined by Peter Zografos, Old Saint Mary's pastoral associate. It does not imply that professional liturgical dance is not pastoral but refers to a dance ministry led by members drawn from among the parishioners. Zografos states, "I want to see beautifully trained professional dancers. I also want to see parishioners dance. I want to hear beautiful liturgical music. I also want to sing!"

Part of the artistry of the dance minister, working with a liturgical team, is to ensure that dance contributes to the uplifting of the entire congregation. The liturgically oriented professional dancer is in a position to nurture untrained members of the parish, who, in turn, witness to dance as performed by ordinary people from within the community. Dance ministry includes encouraging all to dance, leading movement meditation, folk dances, recognizing and supporting indigenous forms of expression, spontaneous praise movements, as well as fine art forms of dance. Serving as ministers (of dance) and as laity, they are in a position to feel, lead, and give expression to the spirit moving among the people. At a training day held for lay ministers at Old Saint Mary's Cathedral, John Hurley, the pastor, urged all to welcome the Spirit, to be proud of a liturgy that was alive, moving, not addicted to sterilized perfection. The ministry of sacred dance was prayed for: Bless those who lead us in holy movement, inspired by the Holy Spirit, for the good of us all." Paul Schmidt reflects, "Shall we dance?" is an important question for our liturgical prayer. Its answer will come through talent and trial and tolerance and the grace of the Holy Spirit. St. Basil says that the Holy Spirit enables us "to dance with the angels."[8]

In a sermon a few years ago, James P. Morton, dean of the Cathedral of St. John the Divine, New York City, pondered what art has to do with the divine, and why art is so vital to our spirituality. He spoke of art as embodiment, the artist teaching us to see, hear, feel, smell. Art helps us receive our sight: "our *insight* into the real world, what Christians call the kingdom. Repeated through art, ideas cease to whisper in our ears, but instead begin to live inside our marrow. God is the artist, which all creation witnesses to." Referring to the burning bush apprehended by Moses, Morton says God's I AM means I (God) will appear in whatever form I want. "All of life is spirit incarnate …. With form, shape, spirit, so we can get it!" Art enables us to take it in, like food, like communion. "The artist embodies Christ's power to remove our blindness, to see with our heart, eyes, flesh …. Art is the way events are turned into memory, and time is made precious …. Art and the sacred are two sides of the same coin … to lead us to God."

Surprises: Prophetic/Healing Ministries

The spirit of freedom is elusive, often ephemeral. One can never fully anticipate what choreography will emerge from the Spirit's inspiration. Having gained acceptance and trust from leaders and their congregations, sacred dancers are beginning to express the field's prophetic possibilities. Sacred dance needs forms which celebrate the diversity of all ages, physical abilities, and races.

> If we wish to challenge our Christian communities to accept peoples of other cultures as brothers and sisters in the family of God, why not use Latin American, Asian, African, or Native American dance in worship interchangeably with dance from the European ballet or the American modern dance tradition?[9]

I asked Kathryn Scarano, director of Kairos Dance Company in Riverside, Calif., what directions were calling her. We started talking about "the millennium" and she remarked: "How do we await the second coming of Christ?" and answered herself saying, "We have to redeem the suffering in the world." Kathryn has been creating dances and rituals around peace and justice themes for many years. We have jointly danced and combined our dance companies in support of nuclear disarmament at the Nevada test site in Las Vegas.

In 1990 De Sola commented:

> Liturgical dance has a healing and prophetic role to play in the church and for the world. It is not 'icing on the cake.' It epitomizes our relation to our bodies and by extension our relation to the earth. Redeeming the body and redeeming the earth are connected. In today's world, our earth is in trouble. The earth is dancing a passion. The vibrations of the earth's dance resound in everyone of our cells and the

liturgical dance calls us to respond to the anguish around us with a reaffirmation of the spirit. The dance and the dancer may shake us from our lethargy to a positive re-engagement to help restore the earth's harmony.[10]

The Need for Ritual Making

Sacred dance as a fundamental urge of the human soul is always finding expression in our midst, with ritual-making a natural avenue of choreographic expression. Those at the growing edge of liturgical dance are poised, ready to explore new forms of ritual, going beyond the cautions and apologetics of traditional mainline churches. One "foot" of the dancer's call is grounded in the Sunday tradition, eager to contribute toward creating beauty as an epiphany of God, grateful to have the skills to be easing the stiff edges of the liturgy, with a procession here and gestures there. The other foot (or call) is being led by the Spirit into new terrain, living out a call to dance is embodiment of the sacred movement of all people and all life. This is the growing field of innovative ritual-making. New movement rituals, outside of a eucharistic framework, are being requested for conferences, prayer services, retreats, social action events, holistic healing centers, and women's groups. Women, becoming increasingly familiar with dance as a way of prayer, experience it as a means to facilitate spiritual development and healing. In the struggle for ordination we glimpse the role dance will play when women's sensibilities are embodied.[11] We are witnessing an exciting development for a culture with a dearth of sacred celebrations to mark special moments in between transitions in life, in addition to traditional public and private ceremonies for birth and death, baptism, confirmation, ordination, marriage, and anointing of the sick.

The Spirituality of the Sacred Dances

A spring wind moves to dance
any branch that isn't dead (Rumi).

Breathing in deeply, my heart expands, my spine stretches. The spirituality of the sacred dancer is multi-leveled and has an affinity with many traditional modes of prayer and spiritual formation. Within these modes its gift may be the ability to begin *where one is* in the practice of prayer, radically referring to a foundation rooted in body/soul unity.

For example, there are many ways for "centering" prayer to be taught. The dancer seeks a still center, yet may remain acutely aware of his or her senses and surroundings, the taking in of these perceptions becoming part of inner attunement. Dwight Judy, trying to describe a "vision of life within divine presence" in a "bodily felt way" arrives at the term "celebrative center": "I described the 'place,' which of course is not a place but a state of mind awareness, as a celebrative center within me."[12]

A liturgical or Benedictine spirituality develops in a liturgical dancer's soul by her work. The dancer enters into the rhythm of the liturgy, embodies the readings and seasons of the church year, imbuing them with the rhythms and imaginations of her life.

The spirit of the dancer becomes informed, transformed, and refined through movement, breath, heartbeat, bones, muscles, flesh, intuition, listening, trusting, knowing form within, becoming present and available for expression in the moment. Interaction of these elements (with guided purpose) produce the "chemistry" which synergizes matter and spirit. Spirit is then no longer disembodied, and matter no longer unconscious. We become more open to experiencing "mysteries" in simple, intuitive, and felt ways—the way of the artist.

For example, a dancer—body curled over, spine and arms creating a protected, inner circle—may experience the dark womb of birth; the arching of a back may lead to a sense of the energy of space or the ecstacy of resurrection; the sound of a chord traveling upward from root source to heart throb, becoming in movement the tree of life. Falling and recovering, opening and closing, the dancer learns of balance and harmony, an ever-renewing cycle of wisdom. Spirit is enabled to infuse matter, now receptive to its inspiration. All the senses are enlivened and are heard in new ways. Our entire body has become a "spiritual organ."

The spirituality of the dancer/artist seems to be particularly attuned, shaped, and woven by the Spirit—as found from the beginning (in Genesis), moving and breathing over all creation. We may think of the spirit of the dancer being fashioned by wisdom, playing in creation, and rejoicing before God (cf. Pr 8:22ff). Wisdom, after all, permeates all matter, she who is "...more mobile than any motion," and who "because of her pureness ... pervades and penetrates all things. For she is a breath of the power of God ... (and) in every generation she passes into holy souls and makes them friends of God, and prophets" (Wis 7:24–28).

For the dancer, to dance is to give expression to who we are, how we see the world around us, and the mysteries of our faith. Despite the ups and downs of belief in our work, and in the adequacy of our body to the task, our faith is not separate from the daily struggles of refining or keeping our body in readiness. The dancer gives expression to the interiority of God through the movements of the soul, and to the omnipresence of God in the movements of the thousand things of the world. All of life is drawn into communion.

Dancers are fed through their own work, serving in partnership within the community. It is an adventure. In rehearsal, our soul becomes strengthened as fears are met and integrated with vision and bodily wisdom. Through movement the senses become heightened; we become attuned, a "tuning fork" for others. In performance, the dancer shares what has been discovered and crafted in an embodied statement about the "inexpressible" part of his or her being, and who he or she has become.

Inner exploration, including improvisation, are usually behind-the-scene steps leading to choreography of the dance. Improvisation catches the spirit on the wing, allowing an unexpected vision of reality that transcends expectations. The dancer perceives the glory and the passion in and through physical engagement. Dance is a language, drawing both performer and onlooker into its story on an intuitive, visceral level. In the absence of words, observers are more integrally affected with their whole being. We are being taught to "listen" in a new, holistic way.

Embodied spirituality is the constant reference point. Both practice and performance include body, soul, and spirit in tandem. You are body, you are spirit. In the process of dancing, you are transforming yourself, enlarging your own soul. A colleague, Cynthia Winton-Henry remarked: "Dance is more than a metaphor—to dance is to have spirit-to-be."

We have begun a new millennium, with expansion of consciousness one of its hallmarks. Two thousand years ago St. Paul reminded us: "the body is one and has many members. If one member suffers, all the members share its joy." Let's flesh this out. What could be better suited than sacred dance for breaking cultures, as we search for the underlying spiritual direction of all humanity for a heaven on earth. "Rite on."

Notes

1. Hugo Rahner, *Man at Play*, quoted in Ronald Gagne, Thomas Kane, Robert VerEecke, *Introducing Dance in Christian Worship* (Washington, D.C.: Pastoral Press, 1984), 61.

2. Gagne, Kane, VerEecke 63; italics mine.

3. Reverend Robert Borg, on a recent visit to the states from New South Wales, Australia, recounted the custom in his parish (in the diocese of Broken Bay) to precede the liturgy with a very quiet and soothing dance, which helps the children quiet down and become more reverential. The dancers then become part of the entrance procession.

4. Carla De Sola, "News of the Cathedral of St. John the Divine," *Cathedral* 2:1 (December, 1986), speaking of her experiences as director of the Omega Liturgical Dance Company touring with Father Thomas Kane in France.

5. While teaching at the Graduate Theology Union, I was privileged to create with Jake Empereur several dances and movement acclamations for the Jesuit liturgies.

6. An inspiring account of mentorship for the dancer is recounted by Howard Thurman in *Footprints of a Dream: The Story of the Church for the Fellowship of all People* (New York: Harper & Bros., 1959), 90–93.

7. *Dance Magazine* (December, 1996): 72–76.

8. *The Catholic Voice*, Diocese of Oakland (Sept. 22, 1997): 13.

9. Martha Ann Kirk, CCVI, *Dancing with Creation* (San Jose, Calif.: Resource Publications, Inc., 1983).

10. Peter E. Fink, SJ, ed., *The New Dictionary of Sacramental Worship* (Collegeville, Minn.: The Liturgical Press, 1990), 318.

11. Feminist theologians have much to contribute to understanding effects of the body/mind split in theology and spirituality. Basic to their consideration is a celebration of embodiment, wherein women refer to their own experiences as a way to relate to and understand theology, while keeping a focus on the interrelatedness of all life.

12. Dwight Judy, *Christian Meditation and Inner Healing* (New York: Crossroad, 1991), 14.

CARLA DE SOLA is director of the Omega West Dance Company in residence at the Center for the Arts, Religion, and Education of the Graduate Theological Union, where she teaches sacred dance courses. She is author of *The Spirit Moves: A Handbook of Dance and Prayer* and *Peace Rites: Dance and the Art of Making Peace*.

Come Dance Sophia's Circle

Martha Ann Kirk, CCVI

In the new millennium, people face challenges of violence and of ecological destruction. Violence is often justified by world views of innate dominance, putting some people over others. Ecological destruction is furthered by consumerism. Dance in ritual is a way of connecting and healing. Women's dance has contributed to transforming role dominance in liturgy and in life. Looking back at some dance in the twentieth century can inspire and focus some uses of dance in worship in the future. The theological term for the activity of the Trinity is *perichoresis* coming from Greek roots meaning to "dance around in a circle." The Trinity dances through the cosmos and the ages. The triune Holy One is not static, but dynamic, delighting in the dancing. Jesus invites people not to be blinded to how Sophia manifests the Christ: "We played the flute for you, and you did not dance .... Yet wisdom is vindicated by her deeds" (Mt 11:17,19). Christ Sophia invites people to the dance, invites them to live an incarnational spirituality, and invites them to live in their bodies. In *Heart of Flesh*, Joan Chittister notes that "Once the body is devalued—as the whole

history of Western civilization, with its pattern of large-scale genocide, enslavement, witch burnings, and holocausts attests—anything can happen."[1] Dance in Christian worship in the twentieth century has contributed towards re-valuing the body. Christian feminist worship in the last quarter of the twentieth century, with its integral use of the bodiliness including movement and symbols can lead other general Christian worship to reclaim the body, to reclaim the Body, and to move toward a more just, peaceful, hopeful, and healthy future.

Judith Lynne Hanna's study of dance performances in the United States in this century, *Dance, Sex, and Gender*, suggests that dance both reflects and shapes gender patterns of dominance and submission in the larger culture. She suggests that late twentieth century America is experiencing in its dance the ambiguity of traditional gender roles. This reshaping of relationships is infuriating for some, exhilarating for others, and confusing for many.[2] In the roots of the Christian tradition, in Scripture, what models for relationships are given? While the biblical tradition is full of examples of dominating power, Jesus said that he no longer called his followers slaves, but rather friends, thus inviting relationships of mutuality rather than domination (Jn 15:15). Joan Chittister writes, "Patriarchy rests on four interlocking principles: dualism, hierarchy, domination, and essential inequality. These are touchstones of the patriarchal world view."[3] This chapter suggests that dance in Christian rituals has contributed to transforming dualisms and dominant power. This dance can bring wisdom to enrich religion and life in the next millennium.

Hanna has explained, "Whether a ritual, social event, or theater art, dance has important yet little-recognized potential to move and persuade us about what it is to be male or female."[4] Being male or female in Christianity and in the world today continues to have many implications. Why should gender be brought into the conversation when looking at the significance of the arts for worship and religious education in the next century? What does it mean to be born and baptized in a woman's body at the end of the twentieth century? In North America in 1900, the majority of women did not live beyond menopause. A large percentage of the women born in the 2000s will live to be one hundred. Length of life for North American women is changing, but is quality of life for the majority of women in the world? According to the International Labor Organization studies, women are one-half the population of the world, receive one-tenth of the world's income, account for two-thirds of the world's working hours, and own only one-hundredth of the world's property. Of the 850 million illiterate people of the earth, women are two-thirds.[5] While the majority of mainline Protestant churches would now accept the ordination of women, the majority of Christians in the world including Orthodox and Roman Catholic would look upon the female body as an impediment to ordination, a channel through which the grace of the sacraments could not come. The study of the World Council of Churches' "Decade of Churches in Solidarity with Women, 1988 to 1998," reported ongoing violence toward women, economic inequalities, lack of opportunities for women both in churches and in society, and the failure of churches to consistently and seriously confront this injustice. A good way of confronting these injustices is through more affirmation of the body and of women's bodies in worship.

Liturgical Dance in the Twentieth Century

J. G. Davies in *Liturgical Dance, an Historical, Theological and Practical Handbook* cited example after example of various denominations using dance in Christian worship in the twentieth century. He concluded, "the facts recorded in this final section reveal a burgeoning of religious dance the like of which has not been seen within Christianity before."[6] Dance is making worship more inclusive, functioning in somewhat the same way as Hanna describes dance in performances, "When moving images created by dancers violate expected male and female roles and their conventional expressions, the novel sign onstage charges the atmosphere and stimulates performers and observers to confront the possibility of altered life-styles. Dances are social acts that contribute to the continual emergence of culture."[7] While in many Christian churches in most of the twentieth century, it was uncommon to see women in the sanctuary as the leaders of prayer and preachers, yet, as liturgical dancers women were leading prayer and revealing God's word. Hanna wrote, "In dance, messages of power, dominance, defiance, and equality usually can be sent without accountability. The same unaccountability may provide a low-risk route to change. What has been historically constructed can be politically reconstructed."[8]

Liturgical dance in Christian and Jewish worship of North America in the twentieth century parallels many of Hanna's observations about dance in relation to gender stereotypes. Liturgical dance has been an area in which women and girls have been within sanctuary space, interpreted Scripture, and led the assembly in praise, intercession, confession, and lamentation, while in regular worship women would have little opportunity for such leadership. A main supporter for the development of liturgical dance has been the Sacred Dance Guild which became a national organization in the 1950s growing out of the roots of the Eastern Regional Sacred Dance Association which nurtured the seeds developing since the 1920s.[9]

Although dance in Christian worship is in continuity with the biblical tradition and the Christian tradition, twentieth century liturgical dance is different in its emphasis on the performance of some, rather than the participation of all. Susan Bauer has written about the communal nature of dance in Christian tradition, "From the early church through the Middle Ages, dance was not a rehearsed event but a spontaneous set of steps and patterns that consisted of simple walking, hopping, or jumping done in lines and circles. The performance quality was pedestrian in nature. The dance steps and patterns came to symbolize more than physical movement for the community or were used to induce an altered state of mind in the performer; dancing was the community's physical expression of its faith and concerns."[10] Communal dance was the norm for liturgical dance until the twentieth century. Later in this chapter, some examples of feminist rituals reclaiming communal dance will be considered.

Ronald Knox in *The Mass in Slow Motion* said that the Roman Catholic Tridentine Mass was like a dance.[11] In that dance the priest had most of the movement. Considering that the congregation was more a passive audience than active participants in the dance of salvation, it is not surprising that most liturgical dance that develops in the first half of the twentieth century is like the "priesthood of dancers" to be watched and not done. Bauer has written that carefully crafted dance to be watched by the congregation in Western Christian liturgy is a twentieth-century phenomenon. It contrasts with the communal, spontaneous, and free dance through the centuries. Of the modern period, Bauer writes, "Dancers are designated by a church community to minister in dance."[12] While much of this liturgical dance of the twentieth century seems to contribute to the transformation of gender patterns of dominance and submission, it has not been explicitly designed for that. The next sections will consider gender.

The Body, Instrument of Sin or Grace?

Despite the incarnation, the concept that the divine took a body in Christ, a contradiction in Christian attitudes toward the body arose. Joan Chittister notes, "The continuing war against the body was a bitter and brutal one. Spiritualities from Gnosticism to Jansenism abounded, far into the twentieth century, intent on the suppression of physical needs, physical pleasure, physical joy, and physical reality. Women's bodies in particular were targeted for ridicule and rejection."[13] Margaret Miles in her perceptive study, *Carnal Knowing: Female Nakedness and Religious Meaning in the Christian West* examines the development of the symbol of woman's body. In the first seventeen centuries of Christendom there is a construction of the idea of woman as symbol for what is finite and material and these are associated with death and evil. In both text and art, patriarchy has constructed woman as the evil object.[14] The pervasive message of female inferiority in Western culture needs to be deconstructed. Women need to be the subjects who define themselves and construct their own images of themselves and of their bodies.[15] Popular media is full of images of women's bodies and women's dance as objects of the male gaze, to please males. Dance in women's rituals is one way of reconstructing body images.

Female bodiliness, considered unclean in ancient biblical tradition, can appear as an integral graceful instrument and also an instrument of grace in ritual. Ann Wagner's extensive study, *Adversaries of Dance from the Puritans to the Present*, focuses on the condemnation of social dancing with men and women by some Christian clergy and groups. She attempts to analyze why dance was criticized and why this raises issues about gender. Wagner writes, "Salvation by grace, in the writings of Luther, stood in opposition to salvation by law and works. Ironically, dance opposition ended during the twentieth century in an unexamined tradition based on law and morality. Had the adversaries of dance followed the more difficult path of perceiving dancing within the social, aesthetic, and theological context of grace, the end result could have been radically different."[16] Since ancient times grace has had both a theological and aesthetic meaning. Grace is a free, unmerited gift. From the Renaissance to the present, the word used most often to describe good dancing is "graceful." Wagner discusses the clergy's prejudice against dance:

> Graceful dancing is, after all, a reference to quality of performance, to that which is first of all pleasing to the eye rather than right or wrong according to the moral law. In the antidance literature, the absence of grace in its theological and aesthetic dimensions, coupled with the presence of law, is striking. The fruits of the law are fear and retribution. The law can produce justice, but not joy. By contrast, a positive affirmation of life flows from the concept of grace. The Greek work *charis* and the Latin *gratia*, as the roots of grace, stand in dramatic contrast to fear and retribution. A gift brings thanksgiving, joy, celebration. And dancing, in its essence, is celebration. It is testimony to God's creation—a human being with an infinite capacity for expression and joy in motion.[17]

In life and in worship, the gift, the grace, the joy of dance are needed to stretch persons beyond law into mystery. The body is not only an instrument of grace, but an image of the divine.

Feminist Prayer, Embodied Prayer

Studies of women's rituals, of feminists liturgies, and of collections of texts from major women's conferences in the last quarter of the twentieth century indicate that gesture, dance, mime, and drama are regular components of women's ritualizing and should be considered as seriously as text. Women's ritual has great power because women take embodiment seriously whether in the use of moment, images, or symbols. Women's bodies, whose bleed-ing has been considered "polluting" and "unclean," are central symbols and mediators of the holy.[18]

Feminist liturgical prayer has developed partially in resistance to patterns of dominance. As with Mahatma Gandhi and Martin Luther King, Jr., non-violent resistance is not an end in itself, but a means to move toward transformation. Marjorie Proctor-Smith notes that groups need to understand how relationships of domination function before they can create "prayers of resistance, prayers that spiritualize sociability, cooperation, and mutuality rather than dominance and submission."[19] She explains that patriarchal prayer "emphasizes the weakness, sinfulness, and ignorance of the one praying, and emphasizes the superior power, goodness, or wisdom of the one to whom we pray."[20] As many forms of liberation theology note, those who have been belittled or humiliated are not called to the same spirituality as the proud. Traditional prayer postures are often examples of submission, such as kneeling, prostrating, or bowing. The postures put one in a vulnerable position. In contrast posture and movement in feminist prayer teach women of their dignity and worth. A good example is Colleen Fulmer's song with expansive, confident communal dance, "We are fashioned in God's image. We are women, radiant glory. Spirit rising, wings unfurled. We are beauty for God's world."[21] Proctor-Smith writes, "Gestures of dominance and submission are the vocabulary of traditional embodied prayer; feminist embodied prayer experiments with, explores, and discovers gestures and postures of mutuality, equality, and community …. To honor our bodies in embodied prayer means to accept our bodies as they are, not as society or religion would have them be; to learn, slowly, to listen to our bodies' changing desires and needs, and to respect those desires and needs; and to honor and respect other women's differing interpretations of their bodies' desires and needs. Above all it means honoring our bodies as inviolable, as holy, as connected, as ourselves."[22]

Ecstatic and Communal Energy

Much of the exuberant movement of large women's conferences in the last quarter of the twentieth century could be associated with the biblical phenomenon of prophetic dance. The dance has not caused an altered state of consciousness, like a trance, but it has transformed the participants' energy. Persons are caught up in a vision and an energy beyond the boundaries of their daily lives. Movement expresses and intensifies that hope and power. In the eighteenth and nineteenth century in the United States, laws against using drums in Christian worship were made because African slaves got too much energy from singing and dancing with them. The dominant group does not know how to control people with that much energy. How often have church men issued directives or laws against dance in worship because women get too much energy from the dance? Such women cannot be controlled. The importance of communal dancing is growing. Communal dancing is in keeping with goals of feminist ritual such as inclusiveness and community building. Feminists are reclaiming the oldest and most pervasive type of dance in religious ritual. Doug Adams writes that "communal dancing in worship resonates with the earliest prophetic practices, the later talmudic and midrashic vision of humanities coming to God, and the history of Hebraic practice. In the early prophetic practice dancing is carried out in a band."[23]

For many national mainline Protestant and Roman Catholic women's gatherings in the last quarter of the twentieth century, dance has been considered an integral part of the worship. Following are some examples of this.

Roman Catholic Women's Ordination Conference

Thanksgiving weekend in 1975, more than one thousand people gathered in Detroit asking why Catholic women couldn't be ordained. Speakers clarified that the theological stones that blocked the way seemed to be placed by men. Carla De Sola danced and the power and freedom of the Spirit seemed to move with her, moving over the stones, filling the room, filling hearts. The ritual leader said, "And those of you who feel called to ordination, stand." As if the dance was leading to the next step, one woman stood, and then another, and another. Catholic

women have not sat down again. They are in the dance.

The second Women's Ordination Conference held in Baltimore in 1978 began with a processional dance. Holding huge chains, people processed from the harbor to the convention center. Chains can bind or chains can link and give strength. Those hoping for women's ordination moved and danced down the streets linked with each other. The momentum grew. The third conference, held in St. Louis in 1985, included the story of the Hebrew people being freed from the slavery of Egypt and Miriam leading them in a ritual of song and dance. The text, one of the oldest fragments of Scripture, seems to come from the tradition of women priests who led ritual in Egypt.[24] All whom God had freed were invited to join in the dance. Doug Adams has reflected on dance associated with freedom, "Dancing in the Judeo-Christian tradition has been associated with the experiences that life is not determined by the past or old self. Bondage to the past may be shaken off by dancing to free attention to feel new intentions. In the Hebrew Scriptures and subsequent Jewish traditions, dance celebrates and effects the end of slavery to the past and the beginning of new freedom to act in the world and create new community."[25]

In early Christianity, circle dances with all the community were popular. This prayer imitated the angels dancing around the throne of God. Dances break down social barriers. In the fifth century as hierarchy developed, the dances began to change. Deacons would only dance with deacons and priests would only dance with priests. Ideas for dance used in the opening service of the twentieth anniversary celebration in 1995 of the Roman Catholic Women's Ordination Conference grew from awareness of this history. About 1,200 women and men from twenty countries gathered for "Discipleship of Equals: Breaking Bread and Doing Justice." The movement of both the leaders and the whole assembly developed integral content of the gathering. In the opening service, persons dressed in albs, cassocks, bishops' miters, and stoles processed in a dance of pomp and prestige. Needy persons huddled cold, hungry, homeless, and lonely, reaching toward the pompous parade. At first the congregation laughed, then they began to grow uncomfortable as the powerful looked over or stepped over those in need. Gradually transformation began—the wearer of a cassock began to use it as a blanket for one who was cold. A miter became a bowl for water to soothe the weary. An alb became a table cloth so the lowly could feast. Stoles began to be ribbons to link friends. Finally, the mighty mitered one, the limping little one, the pompous pontiff, and the pleading pauper were holding hands dancing in a circle, dancing a discipleship of equals. Some of the bishops who attended the gathering met with leadership from the Women's Ordination Conference the day after it ended. One of the bishops spoke not of the words he had heard but of the dance he had seen.

A few years ago in a retreat at the Nevada nuclear test site, I led the Liturgy of the Word with a danced reflection on cherishing rather than destroying our fragile earth. Beside me stood the leader of the Liturgy of the Eucharist, Archbishop Dom Helder Camera of Brazil, frail and in his eighties. At the end of the liturgy, he touched my arm and gestured wanting all of us to do some more dance. The action of Archbishop Camera and the comments of the bishops after the twentieth anniversary gathering, indicate to me that women's position in the Roman Catholic Church is in transition. Women are not the victims begging not to be oppressed and to be let in. Women are the dancers of a discipleship of equals—healing, helping, nourishing, learning, loving, leading, taming, transforming, and doing justice. Crones teach the steady persevering stomps, mothers teach the joyful skips, and maidens run and leap into the future. Brothers want to learn how.

Women Church

Rosemary Radford Ruether used the term "women-church" to explain a growing phenomenon of Christian women recognizing and claiming the power of the Holy Spirit's activity among them as *ecclesia*, church. Traditional male-dominated Christian institutions may or may not recognize them as church. The movement has grown internationally and there was a recognition of this in the inclusion of a workshop "Women-Church: Celebrating Women" at the World Council of Churches Assembly in Zimbabwe in 1998. Ever since the first national Women-Church Conference in Chicago in 1983,

dance has had a significant part in the rituals. Regional and local Women-Church gatherings have multiplied. The Women-Church West Conferences held in Berkeley in the 1980s included many forms of dance. In one, all participants joined in a dance of rising strength, "Mountain-moving women called by justice to awake." At another, an Afro-American midwife, whose work has led her to a profound sense of the sacredness and mystery of women's life-bearing bodies, danced to celebrate these portals to life. For many, especially women who had borne children, this dance was a deep prayerful healing of shame sometimes associated with sexuality. They celebrated their graced reality of bearing children.

The Credo Liturgical Dance Company of Boston, which has continued for more than twenty years, wove dance throughout the content of the 1987 national Women-Church Conference "Claiming Our Power" in Cincinnati. One of the most powerful workshops of the conference was a Jewish ritual dance "Tallit" by Fancon Shur with a huge cloth that was not only prayer shawl for which the dance was named but primal matter, a wedding canopy, and many other things. Dancers moved among participants finally catching up all in exhilarating motion. The closing blessing in Fountain Square was a dance interpretation of Luke 4.[26]

The 1993 Conference in Albuquerque called "Women-Church: Weavers of Change" with about 2,000 people had ritual Native American dances, dance workshops, and keynote sessions with themes carried by dance. The opening talks began with a song, "Blessing of the Sacred Womb," with all doing dance gestures.[27] Arts invite people into mystery, yet keep them grounded in the body. Phyllis Tribble in *God and the Rhetoric of Sexuality* discusses the Hebrew word *rahamim* meaning God's compassion coming from the root word for womb, *raham*.[28] The womb encircles with compassion to nurture life. The conference which began with dance ended outside on the plaza with a "fire dance" to express a passion for justice. An eight-foot tall ritual basket was burned. The ashes were spread on the earth of New Mexico where the first nuclear bombs had been tested and nuclear research continues. The dancing, burning, and sprinkling were prayers to heal whatever in people and in society destroys one's own body, the bodies of others, and the body of the earth.

Critical Mass

Judith Rock has written, "The priestly artist reminds us who we are and where we have come from. He or she affirms our past and offers us the firm ground of tradition on which to stand. As prophet, the artist challenges us with who we were created to be, asks us where we are going, and calls us into the future. The link between priest and prophet is a deep commitment to the community's tradition. The priest reassures us that we do indeed stand within it, and prophet insists that we measure ourselves against it and refrain from idolizing it."[29] Many women deeply committed to the tradition acting as priestly artists and prophet artists have created "Critical Masses." The first Critical Mass was in Oakland, Calif., in 1997 and other such services have been repeated there and spread to other parts of the United States. The first Critical Mass was a prayer experience embodied in dance, drama, and music. It was celebrated at the site of the Oakland Roman Catholic Cathedral which had been substantially damaged in the 1989 earthquake and then demolished. This Critical Mass revealed deconstruction of patriarchal leadership and reconstruction of communal shared leadership. A critical mass of people of faith have been moving toward, dancing toward, worship styles of mutuality and respect for diversity, a model for relationships in everyday life. Jane Redmont reflected on the experience as follows:

> This was a liturgy of bodies: our bodies,
> the body of Christ, the bodiliness
> of God, the body of the Church.
> I wondered briefly whether I
> experienced this as bodily prayer
> more than other participants because
> I danced much of the liturgy as one
> of the ritual leaders. But others told
> me they had the same experience.
> We all moved; we all blessed; we all
> spoke …. A liturgy of the body:
> We learn anew what it means to be the
> body of Christ—to eat it, to touch it,
> to receive it, to share it, to live as a part
> of it—to know the embodied God,

one of the truths at the heart of our Catholic Christian faith. Bodies and breath: at the *epiclesis*, a prayer calling on the power of the Spirit, we breathe as we bless, all of us, breath, arms, words and prayer moving together. Ruach. Breath. Spirit. We hold the loaves of bread and the cups of red wine close to our hearts: This is my body, this is my blood. First in a circle, facing the altar, then facing the assembly, the rest of the wide circle in which we stand. After placing the gifts back on the table, we touch each other's arms. We repeat: This is my body; this is my blood; and move into the congregation to share and spread this gesture and these words. I understand the body of Christ in a way I had not before, at any rate as deeply, with a knowledge inside the flesh. This is my body, I say, touching a woman's arm and shoulder. This is my blood, I say touching another woman, of a different age and race from my own. You are my flesh and blood, we are saying, and Christ's flesh and blood. We know this in the breaking of the bread and the sharing of the cup; we know this in touching each other's bodies.[30]

A type of mystagogia, that is reflection on the experience, followed that first service and the others that have taken place. Good ritual can lead one into probing the mystery of the divine which is much more than the immediate ritual event and the theological explanation of what has happened. Was there, is there, will there be real transformation into the body of Christ? Are the women leading these prayer services leading the Christian community to "life more abundantly"? Are these women like the Hebrew midwives, the mother and sister of Moses, and the Egyptian princess who preserved the lives of the baby boys in Exodus? Such women cherish the ongoing life of the community and will not let fearful people destroy or hold back abundant life.

In Christian Eucharist, is the minister holding and sharing the consecrated bread the climax of the dance? Or is the dance about multiple relationships and interactions—honoring the God ever beyond human images; encircling, touching, noticing the others, bringing pleasure and insight to them; limbering oneself, strengthening oneself, pushing out the tension, claiming the exhilaration, and finding healing? Do people with the movements of their whole bodies make the "Body of Christ" more present than just with words? Is there a critical mass of feminist consciousness that is transubstantiating Christianity, a critical mass of feminist consciousness that is transforming society beyond the patriarchal dominance which has been considered essential reality? In an article considering ritual authority in *Studia Liturgia*, Ronald Grimes has written, "The question we should be asking, then, is not what stands above ritual to authorize it, but what lies below it. The best position from which to answer this question is supine. So if I were forced to answer the question, "What constitutes ritual authority?" without arguing against the question itself, I would have to say something like this: Ritual has (or ought to have) authority only insofar as it is rooted in, generated by, and answerable to its infrastructures—bodily, cultural, ecological, and spiritual."[31]

World Council of Churches "Decade of Churches in Solidarity with Women, 1988–1998"

To celebrate the middle of the Ecumenical Decade of Churches in Solidarity with Women in North America, a conference called "Re-imagining" was held in Minneapolis in 1993. Sue Seid-Martin wrote of some of the goals for the rituals of the conference. The planners had desires for embodied forms, shared leadership and ownership of the rituals, and—a desire to ritualize relationships that emancipate and empower all in the assembly—a desire for a distinctive repertoire of ritual symbols and strategies that critique patriarchal liturgical norms, as well as expand them with images that are more holistic and inclusive. Liturgical renewal, a matter of ecumenical

convergence since the Vatican Council II, specifically upholds the primacy of the gathered people as the first sign of Christ's presence in worship. All perform their priestly function expected of them through their baptism."[32]

Carla DeSola, who ministered in dance at "Re-imagining," said that about fifty women danced with milk and honey in the main ritual in folk dance style weaving around the tables. This expands traditional Christian worship in which there would be gestures over the elements on the altar table. This expands the moment which has gained popularity in women's conferences in the last two decades of the twentieth century in which all the participants gather around many tables and do movements of offering and/or blessing. One of the clearest indications how much the Sophia image was transforming traditional patriarchal Christianity was the backlash to the "Re-imagining" conference. Some reactionary United Methodist and Presbyterians attacked its content after the gathering. The Women's Division of the General Board of Global Ministries was accused of sponsoring heretical teachings. Marjorie Proctor-Smith has reflected on the significance of "re-imagining" as public prayer: "The assertion that the functions of women's bodies are holy, and the celebration of that holiness in symbols of milk and honey, challenged simultaneously the hegemony of Christians praying and the historic Christian hatred and fear of women's bodies."[33]

The World Council of Churches closed the Ecumenical Decade of Churches in Solidarity with Women with a decade festival called "Visions Beyond 1998," in Harare, Zimbabwe, in 1998, immediately preceding the WCC decision-making assembly and fiftieth anniversary celebration. The choice of Africa as a venue was to make Christians throughout the world aware of the gifts of African Christians and also aware of the economic and political challenges that the people of that continent face.

The worship used at the decade festival was an important symbol of Christianity near the turn of the millennium. The festival was attended by about 1,200 women and thirty men from all over the world representing three hundred and thirty some different denominations that belong to the World Council of Churches, as well as Roman Catholics who are not members, but are partners in many areas. People came from the diversity of the free church, spontaneous praise of Pentecostals, to ancient formal ritual of the Orthodox, to the pristine prose of the Anglicans. Some beautiful Orthodox icons were used. Some powerful Protestant preaching was shared. Hymns from around the globe were sung. Creating ways for women from all these worlds to pray together was challenging. The main response to the challenge was for the women to pray together in their tears and in their bodies. Considering the grim reality that more than one thousand people per week were dying of AIDS in the country where the women were meeting, praying in ways disconnected from tears and bodies would seem to be blasphemy against the incarnation. As elderly relatives and church workers struggled to care for the large numbers of children orphaned each day, all longed for the fulfillment of the Gospel, "I will not leave you orphaned, I will send a comforter" (Jn 14:18).

From the opening in which participants processed to a large pot and poured water that they brought from all over the world—symbolic of prayers and desire for unity—to the closing with all joyfully joining in dance to African drums, embodiment was important. One of the most significant uses of dance was in the healing ritual to close the session on violence against women.

Proctor-Smith has written of some of the violence that women know in their bodies, "The existence of pornography, and the prevalence of rape and battery of women, construct the body knowledge of women. Our bodies are not ours to define, to claim, to protect, or to enjoy. Instead, our bodies know fear and threat of harm and invasion. Our bodies are seen as polluting, but in fact what we know is that our bodies are used, abused, and polluted. Our bodies are seen as dangerous, but we know that it is others who are a danger to our bodies. This body knowledge criticizes the patriarchal interpretation of our bodies: not dangerous but endangered."[34] Women need the almost forgotten tradition of lament. Women need rituals of exorcism to deal with the pervasive evils of abuse and degradation on the basis of gender.

For the first time in a World Council of Churches public international forum, acknowledgment of such violence was not just a workshop but a major presentation. Nine women from different regions poured water. They said that they brought the tears of the women of Africa, of Asia, of Europe. Stories of physical, sexual, and psychological abuse were shared. A theologian shared how women's theologies have often been trivialized. Finally all said, "In tears we recognize each other, from continent to continent, from country to country. Through our tears we look at each other. Because of these tears we stay together and move. We will move."[35] And as a commitment to "move," all moved. Dr. Chung Hyun Kyung from Korea led a ritual of healing with liturgical dance by Reverend Kim Jordan from the United States. The type of rainbow cloth used in Korean rituals celebrating that a baby has lived to his or her first birthday was used in the dance. Then all were led in dance gestures to claim the power of healing touch. They sang, "Everything she touches changes." To seal and remember the power of touch, Janis Pozzi-Johnson, an artist, invited each to make a hand print on a large mural which finally said, "I have made a hand print, a sacred one, for I am *imago Dei*—an image bearer of the Divine. We have made our handprints, all sacred ones, for the hands of the Divine have shaped us, creating us, sustaining us, healing us, suffering with us, inviting us into joy, and setting us free."[36]

In the Sunday morning worship of the women's conference, the Scriptures invited a reflection on racism with the story of the Syrophoenician woman. She was a member of a group seen as outsiders in Jesus' culture. Bread crumbs were shared remembering her words that even the dogs get the crumbs that fall from the table. Long pieces of fabric of many colors were danced in as an image of many peoples coming together making a beautiful pattern, and as the many colors of the natural world inviting respect for creation. Dance and symbol were the means of uniting.

Before moving attention away from Africa, a glimpse of the development of women's dance in ritual there will be shared from the morning prayer of the Catholic Poor Clare Sisters at their House of Prayer in Lilongwe, Malawi. To borrow Marjorie Proctor-Smith's term, they "revalorize" women's work such as quilting, cooking, or gardening through using it in ritual. Because women's work is often exploited or trivialized, liturgical use affirms its value. "Women-made objects become prayers: when their stories and the stories of their makers are told;

when the silence that normally surrounds woman-made things is broken; and when the anonymity of the maker is overturned, and her works praise her."[37] For the feast of Our Lady of Africa, the Sisters begin prayer creating a rhythm with the type of mortar and pestle used for grinding grain and the sounds of sifting grain. In their villages before the sun rises, the young women would have heard this work of their mothers. The dance gestures of bending down, left, and right suggest women's work of grinding and bread making. They begin the day remembering Mary whose body brought forth Jesus who nourishes with the bread of his body. These Sisters have developed extensive choreographs for the various services and seasons of the liturgical year.[38] While African cultures may discriminate against women in some ways, goddesses, women shamans, and healers have been significant in spirituality there. Within African Christianity women have been very active as evangelists and ministers. Dance has been an integral part of spiritual traditions in Africa.

Dance As Healing

These examples of women's liturgical dance indicate that its use positively contributes to healing some dualisms, such as soul and body, spirit and matter, male and female, transcendence and immanence, individuality and community. Dance can continue to heal some of the splits in our culture. Choreographies derive from and contribute to evolving culture. As Judith Lynn Hanna suggests, there are at least six factors that make dance a potentially potent form of gender modeling. Dance is "captivating, languagelike, open-ended, multisensory, persuasive, and accessible."[39]

Contemporary North American culture continues to be uncomfortable with women whose bodies are larger, stronger, or freer than men's bodies. Some contemporary studies are exploring images of the male body in relation to dominating power. In *The Stronger Women Get, the More Men Love Football*, Mariah Butron Nelson, a Stanford University and professional basketball player, does a careful study of women's growing liberation and the cultural reaction of males seeking larger and larger bodies in the nineteenth and twentieth century. As women wore bloomers, participated in sports, rode bicycles where they wished, men sought body building, violent sports, and "he-man" images. Nelson traces the huge attraction of football, the male-only sport, as women have entered almost all fields.[40] *Boys Will Be Boys, Breaking the Link Between Masculinity and Violence* documents the dangerous cultural stereotypes that say for a boy to grow into a "man" he needs to de-sensitize himself and accommodate violence, whether this is mildly suppressing his emotions, taking tackles and not wincing on the football field, or going into war.[41] This study written by Myriam Miedzian, who had many relatives die in Jewish Holocausts, invites examination of elements that de-sensitized Nazis to human feelings and of things that desensitize people today. Considering the popularity of the male image of the Iron man and the female image of the Barbie doll, Joan Chittister has written that, "Men learn to garner their gains by force. Women are left to make their way by seduction, both public and private."[42] This leads to an unhealthy world for all. In contrast to these images, stereotypes, and distortions, dance can help clarify, integrate, and heal. Dance invites men to be sensitive. Dance invites women to be strong. Dance moves beyond bodies as domineering or dominated and shows them as relational. Dance reveals strength, beauty, and freedom.

Dancing to Heal the Earth

Dance has been used not only to heal some of the splits between soul and body but some of the splits between humans and the earth. Father Luis Vitale, a Franciscan priest of the Santa Barbara Province, started prayer vigils at the Nevada nuclear test site near Las Vegas in the 1980s to protest the testing and to heal the earth. Vitale has described nuclear testing as an ultimate form of rape saying that the perpetrator forces his way into the earth. The shocks of underground testing are so great that they can be detected by seismographs in China. Vitale suggests that the perpetrators are like those who rape women and say, "It only lasted a few moments and it doesn't really hurt." People rape to reassure themselves of power over the others.

Archbishop Dom Helder Camera has called the test site the most evil place in the world because it has the potential to destroy all life on the planet. Organizers of prayer vigils there, especially the Franciscan friars of the Santa Barbara Province, sense that embodied prayer is needed for the healing of the earth which has been raped by nuclear tests. Kathryn Scarano, director of Kairos Dance Company in Riverside, Calif., Carla DeSola with Omega West Dance Company of Old St. Mary's Cathedral in San Francisco, and I have all contributed dance and led rituals with movement in prayer vigils and retreats on that wounded earth.

Sophia's Invitation to the Dance

In Scripture people slowly start to move from the concept of God as warrior to God as wisdom. They were invited to see beyond a tribal God to a universal God. Contemporary Christians have been reclaiming the figure of wisdom, personified as feminine in Hebrew Scriptures. In Christian Scriptures Christ is identified as wisdom and this rich image is being pondered in Sophia Christology. The personified figure of wisdom was danced both before and in the history of Israel.[43] Christ keeps inviting people to deeper insight, "We played the flute for you, and you did not dance" (Mt 11:17). Do Christians dare dance and reclaim their bodies? Consciously living in one's human body invites one to reexamine relationships with the body of the earth. The human family dances in the womb of earth, water, and air. Polluting them will lead to destruction of the human body. The ecological challenges of the new millennium call for a more integrated, holistic approach of respect for the earth. Dance in liturgy, greater embodiment with the multivalent richness of art, can help bring integration, vision, and hope.

So called white people are less than fifteen percent of the population of the earth. The white people need to learn more about dance from the others. The over consumption and warfare of the whites will irreparably destroy the resources of the planet by 2050, if we do not learn how to step more gently on the earth and in rhythm with its cycles. Christianity speaks of itself as a religion of incarnation which values the material of the earth. Christians who are less than

twenty percent of the population of the globe could learn from the dance of indigenous peoples of Africa, the Americas, and Australia that the dance can keep one in touch with the earth. Christians could learn from Hinduism, which is a few thousand years older than the Judeo-Christian tradition, that dance is an energy for survival. Liturgy is a rehearsal for life. In it relationships are laid out. Though dance can be embellished by costumes and supported by music making, dance in itself is not consuming the goods of the earth. Dance is finding delight in oneself, in community, and in the earth.

In the twenty-first century, war and violence as normal human modes of relationship could become obsolete as slavery and colonialism have become in the twentieth century. Though the global family bear the scars of these demeaning institutions, slavery and colonialism are not publicly and deliberately embraced by governments as effective institutions. Dance has a part to play in weaning human consciousness from war and violence. Dance uses elements that have been perverted by warfare—energy, emotions, and the body. Planning dance involves a healthy use of some of the dynamics so twisted in planning war—deliberate and repeated patterns of movement—and yet the space for spontaneity and surprise. Dance recreates these in contrast to war's destruction.

The Hebrew tradition had dances that celebrate some sort of victory, such as Miriam's dance, the dance of the daughter of Jephthah, the women's dances for Saul's and David's victories. In the new millennium people of faith are called to dance Sophia's circle. They will not dance to celebrate that some have won, *while others have lost.* They will not dance to celebrate that some have been killed or defeated. They will not dance as Jephthah's daughter to celebrate a military victory because she then becomes the victim sacrificed for it. People of faith will dance to recognize that the lives of all the peoples of the earth are sacred. They will dance in circles around the globe. The old dances may have celebrated the "victories," the deaths of the "enemy," the other, whether they be Egyptians, Ammonites, Germans, Japanese, Viet Cong, or Iraquis. People of faith are claiming the new dances, the dance that recognizes and celebrates that all life is one. Women have danced with their sisters in Mexico City, Nairobi, Beijing, and Harare. They can no longer dance to celebrate violence toward any of the children, they can no longer celebrate victory over, only solidarity with.

Humanity has been invited to dance Sophia's circle delighting in and valuing all parts of creation. Wisdom knows how to play. Wisdom nourishes. Are the end times the cosmic battle of Armageddon or is the end being led into the eternal dance? Will the saved be standing there as warriors with the blood of their enemies dripping off their hands or will the saved be holding the hands of the others in an endless dance of jubilation? Will we join the Trinity who dance? Christ invites, "Come dance Sophia's circle."

Notes

1. Joan D. Chittister, *Heart of Flesh, a Feminist Spirituality for Women and Men* (Grand Rapids, Michigan/Cambridge, U.K.: William B. Erdmans Publishing, 1998), 81.

2. Judith Lynne Hanna, *Dance, Sex and Gender, Sign of Identity, Dominance, Defiance, and Desire* (Chicago: University of Chicago Press, 1988), xiii–xviii.

3. Chittister 25.

4. Hanna 3.

5. Chittister 164.

6. J. G. Davies, *Liturgical Dance, an Historical, Theological and Practical Handbook* (London: SCM Press Ltd., 1984), 8.

7. Hanna xiii.

8. Hanna xvi.

9. Doug Adams and Diane Apostolos-Cappadona, "Changing Biblical Imagery and Artistic Identity in Twentieth-Century Dance," *Dance as Religious Studies*, ed. Doug Adams and Diane Apostolos-Cappadona (New York: Crossroad, 1990), 5.

10. Susan Bauer, "Dance as Performance Fine Art in Liturgy," *Dance as Religious Studies*, 167.

11. Ronald Knox, *The Mass in Slow Motion* (New York: Sheed and Ward, 1952).

12. Bauer 167.

13. Chittister 23.

14. Margaret Miles, *Carnal Knowing: Female Nakedness and Religious Meaning in the Christian West* (Boston: Beacon Press, 1989), passim.

15. For more information on women defining themselves see Apostolos-Cappadona, "Martha Graham and the Quest for the Feminine in Eve, Lilith, and Judith" and Kirk, "Biblical Women and Feminist Exegesis: Women Dancing Men's Ideas or Women Dancing Women" in *Dance as Religious Studies*, 118–149.

16. Ann Wagner, *Adversaries of Dance From the Puritans to the Present* (Urbana, Ill.: University of Illinois Press, 1997), 395.

17. Wagner 396.

18. This is by no means an exhaustive list, but some of the persons not mentioned in the chapter or other notes contributing to this expanding collection of feminist liturgical literature and literature on women's dance are Barbara Bowe, Charlotte Caron, Mary Collins, Melva Wilson Costen, Shelia Durkin Dericks, Carolyn Deitering, Denise J. J. Dijk, Ruth Duck, Heather Murray Elkins, Elisabeth Schüssler Fiorenza, Ruth McDonough Fitzpatrick, June C. Goudey, Kathleen Henry, Kathleen Hughes, Mary E. Hunt, Ada Maria Isasi-Diaz, Sharon Karam, Eileen King, Patricia Malarcher, Bridget Mary Meehan, Rose Mary Meyer, Rosemary Catalano Mitchell, Diann Neu, Lesley Northup, Carolyn Osiek, Shelia Redmond, Gail Anderson Ricciuti, Marian Ronan, Victoria Rue, Christine M. Smith, Karen Schwarz, Janet Walton, Margaret Moers Wenig, Delores S. Williams, Miriam Therese Winter. While the divine is always beyond human grasp, people have been exploring images of the divine in dance. A dance called "Trinity" by Judith Rock, Cindy Winton-Henry, and Phil Porter (*Dance as Religious Studies*, 191) is a delightful, surprising, energetic interpretation of a central theme of Christianity which breaks open stereotypes of not only gender but also solemnity. Dances based on biblical female images are explored in Martha Ann Kirk, Colleen Fulmer, and Rufino Zaragoza, *Daughters Who Image God, Weep with God, and Sing God's Praise* (Kansas City, Mo.: Sheed and Ward, 1987), videocassette.

19. Marjorie Proctor-Smith, *Praying with Our Eyes Open: Engendering Feminist Liturgical Prayer* (Nashville: Abingdon, 1995), 14.

20. Ibid. 48.

21. "Wings Unfurled" in Colleen Fulmer and Martha Ann Kirk, *Her Wings Unfurled* (Albany, Calif.: Loretto Spirituality Network, 1989), 68.

22. Proctor-Smith 64.

23. Doug Adams, "Communal Dance Forms and Consequences in Biblical Worship" *Dance as Religious Studies*, 36.

24. Martha Ann Kirk, *Celebrations of Biblical Women's Stories: Tears, Milk, and Honey* (Kansas City, Mo.: Sheed and Ward, 1987), 26–34.

25. Adams 39–40.

26. The passage of Luke in which Jesus said that the Spirit is "upon me" was an appropriate closing for a conference called "Claiming Our Power." Colleen Fulmer and I developed music and choreography.

27. Colleen Fulmer, "Blessing of the Divine Womb" in *Dancing Sophia's Circle* (Albany, Calif.: Loretto Spirituality Network, 1995).

28. Phyllis Trible, *God and the Rhetoric of Sexuality* (Philadelphia: Fortress Press, 1978), 31-59.

29. Judith Rock and Norman Mealy, *Performer as Priest and Prophet: Restoring the Intuitive in Worship with Music and Dance* (San Francisco: Harper and Row, 1988), 93.

30. Jane Redmont, "Women Stake Claim to Rites," *National Catholic Reporter*, Vol. 33, No. 44 (October 17, 1997): 4.

31. Ronald Grimes, "Liturgical Supinity, Liturgical Erectitude: On the Embodiment of Ritual Authority," *Studia Liturgia 23* (1993): 67.

32. Sue Seid-Martin, "Ritual for Re-Imagining," *Theological Markings* (Summer 1994): 19–10.

33. Proctor-Smith 34.

34. Ibid. 36.

35. Text of the ritual "Violence Against Women" distributed by the World Council of Churches at the Decade Festival, Harare, Zimbabwe, November, 1998.

36. Ibid. Poem by Janis Pozzi Johnson.

37. Proctor-Smith 67.

38. The dance can be seen as documented by Thomas Kane, *The Dancing Church: Impressions of the Church of Africa* (Mahwah, N.J.: Paulist Press), videocassette.

39. Hanna 13–23.

40. Mariah Butron Nelson, *The Stronger Women Get, the More Men Love Football: The American Culture of Sports* (New York: Harcourt Brace & Company, 1994).

41. Myriam Miedzian, *Boys Will Be Boys, Breaking the Link Between Masculinity and Violence* (New York: Doubleday, 1991), 61–62.

42. Chittister 76.

43. Othmar Keel-Leu, *Die Weisheit Spielt vor Gott* (Gottingen: Vendenhoeck and Ruprecht, 1974) as cited in Hal Taussig, "Dancing the Scriptures" in *Dance as Religious Studies*, 75.

MARTHA ANN KIRK, CCVI, is professor of religious studies at the University of the Incarnate Word. She is author of *Dancing with Creation: Mexican and Native American Dance in Christian Worship and Education, Celebrations of Biblical Women's Stories: Tears, Milk, and Honey,* and *Women of Bible Lands: A Pilgrim's Guide to the Inner and Outer Journeys*.

Why Are They Writing All This Music?

Reflections on the Popular Liturgical Music Market

John Foley, SJ

Why are they writing all this music?"[1] liturgist Mark Searle used to ask. "Who is it for?" He saw that the amount of liturgical music published in the United States had been doubling and tripling, including not only sheet music but recordings and music books filled with it. The submission, editing, "engraving," and printing of music is now greatly streamlined by computers, making possible publication of more liturgical music than ever before in history. One church publishing company, Oregon Catholic Press, puts a brand new hymnbook into the hands of its client parishes every year, thus providing a self-replacing repertory, with only some music staying on through the decades. Publication of music via the internet, of course, lies just over the horizon. Surely this is the most remarkable liturgical development of the last thirty years: Music publishing is now a major industry and shows no signs of stopping. We are in the midst of a composing and publishing explosion.

It seems fair, therefore, to pose Dr. Searle's question in business terms. Does the market really need all this new music? Or are composers and publishers (self-indulgently) filling their own personal needs to write and to sell product? Are they not in danger of drowning the market, producing so many pieces that no one will even want to look at a catalog? Bishop Rembert Weakland told me fifteen years ago that it was time to stop composing new music and to write musical variations (for example, for organ) on already existing pieces. Was he right?

I want to pursue the question first by locating the problem within the contemporary American liturgical scene. Then I want to compare the present situation with a historical precedent, to show what has happened in the past when the need for new pieces has been filled completely. Finally, I will outline ways I think market exhaustion is being staved off, at least for the time being.

The Context

Creativity is a vital and indispensable element of the church through history. Throughout church history authentic liturgical needs have stimulated the creativity of liturgical composers, which then responds to the needs. There has never been a time when creative individuals have desired to just leave the liturgy alone, to just enjoy what liturgy has and add nothing more. Those who wish to "save" liturgy from the meddling of liturgist/composers will have to take this fact into account, and will always have to bow to it. Let human beings into liturgy and you have let in creativity. This is part of the reason why "they are writing all this music." But who are "they"?

To answer I must speak about "paradigms" of American Catholic church music. M. Francis Mannion has pioneered the paradigmatic approach, presenting six different types of liturgical music and their surrounding liturgical clusters. There is not space here to relate all six prototypes, but a brief view of several will help.[2] Note that paradigms are not descriptions of actual parishes or people; they are "models" that help us to understand actual situations by comparison. Secondly, many liturgical values permeate each paradigm, but no paradigm can give primary stress to all of them. Therefore each paradigm receives its identity from the specific value it stresses over other values, though never to the exclusion of the others. Third, these paradigms are each an approach to the church's mandates. No one of them is "true" as opposed to others that would then be "false."

> We do a disservice to musical values ...
> when we confuse the judgment of music
> with the judgment of musical style.
> Style and value are two distinct
> judgments. Good music of new styles
> is finding a happy home in the
> celebrations of today. To chant and
> polyphony we have effectively added
> the chorale hymn, restored responsorial
> singing to some extent, and employed

> many styles of contemporary
> composition. Music in folk idiom
> is finding acceptance in eucharistic
> celebrations. We must judge value
> within each style.[3]

To put it differently, each paradigm responds in its own way to the three fold liturgical judgment of *Music in Catholic Worship*—musical, liturgical and pastoral—and each is therefore a valid approach.

A first type is the very influential paradigm titled "functionalism and scholarly constraint." It takes seriously twentieth-century gains in theory and history of the liturgy. It says that music has a main function: to accompany ritual action and/or set its words. By doing this it enlarges the rite and makes it more affectively prayerful. As a result of twentieth-century scholarship, ceremony has been pruned, simplified, and corrected by the reforms of Vatican II; music—like the rite—should be short, clear, and free from useless repetitions. Music in this paradigm therefore subordinates general poetic and spiritual expressivity to more purely ritual values.

A second type is what Mannion refers to as "modern classicism." The ruling value here is aesthetical beauty and tradition. This paradigm places great stress on maintaining excellence in composition and performance, together with high regard for the choral dimensions of liturgy. Trained musicians and composers perform traditional sacred music and write new music that is based on the normative contents of the classics. Cathedral music would largely conform to this type, though it is by no means limited strictly to it. Neither paradigm, "functionalism and scholarly constraint" nor "modern classicism" would be particularly vulnerable to over-crowding the market.

Mannion identifies a third paradigm "folk movement and popular culture."[4] The Roman Catholic Church's switch from Latin to vernacular opened the gates to new composers. Many felt that only music in English would now suffice for the church in America, and that therefore the older Latin music repertory was no longer useful. Vatican II's emphasis on full, conscious, and active participation by the people in the liturgy suggested a new path: Liturgical compositions not only in English but also in a form that pleased the people. Popular tastes could at last receive satisfaction.

Because Dr. Searle's question concerns mainly the "popular" paradigm, I want to spend a moment more describing this prototype. The "popular" paradigm aims for simplicity of form, melodic attractiveness, ease of performance, and congregational accessibility. With its emphasis on broad, widely shared values, it took among its early goals the establishment of intimacy and personalism, in place of the perceived formality and institutionalism of tradition. It has strongly emphasized spontaneity and emotional warmth. In certain ways this paradigm borrows facets from the burgeoning popular music industry in the United States. Estimation of future sales, for instance, help determine whether a collection will be selected by the publisher. And unlike traditional church music, a publication includes normatively a recording of the music, not just a written version. As a result, a new type of publication now became possible: replaceable music that enjoys wide popularity during the time it is in use, but then goes out of use. Continuing ready dissemination of new music is based on this ever-changing market. New is replaced by newer, and so on. The "popular" paradigm presents a second answer to Dr. Searle's initial question. Composers write all this music so that congregations may have a continually refreshed repertory of music for use in their assembled prayer, especially as they grow weary of what they are singing now.

But for two reasons the initial question comes back to haunt the popular tradition anyway. First, a problem occurs when certain pieces from the circulating repertory begin to stay in the repertory instead of being replaced. *Mass of Creation*, for instance, has been very popular for almost fifteen years and shows few signs of slowing. "Be Not Afraid" and "Here I am, Lord" are in the same category. Are assemblies engaged in a lengthy sifting process, choosing in the very long run those pieces that will remain permanently in the repertory? To the degree that they are, newly written and published music will gradually become unnecessary, and the question "Why are they writing all this music?" will again recur.

Second, the number of pieces published in this paradigm already outstrips the ability of any assembly to sing or even to sample all the new music. There is no end in sight. For example, if only half of the Catholic Church composers—conservatively estimating around one hundred—each published a "collection" of new liturgical music during the coming year, with perhaps ten numbers in each collection (again a conservative estimate), there would be five-hundred more new liturgical pieces next year than there are today at this moment. How many thousands can be added before music directors not only stop buying but also stop even reviewing the new literature? Questions such as this are beginning to haunt publishers and composers in the still very new "popular" paradigm. What happens when the amount of liturgical music begins to fill and surpass the need for it?

The Winnowing Process

To move toward an answer I want to sketch briefly an instance in which I believe something of the same thing happened: the development of chant. The following reading of history of course would have to be developed and proved, but it is worth stating here in summary form because of the light it might shed on popular church music. The story is the more interesting because anonymous composers took from six hundred to one thousand years to fill the whole chant repertory, while the "popular" paradigm is a scant thirty years old.

Plainsong, often also called Gregorian chant, developed idiosyncratically in various locales in Western Europe. Though we do not possess examples of the music from Christianity's early centuries, surely the references found in documents, paintings, murals and bas-reliefs suggest strongly that local churches had their own versions of chants perhaps heard elsewhere and adapted for local use.[5] Whole families of chant seem to have developed. For instance, in Mozarabic chant, Roman chant, and the music attributed to Hildegard of Bingen, we see sharply divergent stylistic features. Some landmarks from history can be mentioned as illustrating the journey from diversity to uniformity: Pope St. Leo the Great (440–461) instituted the *cantum anni circuli*, or "yearly chant," an ordering of the melodies for each day of the liturgical year. Pope St. Gregory the Great (590–604) ordered and codified the chant according to the liturgical year, resulting in the name we still give to plainsong: Gregorian chant. A grand impetus toward uniformity came at the hands of Charlemagne (742–814). In his quest to unify the church in the Frankish kingdom he sent for what liturgical rites had been written down in the Roman liturgical books. He began to suppress local chants and families of chant in favor of the Roman type, not out of enmity but in order to establish universal practice for his kingdom. During his reign came *Scholae Cantorum* in cathedrals and monasteries, founded to teach the more and more diversified repertory of chant for the whole church year. Since notation of chant did not yet exist, a cantor had to memorize the entire body of chant for use in his church. Markings began to be sketched on manuscripts (formerly containing words only) to remind the singer of a particular turn or a special quirk of the melody. Still total uniformity did not exist. As late as the ninth century an anonymous monk of St. Gall emphasized the great difference between "our cantilena and that of the Romans."[6]

Around the thirteenth century true notation had come into being in order to transcribe accurately the pitches and the rhythm of chant. This allowed further uniformity of the repertory, since chanters could now learn and sing the exact melody instead of merely what they remembered. Composition of new chants became less necessary because so many were already provided. Even the extensive calendar of saints and the large number of daily liturgies could not supply an inexhaustible resource. As the possible texts that had not yet been set to music became ever fewer and finally were exhausted, the creativity of musicians began to seek out crevices where they could still fit in some music. The interesting practice of "melisma" gave new room: syllables of the text were "stretched" by giving one syllable a short melodic phrase of its own.[7] In this way, more music could be written for the same amount of text. It is thought that the practice began in earnest with the last note of the word "Alleluia," which addition was then called the *Jubilus*. From the development of long melismatic passages came the next phase, adding new extra-liturgical text to various melismas. Finally there came composition of new melody as well as new text to be interpolated before, after, and/or in the midst of traditional, rubrical chants. These creations began to take on an autonomy of their own and were called *tropes* (sometimes referred

to as sequences), of which "Dies Irae" is the most famous example.

Robert Taft has suggested a theory of "soft spots" in the liturgy, that is, portions of a rite that have not been formalized and therefore are available for new, creative insertions of this type. Sooner or later the soft spots are filled in and hardened.[8] To use metaphorical language, the practice of *tropes* was an attempt to expand the *horizontal* space available for compositions. It was as if only one story buildings had been allowed and these were beginning to fill the plots of land ("soft spots") available for them, no matter how cleverly they were wedged together. Creativity, attracted by the beauty and transcendence of liturgical prayer, had to redouble its search for new places where it could contribute.[9]

The solution was to add new floors above the already finished ground floor. The new place *par excellence* was not in a horizontal line with the existent chants at all, but above them, in a new layer. Without being able to attempt an adequate study of Taft here, I want to give the vertical soft spots a working name, "soft layers." When one stratum is full, another layer is added on top of it instead of within it. In the present analysis this is the practice of "counterpoint," or "polyphony." Two or more melodic lines are sung or played at the same time as the already fixed chant, all layers in harmony with each other. The chant setting becomes the "fixed melody" or *cantus firmus* over which fresh and original contrapuntal voices create a new piece. The chant is unchanged but still transformed.

We are so used to counterpoint by now that we do not notice the new arena added by its practice. The entire yearly cycle of chant could stay in place if music were added not into it but above (or below) it, in harmony. How did this interesting practice come about? At first, in certain places, the method was for a second choir to repeat a musical phrase already sung by one choir, but doing it a fifth higher, to accommodate high and low voice ranges.[10] It was a small step to sing them both at the same time, resulting in parallel fifths or fourths (that is, the melody is sung along with itself, from different though simultaneous starting points), a practice called *organum*.[11] Gradually one of these voices became free and decorative, needing only to harmonize with the *cantus firmus*. This brilliant solution lasted for centuries while the various contrapuntal voices became more and more florid. Finally composers did away with the *cantus firmus* altogether, and wrote just counterpoint. The era of chant was over.

This quasi-historical overview suggests several points about liturgical music. First, creativity is normally a strong force in the church. Such creativity will operate within the boundaries of the historical situation, but will always and ever search for a way to contribute to the worship ceremony, seeking the most surprising and lovely nooks to decorate. Second, there is only so much room for liturgical compositions in any historical era. The sites needing music are finite in number, even though various layers can be sought out and filled. When all demand is stilled, creative talent finds another way to approach the problem, or else seeks a place outside the church for its contributions.

Third, if it is possible to generalize from chant, the lesson must be learned again that music for the liturgy cannot easily be canonized and fixed. The goal of finally determining the entire repertory, once and for all time, is chimerical. If liturgy is living, the music will be in the process of being created. There is no such thing as a completed, finalized liturgical repertory, in spite of the universal tendency toward uniformity.

Today's Landscape

What light does this analysis throw on today's situation? First, like chant, most of the major paradigm areas do not experience overcrowding except in the very long run. Musicians in the "modern classicism" paradigm are properly concerned with the task given by the *Constitution on the Sacred Liturgy* to "cultivate sacred music and increase its store of treasures."[12] But compositions of this type emerge at a more stately pace, much as "classical" music for the concert hall always has. Composers such as Proulx, Blanchard, or Twynham, fewer in number than those in the popular paradigm, are concerned to contribute music that is "much, not many" to the liturgy. "Functionalism and scholarly constraint" seeks music whose primary characteristic is aptitude for expressing ritual. For this reason the goal of "functional" liturgical music is to set each ritual moment

satisfactorily and then stop. Composers in this paradigm are not in heavy competition and large outputs are not a value for them. Of course a time might arrive when apt ritual compositions have been written for all liturgical possibilities, and then the overabundance question will assert itself for this paradigm too.

Compositions in the "popular" realm, however, face superabundance in principle. Limited lifespan for each composition has to be maintained so that there is room for more music to be published each year. Even so, wherever the market is smaller than the number of products being produced, marketers must either refine their niche or lower their output. I believe the former to be happening at the present time in the popular field.[13]

How are composers refining their products? What I am about to present may not seem like an answer to this question at all, but I hope to show that it is. I will draw up a list of straightforward qualities that have to be found in any good liturgical music whatsoever. I will call these qualities "marks" of liturgical music. I will say that liturgical music should aid ritual, promote prayer, be at the service of a culture, foster creativity and aesthetic quality, make participation easy, and be popular at least in the root meaning of the word. Whether one samples music in a cathedral or in a rural church each piece would either display each of these marks or violate them. It is like a checklist for composers who are serious about contributing to the church's liturgy.

These marks serve to refine the "product," the ritual music that is for sale. Instead of a merely nice religious piece, the liturgical piece becomes more specifically, for example, a vehicle for community prayer or an apt ritual moment. In this way it meets a more refined need. The marks help the composer and publisher target more precisely the needs of the liturgical assembly, thus promoting more sales.

Some readers may believe that marketing values predominate in the popular paradigm to the detriment of more properly church-derived goals. Without trying to refute that judgment here I still contend that structural values are able to co-exist with business concerns of the publisher and popular composer. "Shepherd Me, O God," to name one piece, developed within a complex situation of values. Even though it does add to the composer's income, no one accuses it of crass commercialism. I take it for granted, then, that popular, liturgical music can be written and used for properly religious and ritual reasons even while making money for the composer and publisher.

Analogous Values for Liturgical Music: Burrowing into the Market

Ritual Effectiveness: Setting and Accompanying the Rites

Ritual efficacy, as we have already seen in the "functional" prototype, highlights music's ability to support ritual texts and actions. It is not supposed to draw attention to itself. Ritual effectiveness dictates that music be regarded and performed in the closest possible relationship to rite so that the cleavage between the rite and music that is a reoccurring problem in liturgical history be assiduously avoided.[14]

"Modern classicism" has been affected strongly by such ritual values, since the historical repertory that was written for the Tridentine Mass has had to be adapted or edited for the Vatican II format and purpose. New music in the classical tradition can be designed specifically for the reformed Mass.

Musicians in the "popular" paradigm also have been attending to ritual function, though this value took time to develop. Earlier in the paradigm's history, because there was very little music for the newly "Englished" liturgy, almost anything for use in the revised rites found success. Popular compositions tended to be topic-driven, for use in the Mass wherever prayerful music was needed. For instance, "On Eagle's Wings" (1979) might be sung during an entrance rite, at the preparation of the gifts, during communion, or even as a closing number. It is a general piece. As time went by, publishers grew larger, more composers began to write, particular attention was paid to the use of Scripture, and ritual-specific pieces began to appear.[15] The "Holy" by Dan Schutte and Bob Dufford was in wide use by the late 1970s, well before the same composers wrote a memorial acclamation to go with it.[16] "Mass of Creation" by Marty Haugen, first published in 1984,

edged beyond the Dufford/Schutte composition in popularity and both are now used around the world. Haugen and David Haas produced a collection titled *Psalms for the Church Year* (1983), settings aimed specifically toward parish usage as the responsorial psalm. Many volumes have followed, by diverse composers. Finally, in the present, liturgists and popular composers have been working toward settings of entire ritual units, especially as these relate to proposed changes to the sacramentary.[17]

This development of ritual aptness does not mean that the "popular" prototype has become identical with "functionalism and scholarly constraint." It means that "functional" or ritual purpose has provided additional and more nuanced space for the contributions of popular paradigm composers without giving up stress on other popular values.

Communal As Well As Personal Prayer

It has been a mainstay of the liturgical renewal that liturgy should not provide simply another time for private prayer. Images of congregations before Vatican II come to mind, some people saying the rosary, some reciting personal prayers, the majority focusing on the liturgy only at the words of consecration and at communion. This type of prayer clearly diverged from the participatory model proposed by Vatican II. A distinction has to be made, however, between prayer that is called "private," excluding others, and that which is called more properly "personal" prayer. Every community activity is rooted in the participation of individuals. If the individual is not "personally" involved then the larger activity becomes empty or perfunctory. Liturgy and its music therefore has to be personal *to some degree*. Theoretical justification of this value can be found in a theology of the Trinity in which the Holy Spirit is not an autonomous unit but is in fact the interrelating reality of the persons of God's Trinity. In such a theology the individual in a liturgical assembly simultaneously comes to be with the others by being with him- or herself first and foundationally. The spirit of each person is a "temple of the Holy Spirit," the spirit of interrelated love. In this view, music must serve the personal level in order to be truly communal. Music which allows no contemplative depth may lure people into an excitement without foundation.

Gregorian chant can be seen as an ideal of this value. The sound of many voices intoning the single melodic line of chant exhibits what the early church called *una voce* or singing with "one voice,"[18] a symbol of the assembly's peaceful unity. "Modern classicism" (including chant) perhaps needs work in this area, since the aesthetic beauty of its music can at times force prayer to the sidelines. "Functionalism," because it serves the ritual so well, stands in possible danger of promoting the liturgical action to the detriment of the praying persons. "Popular" music, as I have said before, can be accused of the opposite, of promoting intimacy and personal values to the detriment of community prayer. "Intimate" music can arouse needs that are not always open to others.[19] But in its various stages of development, the popular paradigm perhaps has served the full, conscious, and active prayer of both the persons and the whole assembly more than has ordinarily been thought. Insofar as it does this, it further refines and adds to the assembly's need for prayerful ritual music.

Service of a Culture

This mark can be illustrated by a prototype I have not yet mentioned, called by Mannion, "the development of ethnic expression." In his typography this music's roots are outside the mainstream of American culture, notably within the African-American and Hispanic ethnic tributaries. Growing multicultural consciousness in the United States provides a backdrop for such music. Publishers of popular liturgical music are actively developing Latin American composers; the hymnal *Flor y Canto* (Oregon Catholic Press) provides a good beginning. African-American composers have been major contributors from the beginning of the reformed liturgy, especially Clarence Rivers, and there has long been a hymnal for contemporary Black Catholics entitled *Lead Me, Guide Me* (GIA).

A broad statement can be made that every paradigm does in fact serve a more or less well defined culture of its own. "Modern classicism" developed in Europe and even today's newly composed "classical" music for liturgy serve a certain more formal, indeed classical church assembly. In contrast, the "popular" prototype, at least in its first period, sought to bring church music and liturgy closer to popular American culture—with that culture's eclecticism, mass-production, equality instead of hierarchy, simple melody, and participation by anyone who wants to. It would be interesting but beyond the scope of this chapter to develop each paradigm's attitude toward emotion and feelings in the liturgy, sometimes thought to be a fault in the "popular" paradigm.

Service of cultures does provide another, more refined niche for popular liturgical music. Because it readily assimilates various influences, the "popular" paradigm can seek and create music specifically marked for certain cultures but attractive to the mainstream. African-American music, for instance, by Grayson Warren Brown or Leon Roberts, now is becoming current within the "popular" style.

Creativity: Two Kinds

Creativity of composers through history, as indicated before, represents a mighty force in liturgy. Composers seek out the soft spots in part because the creative urge within them desires to contribute to the God-oriented ritual. I want to note here two different modes of liturgical creativity. First, there is contribution of new pieces to a style of music whose parameters are already specified. "Modern classicism," for instance, explicitly cultivates a conscious continuity of new compositions with inherited tradition. Gregorian chant from the first millennium together with renaissance polyphony and organ accompaniment from the second provide a foundation and model for newer compositions, which bring elements such as harmony and rhythm up to date with the current times. The idea is not to invent a new style or to innovate by use of new or different instruments, but rather to contribute a new musical child that is fresh and incomparably new even though it has all the same equipment as the last.

Second, there is a kind of creativity that continues to invent new forms, styles, and instrumentation as a part of its evolution. It could be said that the "popular" prototype has done this from its beginning. The older custom of adapting a popular tune to sacred style and giving it new, religious words—"O Sacred Head Surrounded," for instance—is an honored tradition.[20] But in the popular paradigm composers are bringing not just melodies into the paradigm's style, they are bringing the popular style itself. This is a huge departure from Catholic liturgical music custom. Various other innovations have been brought in. Ray Repp and Joe Wise started with simple, more childlike music. The St. Louis Jesuits began the practice of adapting scriptural texts for words to liturgical music written in varying styles. David Haas in particular brought fuller orchestrations and an overtly "pop" style to his recorded collections. Michael Joncas and Rory Cooney have borrowed heavily from Broadway-style musicals. And currently new composers are bringing the production and style of thoroughly modern popular music to melodies that are expressive and right for the assembly.[21] The normal musical group for the popular style has gone from guitar alone to ensemble, including piano, bass, and "c instruments" such as flute or oboe, and often guitar. To put it simply, the boundaries themselves of the "popular" paradigm are open to the creative force.[22]

I like to think of these two kinds of creativity as evolving phyla, one of which has long since evolved the tools needed to answer the needs of its liturgies, and the other which is still mutating and deriving its strategies as it goes. In any case neither liturgy nor its ritual components are ever inert. Every paradigm has to allow room for creativity, on pain of losing its life. Rigidity, over-rubricizing and a traditional that is too closed can shut the door to creativity.

Aesthetic Quality

"Classicism" has a high traditional regard for aesthetic attributes. We are sometimes tempted to see this regard as an exclusive ownership. A better way of viewing it is that the "classical" paradigm forms an example for other paradigms. Each paradigm emphasizes certain values centrally, and therefore, without any disregard, still assign aestheticism a lower rank on the list. Renaissance composers created great and lasting music (as did the anonymous writers of chant) and therefore the composers who follow that ideal will be solidly based in musical learning and expertise taking pride in being professionals instead of amateurs. Thus these composers are an ideal for others.

Here analogous understanding is important. All the paradigms value aesthetic quality, but do it in their own ways. Standards of musicianship are quite high in some popular music, for instance, but they are based in a different canon of judgment. Certainly the popular paradigm can be faulted for some pieces that do not stand up to musical principles, as the classical paradigm can be for sometimes going over the assembly members' heads. But the question for all paradigms is whether they are consistently following the musical ideals of their style, and whether their program leaves room for increased expertise in music and words.

Ease of Participation

Ease of participation can be found in its details. Does the tessitura of a piece allow people with various vocal ranges all to sing it *with ease*? Or does its performance require effort and training on the assembly's part? Is the melody memorable? Does the transition into a common refrain motivate the assembly (subconsciously) to join in, or is the transition unrecognizable as such, forcing the people to come in late if at all? Does the melody sound good when many voices sing it in unison, or is it more appropriate for solo? Is it sturdy; that is, does it have to be sung "just so" in order to succeed, or can it weather treatment by the amateur voices of the congregation?

These and similar questions can be asked of any piece in any paradigm. But there is a larger issue as well, one which I have already mentioned: the co-existence of multiple values. I think there can be a kind of competition between popular music's ability to let the people sing and classical music's attention to complex musical values. But participation should not drive out aesthetical coherence or prayerfulness. A piece of liturgical music should not be singable *instead of* being apt for ritual, since values are not an either/or reality but both/and. All marks should be present in each prototype, realized according to the particular genius of that paradigm.

Popularity

If popularity is taken to mean "a hit," in the music industry's meaning today (music appealing to the popular taste, as opposed to classical, jazz, or folk music), no paradigm including "popular" fills that meaning very often. But I want to point to a deeper meaning of the word than I have been using thus far in this chapter. In some of its meanings this word does represent a value common to all paradigms. The root of the word is found in the Latin *populus*, meaning people. Music for liturgy needs to be "of the people" in the sense that it fits well the human purpose at worship. People, having sung it within the ritual, should feel satisfied, feel that their human longing for things of God has been, if not satisfied, then at least expressed. "Human" might be another word for this value.

Gregorian chant has always been popular in this sense. It has always comported itself to the praying person, even though the difficulty of most of the chant repertory precludes congregational singing. "Amazing Grace" is popular in a wider sense, since congregations can sing it and do so often; but somehow it also expresses what Christian people desire to confess to each other and to God. "Shepherd Me, O God" by Marty Haugen is widely used, and it also touches the soul deeply. It is of the people. Probably there could never be enough such music, and therefore this mark of liturgical music provides much room for continued composition.

Conclusions

I have attempted a non-exclusive list of liturgical/musical values. These marks stand for qualities that should never be missing from compositions for worship. Though different paradigms will put the values in different orders, each with its own choice of a principle value, diverse emphases help to maintain a broad range of values. If the "classical" prototype's emphasis on quality and training were to disappear, who would call the church to this characteristic important for all? If the emphasis on participation had not been advanced in these years since Vatican II by the "popular" paradigm, how would the church have remained attentive to this value? Certainly the ritual effectiveness of liturgical music would not have become so important a quality in all paradigms were it not for the example of "functionalism and scholarly constraint." The marks of liturgical music interpenetrate and argue strongly against the victory of one or the other prototype at the expense of the others.

I have been arguing throughout this chapter that the publication explosion has urgently made necessary a refinement of the "product." I said that if too many compositions are being published the market has to be analyzed and the product readjusted. Composers and publishers pore over the liturgical values explicated above, specializing their "product" to make it fulfill more detailed needs. In this way the continued high rate of publication can be partially justified and sustained, at least for a time. Beyond this no one can say. It will be interesting to see whether the popular paradigm will cover all the territory possible before too many years have gone by, and that sooner or later satisfied needs will necessitate fewer publications.

As for right now? Creative musicians are "writing all this music" to give people music that encourages participation, accompanies ritual, stimulates prayer both communal and personal, serves its culture well, gives ample room for creativity, registers high in aesthetic quality both within its paradigm and universally, and comes from and fits the souls and bodies of Christians at worship. These make liturgical music popular in the deepest sense of the word.

Notes

1. This chapter is drawn from a talk given to the Liturgical Music Composers' Forum, held at St. Louis University, January 26–28, 1998.

2. All six, in the order Mannion presents them, are: Neo-Caecilianism and the Restoration Agenda, Folk Movement and Popular Culture, Ethnic Expression, Functionalism and Scholarly Constraint, Modern Classicism, Ecumenism and Eclecticism (M. Francis Mannion, "Paradigms in American Catholic Church Music," *Worship*, Vol. 70, No. 2 [March 1996]: 101–128). I believe that a complete list should include also youth music, which is rapidly differentiating itself from "popular."

3. *Music in Catholic Worship*, *The Liturgy Documents: A Parish Resource*, Vol. 1 (Chicago: Liturgy Training Publications, 1991), no. 28, 281.

4. Hereafter referred to in this chapter as "popular," since its so-called "folk" phase has passed.

5. For example., cf. Johannes Quasten, *Music and Worship in Pagan and Christian Antiquity*, tr. Boniface Ramsey, OP (Washington: National Association of Pastoral Musicians, 1983), especially chapter 4. See also especially Edward Foley, *Foundations of Christian Music: The Music of Pre-Constantinian Christianity* (Collegeville, Minn.: The Liturgical Press, 1996), and Jan Michael Joncas, "Ambrose of Milan and Western Metrical Hymnody," in *GIA Quarterly* 9/4, (Summer 1998). A theoretical investigation can be found in Peter Jeffrey, "The Introduction of Psalmody into the Roman Mass by Pope Celestine I (422–432)," *Archiv Für Liturgiewissenshaft*, Vol. 26 (1984), 147–165. A general reference is Willi Apel, *Gregorian Chant* (Bloomington: Indiana University Press, 1958).

6. Quoted by Gerald Abraham, *The Concise Oxford History of Music* (Oxford, Oxford University Press, 1986), 60. See also the *New Oxford History of Music* 2nd ed.; vol 2, "The Early Middle Ages to 1300," edited by Richard Crocker and David Hiley (Oxford; New York: Oxford University Press, 1990).

7. "(N)eumes, or groups of notes, stretch the value of the syllables, giving the text a somewhat different shape than it would have in a purely syllabic chant. The text phrases are still reflected in the musical phrases, but less strongly. The neumes give more weight to musical aspects of the phrasing" (Richard L. Crocker, *A History of Musical Style* [New York: Dover Publications, Inc., 1966], 14; see all of Chapter One, "Before the Beginning: Gregorian Chant").

8. There is "a filling in of the basic common outline of the Eucharist at the three 'soft points' of the service: (1) before the readings, (2) between the word service and the eucharistic prayer, and (3) at the communion and dismissal that follow this prayer. As ceremonial and text rush in to fill the vacuum at the three action points of the liturgy, thus overlaying the primitive shape with a 'second stratum' of introit, preanaphoral, and communion rites, a contrary movement is provoked. The liturgy, thus filled out, appears overburdened and must be cut back" (Robert Taft, *Beyond East and West: Problems in Liturgical Understanding* [Washington: The Pastoral Press, 1984], 160 ff).

9. The Council of Trent (1545–63) abolished all the sequences except *Victimae paschali*, *Veni Sancte Spiritus*, *Lauda Sion*, and *Dies Irae* (adding *Stabat Mater*), thus stopping sequence composition in its tracks. Cf. Robert F. Hayburn, *Papal Legislation on Sacred Music 95 A.D. to 1977 A.D.* (Collegeville, Minn.: The Liturgical Press, 1979), 3–5, 25–31, 33–67.

10. Another speculation about how harmonic treatment of chant began is that the tenor and bass voices created the need for two different ranges to be sung at the same time. Cf. *The New Oxford History of Music*, Vol II: *Early Medieval Music: Up to 1300* (London, Oxford University Press, 1954), Chapter 8, "The Birth of Polyphony," by Dom Anselm Hughes. Dom Anselm holds that tenors and tenor-baritones were used, which would eliminate this theory.

11. Perhaps so-called because the effect was similar to that made by the instrument called the organ.

12. Article 121, *Vatican Council II: The Conciliar and Post Conciliar Documents* (Collegeville, Minn.: The Liturgical Press, 1975), 33–34. Mannion notes that this paradigm uses "Gregorian chant and Renaissance polyphony as *the basis for new developments and expressions . . .* ," having "both conservative *and* creative dimensions" (121, his italics). Edward Foley notes that the term "sacred music" has come to refer generically to "religious music, especially that which is considered art music such as J.S. Bach's *St. John Passion* (1724)" ("Music, Liturgical: Clarification of Terms," in *The New Dictionary of Sacramental Worship*, Peter E. Fink, SJ, ed. [Collegeville, Minn.: The Liturgical Press, 1990], 855).

13. I do not mean to imply that this is the only motivation. Each of the values that follow also has its own rationale, which also just happens to open the market.

14. Mannion 116.

15. Virgil Funk proposes three phases in the development of this paradigm in his article "The Future of Church Music," *Sung Liturgy: Toward 2,000 A.D.*, Virgil C. Funk, ed. (Washington D.C.: The Pastoral Press, 1991). Mannion adopts this schema in his paradigms article. Jan Michael Joncas enlarges the schema and examines compositional strategies since Vatican II in his as yet unpublished article "Where We Have Been: Roman Catholic Liturgical Music in the United States Since Vatican II," given at the 1998 Liturgical Music Composers' Forum, January 27, 1998 (article available from the Center for Liturgy at St. Louis University, 3837 West Pine Mall, St. Louis, MO, 63108).

16. These and settings of all the acclamations were republished in 1994 as *St. Louis Jesuits Mass* (Oregon Catholic Press).

17. This idea has been stressed by Edward Foley and taken up by Robert Hurd, who wrote "A More Organic Opening: Ritual Music and the New Gathering Rite," *Worship* 72/4, (July 1998): 290–315. Two collections have appeared thus far featuring through-settings of the gathering rite: Hurd's own *Ubi Caritas* (Oregon Catholic Press) and *The Church Gathers* (GIA Publications) by Gary Daigle and Marty Haugen.

18. On this usage see Quasten 66–72.

19. Thomas Day has lodged precisely such a critique in his *Why Catholics Can't Sing: The Culture of Catholicism and the Triumph of Bad Taste* (University of Alabama: University of Alabama Press, 1990).

20. David Haas in particular has continued this custom with his adaptation of Hawaiian and Irish melodies to liturgical use with, of course, new words.

21. Tim Valentine's *The Fire of Love* (GIA) came into my office as I was writing this chapter, a thoroughly compelling example of such music.

22. The same differentiation can be applied to the other paradigms. We can ask whether a form is still developing, how its seemingly final style choices serve the demands of liturgy, and finally if indeed a paradigm has gone beyond its time and now no longer handles the needs of the reformed liturgy.

JOHN FOLEY, SJ, is distinguished professor of liturgical theology at St. Louis University and also director of the Center for Liturgy. His *Creativity and the Roots of Liturgy* is a theological aesthetics of liturgy; his latest musical publication is *Like Winter Waiting: An Advent Pageant.*

Three Funerals (and a Film)

John Baldovin, SJ

Funerals are powerful events for they bring us face to face with the most serious issues in life: our own finitude, overpowering grief at the loss of a loved one, solidarity in the pain of our friends and family, the question of life's ultimate meaning, the very existence of a provident God. During the past forty years of liturgical reform and renewal several funeral liturgies stand out as worthy of comment. They will act in this chapter as test cases of the success, failure, and development of that renewal and its adaptation to very different circumstances.

The "three funerals" of the title refer to that of Paul VI in August 1978, Mother Teresa of Calcutta, and Diana, Princess of Wales, both in September 1997. The "film" referred to is the funeral of a gay man in *Four Weddings and a Funeral*. Two of the funerals are Roman Catholic, one Anglican, and another Presbyterian. Three of the funerals were on the grand scale—truly international events, the other a cinematic glimpse of very private grief. Each of these funerals can be instructive as to the ritualizing of public and private grief. Moreover, they each can tell us something about the experience of liturgical reform and renewal. I will comment on each as follows: Paul VI, funeral as ecclesial event; Mother Teresa, funeral as national and ecclesial event; Princess Diana, funeral as national event; *Four Weddings* ..., funeral as event of private grief.

Funeral As Ecclesial Event: Paul VI

The world was captivated by the funeral liturgy of Pope Paul VI, which took place in the piazza of St. Peter's at the Vatican on the afternoon of August 12, 1978. Like most deaths, his came as somewhat of a surprise six days earlier on August 6, appropriately enough the feast of the Transfiguration. One can assume that little had been done prior to that date in terms of preparation. Most funerals, as a matter of fact, need to be planned more or less on the spot. On the other hand, the Pope's will had indicated that he wished a simple funeral. It is rather difficult to have a simple funeral concelebrated by over one hundred cardinals, not to mention patriarchs of the Eastern Christian churches in union with the Church of Rome and a piazza half-filled with international dignitaries.[1] On the other hand, Pope Paul VI's funeral liturgy turned out to be an exemplary demonstration of the eucharistic liturgy reformed during his papacy as well as of the funeral ritual itself.

What made this funeral liturgy so striking and memorable—even twenty years later? First, this eucharistic liturgy was a fine example of the noble simplicity that had been the aim of the Second Vatican Council's *Constitution on the Sacred Liturgy*.[2] Early in the twentieth century the British liturgical specialist, Edmund Bishop, had published a landmark essay in which he had characterized the "pure" Roman liturgy by the nouns "sobriety" and "sense" in contrast to the tendency toward verbosity and ceremony in transalpine liturgical forms.[3] Less than ten years after the missal of Paul VI had been promulgated, here was an example of a reform that had been undertaken at the inspiration of historians like Bishop. To be sure, our reflections on the other funerals will show that liturgy cannot rest for long in such a pristine state. Sooner or later the "local" will have a significant effect on how the liturgy is celebrated. We have come to think of this process as inculturation—but few perceived the need for a serious dialogue between liturgy and local culture in 1978.

Second, there was the decision, made by Paul himself, to dispense with a catafalque and have the coffin lying directly on the ground. Surely one of the more memorable moments of the funeral liturgy was the sight of the Book of the Gospels atop the coffin with its pages turning gently in the breeze. Needless to say the sight of so many red-chasubled cardinals was also rather impressive. Many were confused by the choice of liturgical color for the vesture at this liturgy. By tradition red is employed at the funeral of a pope because so many of the early bishops of Rome were martyrs. But even the great number of hierarchs did not rob the occasion of its simplicity—perhaps because of the mammoth scale of St. Peter's square.

A third striking factor in Paul VI's funeral was the presence and activity of patriarchs from the Eastern Christian churches who conducted the commendation at the end of the liturgy. They were a potent reminder (along with the chanting of the Gospel in Greek as well as Latin) of the variety to be found within the church catholic.

A singularly unimpressive feature of the liturgy was the funeral homily, given by Carlo Cardinal Confalonieri, Dean of the College of Cardinals, who also presided at the liturgy. Paul had chosen the text himself—John 21:15–19—about Peter being led where he would not go in his old age. This text was perhaps a poignant reminder of how complex and tortured an individual Paul VI seems to have been. Unfortunately Confalonieri chose to ignore the rather clear instructions about funeral homilies given in the *Praenotanda* to the funeral rite, published in 1970—in Paul's own pontificate:

> A brief homily based on the readings
> should always be given at the funeral
> liturgy, but never any kind of eulogy.
> The homilist should dwell on God's
> compassionate love and on the paschal
> mystery of the Lord as proclaimed
> in the Scripture readings. Through
> the homily, the community should
> receive the consolation and strength
> to face the death of one of its members
> with a hope that has been nourished
> by the proclamation of the saving word
> of God.[4]

Instead Confalonieri chose to eulogize the dead pope, concentrating on his *Credo of the People of God,* which as Hebblethwaite points out was not the highpoint of his pontificate. For reasons which will have to be discussed later, there has been great resistance to preaching homilies at funeral liturgies.

To sum up, the funeral liturgy of Pope Paul VI was a kind of model of the reformed Roman liturgy, a tribute to the vision of Paul himself and to the council he brought to fruition. It was, of course, a far cry from the "ordinary" Roman Catholic funeral, but it still attempted to present the Roman Eucharist in a somewhat pristine form, exhibiting the sobriety and sense that characterize this particular (local) rite. This funeral was a worldwide ecclesial event. Being held in the open-air (even if in the splendid environs of the piazza of St. Peter's) it was a symbol of a man who desperately wanted to be a populist leader, even though he was ill-suited to the role by dint of his personality. A useful comparison may be made with the funeral of Mother Teresa of Calcutta.

Funeral As National and Ecclesial Event: Mother Teresa

Hard on the heels of the tragic death of Princess Diana came the rather more peaceful passing of another woman who had captured the imagination of the world. Despite the possible varying reactions to this woman's ministry, she was widely regarded as saintly and indubitably a major force in Roman Catholicism at the turn of the millennium.

The funeral of Mother Teresa provides a stark contrast to that of Paul VI. In the first place it was a national event—a state funeral—in a mostly non-Christian nation. To non-Indian observers (perhaps even to a number of Indians) the sight of her coffin on a gun carriage, covered with the Indian flag and accompanied by soldiers, seemed a bit incongruous for the funeral of a woman who devoted her life so selflessly to the poor. There was a poignancy, however, to the fact that the same gun carriage had carried Gandhi to his funeral. Moreover, the funeral liturgy itself obscured the clean classical lines of the Roman rite.

The eucharistic liturgy began with a rather long welcome from the Archbishop of Calcutta, Henry D'Souza. It had little place in the normal funeral liturgy (if there is such a thing as a normal funeral liturgy). From the ecclesiastical side it was an example that this funeral was somewhat of a political "football"—balancing the interests of the local church with that of the church universal. Angelo Cardinal Sodano, the Vatican Secretary of State "stood in" for the pope, preached, and presided over the Eucharist. From the point of view of the author, who regularly teaches liturgical presiding, Cardinal Sodano conducted himself with great dignity and grace. This is remarkable especially given the crowded conditions of the platform where the Eucharist was celebrated.

As with the funeral of Paul VI, the venue was not a church building but rather an indoor stadium, which held from 13,000 to 15,000 people. Scripture readings were proclaimed in the main languages of the nation: Hindi, Bengali, and English. Mother Teresa's own Missionaries of Charity formed the choir.

The coffin of Mother Teresa lay half open. The bottom half was draped with the Indian flag while the upper half revealed her face and sari-covered upper torso. During the funeral liturgy flies alit on the coffin and her corpse—to this viewer, at least, a symbol of the simplicity with which she lived and the destitute whom she served. Representatives of those same destitute participated in the procession of gifts to the altar.

The music at this funeral was rather unremarkable but very populist. Most of it could be heard in Catholic churches throughout the United States on any given Sunday. The homily once again skirted the norms laid down in the *Order of Christian Funerals*. Along with Archbishop D'Souza's welcoming speech at the beginning of the liturgy, Sodano's was far more of a eulogy than the kind of homily prescribed above. In fact it was a message from Pope John Paul II. In a sense neither of these clerics could be blamed for eulogizing someone for whom the term "eulogy" could have been invented.

The final commendation was perhaps the best example of needlessly complicating the funeral rite. Each of the five bishops on the platform took turns circumambulating and sprinkling the coffin. Like having a cardinal instead of a deacon read the Gospel, the concern with this funeral was far more the showcasing of the ecclesiastically and politically powerful than the celebration of the Roman rite. One cannot fault the church officials for the post-liturgy testimonials given by other religious leaders as well as representatives of the world's nations. After all this was a state funeral. Perhaps events made it impossible to observe the technicalities of the Roman rite, but there is a sense in which Mother Teresa's funeral, watched by millions, was a lost evangelical opportunity in terms of demonstrating the beauty and power of the Roman liturgy. However, a bishop reading the Gospel is a good example of ignoring the fundamental distinction of roles within the Roman rite in favor of parceling out liturgical roles so that important persons will be noted.

On the other hand there was a power in this event which transcended the breaking of liturgical rules.

I would venture that the power was more evident on the streets than within the stadium. Reports after the event claimed that the most moving aspect of the funeral was Mother Teresa's burial at "motherhouse," the headquarters of the Missionaries of Charity. There was a truly populist character to this funeral—but it was among the destitute and the "ordinary" people of India as well as Mother Teresa's sisters, not necessarily among the internationally and ecclesiastically powerful at the funeral liturgy.

Funeral As National Event: Princess Diana

From the late hours of Saturday, August 30, 1997, until Saturday, September 6, the world was gripped by the tragic death of Princess Diana, former wife of the Prince of Wales. Her funeral liturgy marks the third and last of the services on a grand scale to be dealt with in this chapter. Unlike the funerals of Paul VI and Mother Teresa, this liturgy was not a Eucharist but rather a memorial service that basically followed the lines of the Church of England's *Alternative Services Book 1980* and *The Book of Common Prayer 1662*. It would be unfair to judge it by the standards of Roman liturgy, but it certainly can illuminate our understanding of ritualizing death in the late twentieth century.

The structure of the ASB service is straightforward. It begins with introductory scriptural sentences from the Gospel of John, 1 Timothy, and Job followed by an opening prayer. For Diana's funeral, the procession being quite long, a number of other sentences were added—all sung to the settings of William Croft and Henry Purcell by the Westminster Abbey choir. A bidding, instead of a prayer, by the Abbey's dean, Dr. Wesley Carr, followed the sentences. Normally in the ASB a psalm and reading from Scripture would follow. At this funeral, however, the bidding was followed by a hymn, "I Vow to Thee, My Country," apparently a favorite of the late Princess. The hymn has the virtue of transcending national pride to sing of "another country," perhaps an adequate allusion to the fact that the event was a funeral, but hardly a text that would remind one of the paschal mystery at the center of a Christian's life and death.

In another departure from the ASB order there followed a poem by the Princess's elder sister, Lady Sarah McCorquondale, and then the "Libera me, Domine" from Verdi's *Requiem*. Another poem was read, this time by another sister of the Princess, Lady Jane Fellowes. Then all stood to sing the hymn "The King of Love My Shepherd Is." Adapted from Psalm 23, this hymn corresponds to the recommended psalm in the ASB. 1 Corinthians 13, the great hymn on love by St. Paul, was then read by Prime Minister Tony Blair. (Rather powerfully, one might add.) Next came what for many must have been the highpoint of the ceremony, Elton John's revised version of his song "Candle in the Wind." As one liturgical colleague put it, "Now everyone will want that song at their funeral." (One can imagine further revision to the song, "Goodbye Polish Rose ....")

Instead of a sermon or homily, indicated by the ASB, the congregation heard a tribute to the late Princess by her brother, Charles, Earl Spencer. The tribute was angry but elegant, hardly a homily. The only mention of God came at the end, when the speaker commended his sister to God. One can certainly question whether a brief homily on the participation of the Christian in the passion, death, and resurrection of Christ might not have been an ideal evangelical moment for the millions who watched or listened to the funeral. If so, to say that this was a lost opportunity is an incredible understatement.

The ASB directs that verses from the *Te Deum* or a hymn may be sung after the sermon. The choice was Sebastian Temple's "Make Me a Channel of Your Peace," adapted from St. Francis of Assisi. No doubt this hymn was chosen because it reminded everyone of Princess Diana's wholehearted commitment to a large number of charities. (The charity workers who had followed the cortège had been shuffled off to St. Margaret's Church, near the Abbey, to listen to the service.) One is tempted to be extremely critical of this song which is so musically weak and sentimental. On the other hand, to see the huge crowd gathered in Hyde Park to watch the funeral on large screen TV or the thousands in the streets around Westminster Abbey, singing along as the television cameras panned during the singing, was to be mightily impressed by both the power of a popular tune and the ardent desire of so many to participate in some way in this event which so obviously touched their hearts.[5]

At this point prayers were led by the Archbishop of Canterbury, Dr. George Carey. The prayers are well written and cover the basic themes one would want to acknowledge in a funeral service. The choir then sang Petrie's "Air from County Derry" commonly called "O Danny Boy."[6] There followed the Lord's Prayer (in whatever language one spoke), the blessing by Dr. Carey, and final commendation, led by Dean Carr. The recessional was accompanied by the choir singing the haunting "Song for Athene," a combination of lines from Shakespeare's *Hamlet* and the Orthodox funeral service. After one minute of silence throughout the church and the country the coffin was placed in a hearse for its journey to Diana's place of burial north of London.

A number of features of this funeral liturgy deserve further comment. First, the service was a fine example of the British love of ceremonial precision. From the ringing of the bells at exactly eleven A.M. when the coffin was carried through the west door of the Abbey until just a little over an hour later when it was carried out everything went like clockwork. The British sense of ceremony is precise, well rehearsed, and made-for-television. Second, there was a deep emotional tone to the funeral, since the entire nation had in a way participated in its construction as an expression of its extraordinary outpouring of grief. In this sense, the funeral was but a moment in the national ritual of mourning that had brought so many people to the streets and with flowers to the various royal palaces. Third, the liturgy itself was an example of adaptation to the wants and needs of both grieving families, the Spencers and the Windsors, not to mention the British and worldwide public. Fourth, there were a number of Christian elements in the funeral liturgy. Some of them had more to do with the predilections of the princess; others were taken directly or adapted from the ASB funeral service. Roman Catholics found it odd, of course, that the funeral lacked a eucharistic liturgy. It should be noted that the ASB first gives the funeral service without holy communion and then provides a service with the Eucharist. My British informants tell me that normally only the very "high church" Anglicans would have a Eucharist at a funeral.

Perhaps it would be better to understand the funeral of Diana, Princess of Wales, as a national event of mourning rather than an ecclesial event. To be sure, the funeral took place in the context of the Anglican Church, the state church of England,[7] of which Diana was a member. In a sense the event was too large to be confined to Christian liturgy. The funeral of Diana had to be a national event—one that responded to the grief of the British public.

Funeral As Event of Private Grief: A Film

The last funeral I have chosen to analyze was not "real." It takes place in the film, *Four Weddings and A Funeral*. This film is a romantic comedy, directed by Mike Newell, in which the main character, Charlie (Hugh Grant), fumbles his way into a commitment to Carrie (Andie McDowell) through a series of weddings of friends. The weddings themselves might provide the basis for a liturgical and social analysis given their varied "churchmanship" and social location, but the funeral stands out as an emotional highpoint of an otherwise comic film. Among the group of friends (mostly university classmates) who turn up at the weddings are Matthew and Gareth, gay lovers. At the film's third wedding, which takes place in a Scottish Presbyterian church and a Scottish castle, Gareth drops dead of a heart attack during the toasts. The scene shifts to his funeral, a bleak event with clearly confused parents and shocked mourners. We are not shown the funeral liturgy as such. Rather, the vicar introduces Matthew, Gareth's friend, to say a few words before the service begins. Matthew pays eloquent tribute to the ebullience, charm, eccentricity, and lovableness of Gareth and then—as an expression of his own unmitigated grief—reads W.H. Auden's "After the Funeral." The scene shifts to the cemetery and burial as Matthew (John Hannah) finishes reading the heart-rending poem. In the film's vocabulary it is as if the liturgy were of little or no consequence to the event. I may well be reading unfairly into the director's intentions, but I believe that one can draw the lesson that the funeral liturgy needs to provide a space for the public expression of private grief. In fact the Roman Catholic *Order of Christian Funerals* does just that both at the funeral vigil and after communion at the funeral Eucharist.

Most funerals, after all, are not national or international events like those of Paul VI, Mother Teresa, and Princess Diana. Most (Christian) funerals are an occasion for combining private grief with the faith tradition.

Conclusion

I set about writing this chapter with some very clear presuppositions about the theology of the paschal mystery and how little it seems to affect the celebration of Christian (even Roman Catholic) funerals today—by analyzing four very different funerals. I must admit that at the end I come up with different conclusions than I had supposed at the beginning.

The Homily

The homily, as a means of interrelating the life and death of the individual with the paschal mystery, is a difficult exercise. Regardless of the liturgical directives, most preachers seem to center on the eulogistic, since that is precisely what the congregation expects. I would have to admit that, in the case of the "generic" funeral in which the presider of the assembly has no acquaintance with the deceased, a homily that relates in no way to the dead person is most unsatisfactory.

On the other hand, eulogies are not always possible. Some people's lives are tragic on any number of levels and often well-meaning eulogizers offend against the basic truthfulness that ought to characterize worship of the God who is truth. (I have heard tell of the funeral of a prominent attorney, who was to say the least a rather complex individual. The preacher began by saying that this man was the person most like Jesus Christ whom he had ever met. Not a few of the man's law partners were forced to stifle their guffaws.)

None of the homilies at the funerals analyzed here was able to strike that delicate balance between eulogizing and preaching the (literally) life-and-death importance of Christian faith. The difficulty of achieving this balance should probably caution tolerance of those who cannot do it, even as it is recognized as ideal.

Funeral Liturgy

There is no such thing as the "correct" funeral liturgy. How such a liturgy unfolds will depend on a number of factors: the meaning of the event for the church, or its significance for a nation (or even internationally), the faith of the mourners, the composition of the congregation, and the willingness of someone to express private grief publicly. The aesthetics of each of these funerals differed greatly—and appropriately according to the situation and the genius of the particular culture. There is no one Christian aesthetic, just as there is no "generic" funeral liturgy.[8]

Personal Material

The inclusion of material of a more personal nature into the funeral liturgy is, like the question of the funeral homily, a rather delicate matter. In the funeral of Princess Diana, for example, Elton John's "Candle in the Wind" represented a significant moment in the service. Perhaps there is no way to avoid the inclusion of such elements—provided they are balanced by the expression of ecclesial faith.

Paschal Mystery

What is meant by celebration of the paschal mystery may at times be more implicit than explicit in the funeral liturgy. After all, funerals are the occasion for a wide variety of thoughts and emotions: grief, sadness, loss, gratitude, regret, faith, hope, love, and even humor. These varied thoughts and emotions cannot be so much programmed as allowed a space within the framework of the church's fundamental faith in the meaning of the death and resurrection of the Lord. All funerals call for a judicious (and at times serendipitous) combination of the personal and the public.

Notes

1. Most of the facts contained in this section are taken from Peter Hebblethwaite, *The Year of Three Popes* (New York: Collins, 1978), 7–9, plus the author's own recollection of the televised event.

2. *Constitution on the Sacred Liturgy* 34; see also 21.

3. Edmund Bishop, "The Genius of the Roman Rite," in *Liturgica Historica* (Oxford: Clarendon Press, 1918), 1–27.

4. *Order of Christian Funerals* 141.

5. This observation is made possible, of course, thanks to modern technology and the superb BBC coverage of the event, transmitted in the United States by C-SPAN. CNN did not fare as well in its coverage of Mother Teresa's funeral liturgy. One might venture that the scale of the latter event, not to mention technical conditions, made it virtually impossible to cover it as well as an event in Westminster Abbey, which seems like a set made for television.

6. After years of suggesting to students that this song might not be the most appropriate for a funeral liturgy, I fear I may have to admit defeat. The lyrics used ("I would be true for there are those who love me ...") might at least be more suitable than those normally chosen.

7. One cannot say the United Kingdom or Great Britain here, since Presbyterianism is the state religion of Scotland.

8. An edition of *La Maison Dieu*, no. 213 (1998) Les Funérailles arrived too late for inclusion into this essay, but three of the articles seem worthy of note: Joël Morlet, "L'Eglise dans le champ social des funérailles" 7–32; Louis-Michel Renier, "Rôles et fonctions dans la liturgie des funérailles" 97–111; and Jean-Louis Angué, "Ponits de repère pour la pastorale des funérailles" 123–127.

JOHN BALDOVIN, SJ, is professor of historical and liturgical theology at Weston Jesuit School of Theology in Cambridge, Massachusetts, and president of the Societas Liturgica. He is author of *The Urban Character of Christian Worship, Liturgy in Ancient Jerusalem,* and *Worship: City, Church and Renewal.*

Part 3

Educating for Inculturation

Reasons Why the Arts Cannot Be Ignored

Eduardo C. Fernández, SJ

*B*ack in 1991, while studying at the Jesuit School of Theology at Berkeley, I enrolled in a class entitled "Celebrational Style." Team-taught by Jake Empereur, it introduced us to the essentials of good liturgy preparation and presiding. I decided that my practice Eucharist was to be an example of an inculturated liturgy in the Southwest. I soon found myself gathering not only energetic symbols and images, such as that of Our Lady of Guadalupe, but also colorful fabric and joyful music. To suggest the history of the early evangelization in these Spanish borderlands, I asked one of the Vietnamese men in my class to do a Native American processional dance. Behind him walked another friend, an Irish-American from New York, dressed as a Franciscan Friar. A woman in a bright print blouse proclaimed the first reading and my stories about growing up in a little mission town in West Texas helped take us back to Ysleta, my home faith community, which had been founded in 1682.

I discovered two aspects of this celebration particularly striking: one, how authentic it felt; and two, how much art played a role in making it authentic.

Through the use of color, movement, storytelling, and the beauty of eucharistic ritual, we entered a sacred space which not only helped us to appreciate cultural diversity of expression and celebration but which also brought us closer together as a community.

I am not so naive as to think that inculturation is simply about replacing traditional altar cloths with colorful sarapes or asking my Vietnamese brother to dance as a Native American. If our aim is to work towards an authentic inculturation, we must be sensitive to its deeper manifestations. A new found appreciation for Hispanics' popular religion, for example, reveals that there is always "much more there than meets the eye." The writings of Virgil Elizondo and Andrés Guerrero broke ground in calling attention to the centrality of Guadalupan devotions for Mexicans and Mexican-Americans.[1]

In this chapter, after I demonstrate the close historical relationship between art and theology, I will explain what I understand by inculturation and why art is one of the key factors in its attainment. My reasons for valuing the arts in educating for inculturation stem largely from what has worked for me as a student, as a teacher, and as a leader of worship. In this matter, I find it helpful to reflect on the ways in which I have learned best.[2]

Diane Apostolos-Cappadona defines art as "the application of skill, dexterity, knowledge, and taste to the aesthetic expression of beauty, feeling and emotion through the media of color and form."[3] Throughout the church's existence over the centuries, art has not only reflected but also shaped the faith life of Christian believers.

Apostolos-Cappadona describes four ways in which art has functioned in this context: 1) symbolically, that is, engaging and/or transforming the viewer through a minimal use of forms; an example would be the art found in the catacombs, 2) didactically, as when an event is visually narrated in an edifying manner; here endless drawings and paintings of biblical scenes come to mind, 3) devotionally, as types of "gateways to the sacred"; for example, icons or statues, and 4) decoratively, as "when the visual images are pleasing to the viewer's aesthetic sensibilities but otherwise incomprehensible because of their abstract or geometric nature"; her example being calligraphic lettering of medieval manuscripts.[4]

Going beyond Apostolos-Cappadona's functional description of the close, dialogical relationship between art and theology, Michael Moynahan, incorporating some of theology's key components, says that liturgy, art, and spirituality converge in a number of ways.[5] They each share at least four common characteristics with the others: 1) Each attempts to name mystery; 2) each calls us to see in new and fuller ways; 3) each is grounded in the incarnation; and 4) each is a catalyst of conversion. Our "Berkeley-West Texas" practice liturgy reflected each of these four characteristics. The celebration of the paschal mystery revealed God's incarnation, both in the person of Jesus and in the history of that particular faith community. This revelation, this grace to "see in new and fuller ways," served as a catalyst for conversion, for only by embracing its diversity was this community able to work towards further unity in Christ.

In the above discussion of liturgy, art, or spirituality, as general as I have tried to make their applications, I have only been able to do so from a personal experience of the particulars. My introductory example of preparing a practice Eucharist in Berkeley comes from a specific place, time, and culture. In fact, there is a growing awareness that all of our theologizing is done within a particular physical and mental context. Currently, much is being written about constructing contextual or local theologies.[6]

Art constitutes an important component of that context, that culture. Current theological writings, in fact, place a great deal of emphasis on the role of culture in the theological enterprise. As anthropologists and art historians remind us, art not only reflects aspects of that culture but also helps to shape it. This dialogical interpretation of art and culture adapts easily to the ongoing relationship between faith and culture, indeed what many mean by the use of the term "inculturation."

Although I prefer to use the terms "contextual theology" or "local theology" to describe this phenomenon because they are, in my opinion, more descriptive of what is actually taking place, I use "inculturation" because the word is more widely known and used. In the following definition formulated by the missiologist, Arij Roest Crollius, we note the formative play between theology and culture.

> Recapitulating, we can describe the process of inculturation in the following way: the inculturation of the Church is the integration of the Christian experience of local Church into the culture of its people, in such a way that this experience not only expresses itself in elements of this culture, but becomes a force that animates, orients and innovates this culture so as to create a new unity and communion, not only within the culture in question but also as an enrichment of the Church universal.[7]

Robert Schreiter, who prefers to use the term "local theology" for the same phenomenon, acknowledges that the word "inculturation," which is now widely used in Roman Catholic circles and appears in many ecclesial documents, "is a combination of the theological principle of incarnation with the social science concept of acculturation (adapting oneself to a culture) …"[8] In presenting the following ten reasons why the arts play an essential role in educating for inculturation, I am working from an understanding of inculturation described above by Roest Crollius and Schreiter.[9]

1. Art best reflects the revelation that the Word became flesh.

Over the centuries, countless heresies have arisen which have attempted to make less of this revealed truth. Whether referring to those which denied Christ's divinity or his humanity, or those which set up manichaean dichotomies of matter versus spirit, they distort God's way of creating, redeeming, and sustaining us. Creation, matter, the human body—all are good. Art celebrates this biblical truth already evident in Genesis.

I once heard of a pastor who commissioned a group of women parishioners to choose a new statue of Mary for their parish church. He confessed to being somewhat struck by the femininity of their chosen figure. Renaissance painters understood the corporeality of God when they depicted lifelike images of Christ, of his mother, or of the saints. Some art historians have noted the importance of depicting genitalia in the case of images of the Christ Child. What better way of making the point that Jesus became man and dwelt among us than in depicting such visual representations?[10]

2. Some cultures are more literary than others. A more oral or visual culture demands greater use of these means of proclaiming.

I am often struck by the differences in how I preach depending on whether I am preaching in Spanish or English. Even in the case of preaching at the same parish, and consequently to people of the same socio-economic class, I find myself using a much more literary approach if I am preaching in English. Walter Ong's book, *Orality and Literacy: The Technologizing of the Word*[11] has helped me to understand why. The consequence of using art in this environment, therefore, is that it gets us out of a strong literary cultural focus to one which is more oral or visual. In this manner, we are better able to enter other cultural worlds. Traditional cultures often use song, dance, and symbolic objects in their rites of passage. Such use of art forces more modern, literary cultures to look beyond the written or spoken word to the world of meaning these objects represent.

3. As theology moves from a more linear, analytical, deductive way of proceeding to a more circular, experiential, inductive mode, art often functions as the embodiment of this theological reflection.

In the case of popular religion, people are not always able to explain their way of worship rationally. Yet, the more one enters into the immediacy of the mystery through ritual and symbol with them, one gradually experiences "the reasons of the heart." As an adolescent, I often did not understand rationally such Hispanic popular religious practices as *posadas* (the re-enactment of Joseph and Mary in search of lodging around Christmas) or why so many of our parishioners had such a strong devotion to Our Lady of Guadalupe or to Cristo Rey (Christ the King). Years later, only through reflecting on my experience as a participant, whether that of walking in candlelight processions on cold, December nights or getting up at the crack of dawn to serenade the *Virgen* on her feast day, or hearing my Father sing hymns to Christ the King (all of which involves some form of art, by the way), did I come to a realization that love demands sacrifice, that we are part of something much bigger than ourselves, and that, in a world of uncertainty, our only rock of strength is Jesus, the king of peace. I now know these truths because I have experienced them inductively in a loving context of beauty, not through complex, disengaged, analytical reasoning.

4. In the formation of the Christian tradition, artistic expression has often come before doctrinal definition.

Margaret Miles describes how during the time of fourth-century trinitarian and christological controversies, the appeal for the masses was not linguistic analysis or creedal definitions but rather, for pagans-becoming-Christians, the appeal was the Christian faith's visual splendor; within its embrace, "they were instructed by its imagery, a visual program that deliberately and skillfully included and set in a new context of meaning a broad spectrum of cultural inheritance."[12] She adds

> The curling vine tendrils of Dionysius adorned Eucharistic chalices, where

they symbolized the blood of Christ, the fruit of the vine. Christ rides a chariot across the sky as the sun god in one fourth century mosaic. The ability of the new churches of the fourth century to provide a vivid new context for ancient symbols, a context that guaranteed their interpretation in ways compatible with Christianity, is probably the most striking aspect of fourth-century visual evidence.[13]

It was within this context of diverse cultural traditions that creedal formulas eventually were able to be ironed out. In light of this historical reality, therefore, it is no wonder that the arts play a key role in educating for inculturation.

5. Art often acknowledges that the environment belongs to the people, not exclusively to the clergy.

As the above example reveals, when the differences in the trinitarian and christological controversies were being formulated, people voted with their feet. By choosing to support or attend a certain church or devotion, they help determine its character. Clergy who are insensitive to the people's felt needs soon find themselves isolated. Allow me to present an example. In another little West Texas mission town, Socorro, the official patron of the church is *La Purísima* or "the Immaculate Conception." A beautiful, carved image of the Virgin can be seen in the sanctuary.

Yet, for over a century, a much more popular devotion has been to *San Miguel* (St. Michael), whose historic statue is also located in the old mission church. If one inquires among the older families of the town, there are at least three major stories about how St. Michael has saved their town on numerous occasions since the founding of the town in the late seventeenth century. With changing demographics and neighboring El Paso's urban sprawl, the town is becoming much more Mexican replacing the older Mexican-American and Spanish-American population. The devotion to Our Lady of Guadalupe, therefore, is quickly becoming the people's choice.

6. Art is a concrete way of affirming cultures that have been oppressed and do not value their own heritage.

I recall the impact visiting the interior of Mexico had on me when I was seventeen. Having grown up on the U.S.–Mexican border, I was familiar with many of the darker aspects of large border cities, such as crowding, economic exploitation, and lack of identity. The pre-Columbian pyramids, murals, architecture of old Mexican cities, together with their food, folklore, hospitality, and even technology affirmed that I had descended from a people with great abilities. After that trip, I looked at Mexican culture very differently. The cultural elements which I saw being used in liturgies, for example, the realistic images of the crucified Christ, became signs of a people who not only identified with the suffering Christ but also drew their strength from his victory.

At the same time, living in the deep South for more than ten years, I imbibed the rich cultural traditions of Euro-Americans and African-Americans. I found myself particularly attracted to the study of American folklore, especially in terms of the creative national blends which it represented. I discovered that other national groups also struggle to embrace their own backgrounds, unfortunately often tainted with derogatory stereotypes.

7. Art can be a tangible reminder that we belong to a church much bigger than our region or even our time.

A few year years ago, I went to meet a friend from the Slovak Republic who flew into Kennedy Airport in New York City. As we toured around the vast metropolis, I noticed that he was a bit apprehensive. Aside from taking note of what seemed to him like very large cars, he asked me if many of the people there carried guns. "Ah," I said to myself, "thank you, Hollywood, for shaping the international community's negative image of us!"

Once inside St. Patrick's Cathedral on Fifth Avenue, he seemed more relaxed. Within the massive church interior, he was delighted to spot marble statues of Saints Cyril and Methodius on one of the side altars. "I now feel at home here," he remarked, "for these two saints are very dear to us in Eastern Europe." When visiting a church for the first time, I often find myself contemplating its religious art. Who put it there and why? What does it reveal about that faith community's history? Like my friend Josef, the many immigrants from Eastern Europe around the turn of the century, seeing such familiar art in their churches, must have known that they had found a new home.

8. Good, indigenous art affirms the sacredness of the local community.

As our economies move toward rapid globalization, industry threatens to stifle the creativity of handmade, indigenous crafts. Mass-produced religious art, for example, does not take into account a particular faith community's religious history and culture. In an era of uniformly produced commercial artistic goods, the specificity of a handmade religious article, whether it be a candle holder, altar piece, tapestry, eucharistic vessel, or tabernacle, speaks infinitely of a unique giftedness put at the service of the wider community.

As the foregoing quote from Miles illustrated, each culture has its own visual language and symbol. Their incorporation into worship via inculturation brings together the Gospel message and the best of that culture, art often being foremost. When I first saw Pueblo Indian pottery used in the Eucharist at my home parish, one graced with the presence of Native Americans since the seventeenth century, I realized how much they had contributed to our entire community over the centuries. Another example of the dialogue between Christianity and native cultures as expressed in art is Robert Lentz' "Apache Christ," which he painted for the Mescalero Apaches in New Mexico.

9. Art, especially as used in good liturgy, is transformative.

My own experience of visiting Mexico as a teenager is an example of how encountering such cultural treasures there changed me. I no longer was ashamed of calling myself Mexican. By the same token, recently experiencing the Easter vigil in our San Francisco parish in four languages—English, Tagalog, Vietnamese, and Spanish—brought our largely urban, poor, multicultural community closer together. The persons planning the liturgy took great pains to include members of the different communities as well as to incorporate diverse musical rhythms and gestures familiar to each group. That Saturday night of ancient hope found us celebrating the fact that though we may be economically poor, we are richly blessed when we work to create a Christian community of diversity and inclusivity. It transformed us to the point of no longer seeing ourselves as members only of our particular ethnic, linguistic, or economic group but now as members of a church universal, or as we used to say on the U.S.–Mexican border, as *una iglesia sin fronteras*, "a church without borders."

Often societies or cultures which are not affluent have a very developed sense of art. The example of India and Latin American countries comes to mind. This fact shatters the notion that good art and wealth always go together. As twentieth-century Mexican muralists have sought to demonstrate, our history, our color, our beauty, belongs to *all* of us, not only to those who can afford the price of an education or a museum ticket. Incorporating art in our attempts at inculturation allows us to view not only the suffering and struggles of a people but also their graced artistic achievements, two elements not the least unrelated. These achievements are not something foreign to that culture but something which exists in their midst. I am convinced, in the phrase used by Moynahan, that this sacred encounter thus serves as a "catalyst for conversion." Once we come to the true realization that we are the people of God, holy because God is holy, anything foreign to that dignity seems inappropriate.

10. At a time when there is so much which divides us, art can help make us whole.

One of the major principles in art appreciation is the alternation between the whole work and a particular detail. A continual recourse to both is essential for contemplating the beauty of the entire work.

A group of people engaged in art as prayer will often find that there is a certain unity, a commonality of focus, perhaps, which comes from musing on art together. My point is simply that art can be prayerfully contemplated either individually or as a group. But whatever the case, each is a different experience. In exposing students to art, I have often experienced a unity similar to that found in a good liturgy. The laughter, tears, silence, or interchange which followed revealed our common humanity. And if inculturation, as defined by Roest Crollius, is about that process which "create[s] a new unity and communion, not only within the culture in question but also as an enrichment of the Church universal,"[14] then I have no doubt that in educating for inculturation, the arts must not be ignored.

Notes

1. See Virgil Elizondo, *Guadalupe: Mother of the New Creation* (Maryknoll, New York: Orbis, 1997) and Andrés G. Guerrero, *A Chicano Theology* (Maryknoll, New York: Orbis Books, 1987). More in the area of Hispanic popular religion can be found in Orlando Espín, *The Faith of the People: Theological Reflections on Popular Catholicism* (Maryknoll, New York, 1997), Alex García-Rivera, *St. Martín de Porres: The "Little Stories" and the Semiotics of Culture* (Maryknoll, New York: Orbis Books, 1995), Roberto S. Goizueta, *Caminemos con Jesús: Toward a Hispanic/Latino Theology of Accompaniment* (Maryknoll, New York: Orbis Books, 1995), and Arturo J. Pérez, *Popular Catholicism* (Washington, D.C.: Pastoral Press, 1988).

2. I highly recommend Chapter 4, "If Liturgy Is Art, Then What Is Art?" in Patrick W. Collins' *More Than Meets the Eye: Ritual and Parish Liturgy* (New York: Paulist Press, 1988) as background for some of the points regarding art which I make in this chapter.

3. See "Art" by Diane Apostolos-Cappadona in *The New Dictionary of Theology*, edited by Joseph A. Komonchak, Mary Collins, and Dermot A. Lane (Wilmington, Del.: Michael Glazier, 1987), 59–63.

4. Ibid. 59.

5. Michael Moynahan, "Liturgy, Art, and Spirituality" in *Liturgical Ministry* 5 (Summer, 1996): 108-120.

6. See Stephen B. Bevans, *Models of Contextual Theology* (Maryknoll, New York, 1992) and Robert J. Schreiter, *Constructing Local Theologies* (Maryknoll, New York: Orbis Books, 1985).

7. A. Roest Crollius, "Inculturation and the Meaning of Culture" in *What Is So New About Inculturation?* A. Roest Crollius and T. Nkéramihigo, eds. (Rome: PUG, 1991), 15.

8. Schreiter 5.

9. Aylward Shorter also provides an excellent introduction to issues surrounding inculturation in *Toward A Theology of Inculturation* (Maryknoll, New York: Orbis Books, 1988).

10. See Leo Steinberg's *The Sexuality of Christ in Renaissance Art and in Modern Oblivion* (New York: Pantheon, 1983).

11. Walter Ong, *Orality and Literacy: The Technologizing of the Word* (London and New York: Routledge, 1982).

12. Margaret Miles, *Image As Insight: Visual Understanding in Western Christianity and Secular Culture* (Boston: Beacon Press, 1985), 57.

13. Ibid.

14. Crollius 15.

EDUARDO C. FERNÁNDEZ, S.J, is assistant professor of pastoral theology and ministry at the Jesuit School of Theology at Berkeley and author of *La Cosecha: Harvesting Contemporary United States Hispanic Theology* and *Celebrating Sacraments in a Hispanic Context.*

The Challenge of Cultural Diversity and Liturgical Planning

Sociological and Constructivist Responses

Shane P. Martin

To whom do liturgy and ritual belong? While there is probably more agreement than disagreement among liturgical experts that liturgy is a ritual that ultimately belongs to the people, there are at least two distinct positions present in the discussion of this topic. One position emphasizes the role of the liturgist as knowing what is "liturgically correct," and the other emphasizes the role of popular expressions of religiosity that manifest themselves in ritual.

The question is even more complex in the light of the kind of cultural, ethnic, racial, and linguistic diversity present in the United States today. Responding to the diversity present in the assembly has become an important goal for many churches.

Adhering to the notion of *inculturation* introduced at the Second Vatican Council, many Christian churches are actively engaging the Latina/o community by using Spanish language and Hispanic culture in ways that were never imagined just twenty years ago. While the Roman Catholic Church in the United States has been historically identified as the church of immigrant peoples, that traditional relationship is being called into question by those who feel that the church has not fully embraced newer immigrants, especially Latinas/os and Asians.[1] Increasingly, the U.S. Catholic bishops have attempted to reach out to diverse groups.[2]

Despite the realization of both the actuality and importance of diversity, and despite inculturation, there is still a lack of information concerning the best approaches and methods in responding to diversity. The problems include: (1) confusion about the notions of diversity and culture among liturgists; (2) lamentable practices concerning diversity among liturgists; (3) lack of clarity about the roles of the liturgist and the community concerning liturgical planning and practice; and (4) inadequate responses to cultural diversity.

When I was still an ordained minister serving in a university community in which the Latina/o students made up 23 percent of the undergraduate population, the new liturgist decided to cancel the annual liturgical celebration for the feast of Our Lady of Guadalupe. The tradition of this particular university community had been to move the liturgical and social celebration to the nearest Sunday, usually the Second Sunday of Advent, because celebrating the occasion on December 12 would usually fall during final examinations. The liturgist argued, and not without merit, that the Second Sunday of Advent should take precedence over a Guadalupe celebration. The liturgist prevailed and the Guadalupe liturgy was moved. Consequently, the majority of Latina/o students on the campus felt a deep sense of alienation from the liturgical program of the church to which they had been connected through tradition and history. Although the new liturgist felt she was being professional, the Latina/o students interpreted the decision as another example of oppression from the white power base that controlled the institution. The students did not care about the Second Sunday of Advent; they cared about Guadalupe. The situation was exacerbated when the liturgist, fresh from a master's degree program in liturgy at a prestigious school of theology in Northern California, told the students that she wanted the university to become known for exceptional liturgy, and as long as she was in charge there would be no serious mistakes. End result: an alienated minority group who increasingly became less involved with the liturgical life of the campus.

As unfortunate as the foregoing incident was, it is not isolated. I could recount other incidents concerning the role of the liturgist and the process of liturgical planning in the face of diversity. Some of these incidents involve language issues, some cultural issues, and most often both. Often they involve

a European-American liturgist or ordained minister working in a local context that consists of ethnic and linguistic minority church members.

In the face of such confusion I suggest that liturgists look to other fields that are engaging in similar issues because the challenge of effectively responding to diversity is not unique to liturgy and religious denominations. For example, government, business, and education are engaged in a similar challenge. I see an obvious connection between liturgy and the field of education. The majority of teachers in the United States are European-American, as are the majority of liturgists and ordained ministers. With little training or experience, educators are increasingly asked to work in settings where cultural, ethnic, and linguistic diversity predominates, as are liturgists and other ministers. Moreover, the role of the liturgist and ministry in general may be compared to that of the teacher, at least from the perspective that views a teacher as a facilitator of knowledge construction rather than the absolute bearer of knowledge. Thus, I suggest a dialogue between liturgy and education concerning both roles and responses to cultural diversity. Specifically, I suggest that the sociocultural/constructivist approach from the field of education offers the most positive direction for liturgists and ordained ministers in responding to the challenge of cultural diversity. In this chapter I will examine the limitations of the inculturation model, give an overview of the sociocultural/constructivist approach, discuss its application to liturgical planning and practice, and conclude with a personal reflection.

Limitations of the Inculturation Model

The history of Christian evangelization has been primarily assimilationist. However, Vatican II introduced the notion of *inculturation*, which has implications for evangelization and liturgy. In terms of evangelization, Marcello Azevedo, defines inculturation as "the process by which the Christian message is inserted gradually into a given culture, starting from the assumptions of that very culture."[3] Referring to liturgy, Anscar Chupungco, describes inculturation as the process "whereby pre-Christian ritual is endowed with Christian meaning.[4] Thus, liturgical inculturation implies adaption, accommodation, and experimentation.

The basic tenets of inculturation include: (1) ongoing dialogue between faith and culture;[5] (2) an incarnational foundation;[6] (3) a concern with the anthropological understanding of culture;[7] and (4) respect for local culture and contexts.[8] Lucien Richard states that authentic inculturation demands ongoing and living exchange between the church and other cultures, a willingness by the church to dialogue with other cultures in such a way that the other cultures' identity, values and modes of expression arc respected and accepted, and an openness to transformation.[9]

Inculturation is an important and sound theological construct, yet I offer two areas of critique that reveal its limitations. First, while the Roman Catholic Church has used inculturation in outreach to developing nations and indigenous and marginalized peoples, the church has been unable to inculturate itself in Western, democratic societies.[10] People socialized in democratic societies are accustomed to dialoguing and debating with and dissenting from the structures that govern them. However, the hierarchical structure of the institutional church does not allow the above processes to occur, particularly on issues such as the role of women in the church, same-sex relationships, birth control, and married clergy. For example, the church recently disallowed any discussion on the issue of women's ordination, thus contradicting one of the major tenets (dialogue) of its primary method of evangelization, inculturation.

The second limitation concerns methodology. Inculturation is more accurately a general theological/philosophical principle than a clearly defined method. It is not clear how the successful implementation of inculturation can be empirically evaluated. Although some authors like Peter Schindler have discussed methodology, the language concerning methods of inculturation tends to be general rather than specific.[11] Concerning liturgy, it is not clear how the principles of inculturation should be applied to actual local contexts. While inculturation is useful as a guiding theological/philosophical principle, it does not seem to be an adequate response to cultural diversity and the liturgy. I present the sociocultural/constructivist approach as a more helpful response.

An Overview of the Sociocultural/Constructivist Approach

The literature on the sociocultural and constructivist approaches to learning is not clear concerning the exact relationship between the two constructs. Often they are used interchangeably. Both are based on the work of the Russian psychologist, Lev Vygotsky, and his groundbreaking theories from the *1930s* regarding teaching and learning.[12] While there are subtle nuances between these two constructs, for the purposes of this chapter I will use the term *sociocultural/constructivist approach* to refer collectively to the learning theories that have appropriated the Vygotskian heritage.

The primary aim of the sociocultural/constructivist approach is to provide understandings regarding the social and cultural factors that affect teaching and learning in local settings in order to improve educational outcomes for all learners, especially for those from ethnic and linguistic minority backgrounds. This approach utilizes the anthropological method of qualitative analysis to understand the various complex factors that affect educational success and failure. Of particular importance is the way specific contexts affect learning. The strengths of this approach are its inclusivity in recognizing culture as an important variable in learning, and its flexibility and adaptability to individual contexts. The application of this sophisticated approach is laborious as it requires educators, particularly those in leadership positions, to rethink their basic philosophy of education and to implement integrated full-scale changes in the structure and culture of schools and other learning institutions. Unfortunately, many educators do not look toward administering this approach as they are looking for less complex, "quick fix" approaches.

Tenets of the Sociocultural/Constructivist Approach

Anthropological Basis of Culture/Context

In discussing liturgical responses to cultural diversity, it is important to define the meaning of the term *culture*. There are various ways the term is used, including a popular, everyday notion of culture. The popular view of culture has at least three components: (1) Culture is seen as a static set of traits that can be lined out of a particular context to define a culture. This often leads to generalizations and stereotyping. For example, the notion that Latinos are Catholic, sympathetic to the democratic party, family oriented, cooperative rather than competitive in learning style, and like spicy food, results in a stereotypical portrayal of the community. The danger with this approach is that it decontextualizes culture, which by definition refers to a particular context. (2) Culture is identified with "high culture" and elite status. In this view, a person who is "cultured" speaks European languages, goes to the opera and understands the words in the original Italian, commands knowledge of fine wines and gourmet dining, and is well traveled in Europe. The danger with the high culture approach is that it gives the impression only an elite group has culture, and the rest of the masses struggle to survive without having culture. In this view, the construct of culture is out of the grasp of the average person. (3) Culture is defined as the exclusive domain of particular ethnic, racial, and linguistic minority groups. In this view, African-Americans, Latinos, Native American Indians, and Asians have culture, but the average white person does not. Similar to the second component, this notion is also an elitist view of culture, albeit that the basis for having culture is your connection with an ethnic heritage. In giving workshops to educators I often encounter this view, as when white educators tell me they "don't have a culture."

The anthropological notion of culture contrasts with the popular view outlined above. Although there is divergence as to an exact definition of the word *culture*, anthropologists generally emphasize that culture is: (1) learned rather than innate, (2) shared by a group of people which creates a context for individual activity, (3) an adaptation to new and challenging conditions ranging from the environment to power relationships within society, and (4) a dynamic system that has permeable and changing boundaries.[13]

Of particular importance are the ideas that culture is learned and shared. Children usually first learn their culture from their parents, families, and home communities. Given the relationship that children have with their parents and extended families and communities, culture becomes a sacred construct because it has been taught by those whom a child loves the most. Because culture is shared, it creates a context in which human activity makes sense. The context is especially powerful because of the familial connections. Generally speaking, a child comes to school with a certain set of assumptions concerning what is appropriate about behaviors, values, and beliefs, and the *meaning* of those behaviors, values, and beliefs.

The popular view of culture has serious limitations for academic work for it leads to and manipulates generalizations and stereotypes and has no empirical foundation. In contrast, the anthropological construct of culture is based in ethnographic studies and grounded theory. The anthropological notion of culture and its components are the basis of the sociocultural/constructivist theory of learning and what I propose to be the most helpful to liturgists and educators alike.

To make a local culture/context articulate and explicit, the sociocultural/constructivist approach advocates using the anthropological method. This includes interviews, participant observation, and simply "being with" participants in their home context in order to understand their insider or *emic* perspective. The anthropological method seeks to make explicit the implicit cultural knowledge each person has, and to do so with understanding and without judgement.

Mediation/Assisted Performance

The anthropological notion of culture implies that all human activity, including learning, occurs in a particular context. According to Roland Tharp and Ronald Gallimore, learning in the sociocultural/

constructivist perspective is best accomplished using assisted performance.[14] This involves using *scaffolding* techniques, in which more competent others guide novice learners in problem solving and tasks. Following the traditional apprenticeship model, the task is not diminished for the novice learner, but the level of assistance moves from being substantial in early stages to minimal and none at all in later stages. A real-life example of a scaffolding technique is the use of training wheels in learning how to ride a bicycle. The task of riding the bike is held constant, but the novice learner is able to do so with the aid of the training wheels. As the learner increases in ability the training wheels are removed, but the more competent other (usually the parent in this case) may hold the hack of the bike or run behind until the learner becomes more adept at the task. Scaffolding takes the form of assistance which is gradually reduced until the learner can understand and perform the entire task herself.

Motivation

From the sociocultural/constructivist perspective, motivation is inherent in the human condition. Motivation for learning occurs when learning experiences are structured to be authentic and meaningful, and related to real-life tasks and problem solving. Motivation is enhanced in the social, relational dimension of learning, including the relationship between the learner, the more competent other, and the task at hand.

Learning Communities

Learning does not occur in isolation from the community. A community is based on the core belief that all members of the community are learners, and that the context of learning has no boundaries. The members of the community work collaboratively to support the learning process and value lifelong learning.

Authenticity

Authenticity in the sociocultural/constructivist perspective means that *all* aspects of education— problems to be solved, the curriculum, school envi- ronment, materials, assessment, interactions, and relationships—are rooted in real life. All teaching and learning must be authentic and meaningful. Authenticity refers to the connections between structured learning activities and everyday, prob- lem-solving tasks, mediated by the particular culture and context of the learner and the educator. Learning is holistic, concrete, and contextualized, as opposed to fragmented, abstract, and decontextualized.

Teaching and Learning as a Process

Process refers to the ongoing series of actions, events, operations, and relationships that lead to value-added knowledge and growth. All learning is seen as a process, and the process is as important as the end result. Additionally, the process of learning is transformational, not merely additive. That is, learning is not simply the sum of various parts. Because learning is social and relational, learners come to new questions and tasks with an entire his- tory of experiences that relates with problems to he solved, new ideas, new tasks, and other persons involved in these. The interaction between and among the foregoing transforms the individual parts (the learner, the question, the more competent other) in a holistic, integrative, and constructivist manner that creates something new. The process of transformational learning is ongoing and is lifelong.

Funds of Knowledge

The *funds of knowledge* construct maintains that every learner possess an individual and community- based history and a set of experiences that combined are that individual's funds of knowledge.[15] It can be described as the totality of experiences and home- based knowledge that each learner brings to school or any other learning situation from the home cul- ture.[16]

Such an approach is especially significant for eth- nic minority, language minority, and immigrant learners because they may bring very different funds of knowledge than the dominant majority of students in a school. Using the existing funds of knowledge that learners bring from their families is important for educators. This helps to build a bridge between the home culture and the school culture, and enhances student motivation.

In summary, the sociocultural/constructivist theory of learning maintains that learning occurs in the interaction between the learner, the more competent other (teacher, parent, peer, minister, and so forth) and the problem to be solved. Both the more competent other and the learner bring something to the process, and the result of their interaction is the construction of knowledge. In this view, knowledge is not a given set of fixed ideas that are passively passed from teacher to student, but rather knowledge is created by the interaction of the two.

Thus, this learning theory says:

- ≈ Thinking and learning are social processes, not merely individual processes.
- ≈ Teaching and learning occur in activity settings where more competent others provide guided participation to learners in productive and authentic activities.
- ≈ Learning requires active participation, not passive processing.
- ≈ Meaningful learning is situated in the context of everyday teaching/learning settings and in everyday problem-solving activities these vary by cultural context, socioeconomic status, and other factors.
- ≈ School failure is a product of the interaction of several factors the environment, the student, and the teacher not just the student.

The sociocultural/constructivist approach implies the practice of culturally sensitive instruction, which seeks to build a bridge from a student's experience, home culture, and funds of knowledge to the school culture. In using this approach toward teaching, educators affirm and recognize a student's cultural identity and background. This does not mean that teachers never use abstract, decontextualized instruction; all students must learn to master these areas as well, but that is not the starting point. Students first need to be motivated and excited about learning. Starting with their own funds of knowledge and connecting instruction to meaningful, context-sensitive activities in the everyday experiences of students is a good way to motivate.[17]

Application of the Sociocultural/Constructivist Approach to Liturgical Planning

While a M Div student and chair of the liturgy community at the Jesuit School of Theology at Berkeley (JSTB), I was involved in many innovative liturgies. Upon leaving Berkeley, however, I soon realized that the local context of JSTB was vastly different from the world of inner city parishes. My training in responding to cultural diversity was mostly theoretical and, although solid, did not fully prepare me for the kind of flexibility and adaptability required by the complexities of culturally diverse parishes. I believe this is a major problem for many liturgists and ordained ministers—the challenge of turning theory into practice.

Although the inculturation model previously mentioned is helpful as a general frame of reference, it is another example of a great theory that does not easily manifest itself in a particular local context. The question left unanswered is: How do liturgists and ordained ministers actually turn theories about diversity such as inculturation into concrete practice?

I once worked in a parish in south central Los Angeles near the flashpoint of the Los Angeles civil disturbances of 1992. The parish community had undergone rapid demographic change, moving from a predominately African-American community in the 1970s and 1980s to approximately one-half African-American, one-half Latina/o in the 1990s. The Latina/o community predominately consisted of newly arrived Spanish-monolingual immigrants from Mexico and Central America. Working in the parish from 1992–1996, I was aware of tension between the two communities due to many factors, including the changes in demographics. The division between the two communities intensified during the election about proposition 187, which sought to eliminate the use of public monies for undocumented people. The African-American community largely supported this measure while the Latina/o community did not.

In reality there were two parishes, separated by language and culture. The English-speaking African-American community dominated the parish council and power base, and had little to do with the Spanish-speaking community. There were separate Masses, sacrament preparation programs, and social events, all delineated by language group. The pastor and I agreed to use a model of multicultural liturgy I had learned about at JSTB, in order to bring the parish together for a Thanksgiving liturgy. The model called for two simultaneous ceremonies for the Liturgy of the Word in each language and then an elaborate procession bringing the two communities together for a bilingual Liturgy of the Eucharist. Our idea failed miserably when we presented it to the leadership of each community, who immediately realized that one group would have to start in the parish hall while the other was in the church. Neither group was willing to start in the hall, and both felt the other group should be in the hall. In frustration we went back to our practice of two separate liturgies on Thanksgiving—one in English and one in Spanish.

On reflection, I feel that the pastor and I could have been aided by using the sociocultural/constructivist approach in liturgical planning for the Thanksgiving liturgy. The Thanksgiving case illustrates how I believe the sociocultural/constructivist approach has much to offer liturgists and other ministers in trying to respond to cultural diversity.

Among the tenets of the sociocultural/constructivist approach is the idea that knowledge is constructed in the active interaction between the learner, the more competent other, and the task at hand. Each brings something critical to the process, and each must be engaged in the process. As to the Thanksgiving liturgy, the pastor and I (in this case we could be considered the more competent others) had a vision of what we wanted to happen, but we did not engage the community leaders (in this case the learners) constructively in the task at hand. In using our mouths more than our ears we alienated the community and neglected their collective wisdom.

If we had applied the sociocultural/constructivist approach to this case of the Thanksgiving liturgy, we would have proceeded differently and thus increased the likelihood of a more positive outcome. For example, we did not see the communities as learning communities nor did we see ourselves as learners. We approached the situation as the experts and tried to impose a solution on the community. Although these communities successfully interacted on a daily basis in community life, we never solicited their experience (funds of knowledge) on working together and managing language differences. We never allowed the community learners to "own" the problem (the task at hand) nor did we frame the problem in an authentic, meaningful, and real-life context. Thus, there *was* little motivation for the communities to become actively involved in solving the problem. We did not present the situation to the community and then provide guided mediation or scaffolding to help guide them through the process of solving the problem together. Rather, we presented the entire solution as a finished product. We were not sensitive to the cultures of the people involved and their particular local context.

Using the foregoing example, I believe the sociocultural/constructivist approach has the following to say concerning application to liturgical planning and cultural diversity: (1) liturgists and other ministers need to see themselves in the role of a "more competent other" rather than an authority or expert; (2) liturgical communities should be reconstructed as learning communities in which everyone, including ordained and lay ministers, is always learning from one another; (3) liturgists should approach liturgical planning from the problem-solving perspective as articulated in the sociocultural/ constructivist approach in order to more fully engage the community in ownership of the liturgy; (4) liturgist and ministers should understand, respect, and utilize the funds of knowledge of the community, considering formal and informal modes of education and communication; and (5) liturgists and ministers must be respectful of local cultures and contexts—not in a purely theoretical way—but by actually being with and asking the communities about their realities, following the anthropological method.

Conclusion and Personal Reflection

What distinguishes the sociocultural/constructivist approach from other models responding to cultural diversity is its emphasis on the social dimensions of learning. In this perspective all learning is social in nature, and learning is ongoing and lifelong. The sociocultural/constructivist perspective holds that there is no one method or approach that fits all situations concerning diversity. Like inculturation, the sociocultural/constructivist approach emphasizes the need to he sensitive to local context and cultures. Its particular emphasis on learning, however, distinguishes it from inculturation. Each person involved in the learning process is a co-creator of knowledge, and knowledge is constantly being created and recreated by social interaction. Ultimately, this process happens locally, but the sociocultural/ constructivist approach gives a method (based on the anthropological notion of culture) for understanding and responding to the local context.

This chapter is one in a book honoring Professor James (Jake) L. Empereur, S.J, formally of JSTB and currently of the San Antonio Cathedral parish in Texas. Dr. Empereur's professional life mirrors the sociocultural/ constructivist perspective outlined in this chapter, and I have been in a privileged position to know this. Dr. Empereur was my professor at JSTB for courses in liturgy, the sacraments, ecclesiology and the Enneagram, and spiritual direction.

I have fond memories of those creative and energetic class meetings during the late 1980s and early 1990s. Jake's style was constructivist in the sense that he, as the more competent other, was always pushing the envelope for his students. He challenged his students by suggesting possibilities for seeing things in new and different ways; he pushed me to enlarge my world with ideas and constructs I had never previously imagined. His teaching process was never coercive; Jake invited students to be co-creators in his teaching process. Jake was especially adept at using comments and questions presented by students in class as the basis for a mini-lecture. Although he was always well prepared and focused as a professor, he was willing to allow the class to have a life of its own, at times moving in an unexpected direction to respond to a student's concern.

I am fortunate that I said yes to Jake's invitation to be a research assistant on his 1990 work *The Liturgy That Does Justice*, to be his teaching assistant for two liturgy courses, and to be a reader for his two recent works on the Enneagram and spiritual direction, and spiritual direction and the gay person.[18] Jake was also my Th.M. thesis director and a respondent to a paper I gave on multicultural education at the JSTB Dean's lecture series.

Jake's approach to liturgy and liturgical planning was creative, engaging, and inclusive. Although his liturgies were provocative, he was always respectful of culture, context, and individuals. In working with Jake on liturgical planning, I witnessed the use of the constructivist approach. Everyone involved in the planning process was invited by Jake to contribute something from his or her funds of knowledge, and the end result was a blend of the creative energies of many people. I always learned more about liturgy when I worked with Jake, but he himself was also a learner. Because of the co-creation and inclusivity involved in Jake's process of liturgical planning, liturgy became more meaningful and authentic to the community.

In all of the experiences I have had with Jake Empereur, I have been challenged and invited to grow personally, academically, and intellectually. Jake's sensitivity and concern for culture and context in liturgy was my first introduction to the anthropological perspective, although I was not aware of the full implications this perspective would have for my future professional work. Jake modeled the tenets of the sociocultural/ constructivist approach, always respectful of others. His present work with Hispanic liturgy in San Antonio is a testament of his adaptability and flexibility. It was no small feat for him to begin to learn Spanish in his late 50s, and master it enough in a few years to be able to preside meaningfully at Spanish-language liturgy.

Although the sociocultural/constructivist approach is not directly discussed by Jake in his works on liturgy,[19] his professional perspective is notably congruent with the approach. I offer my reflections on the sociocultural/constructivist approach, liturgy, and cultural diversity in tribute to a man who was my mentor, having a major influence on me and so many others.

Notes

1. See, for example, Allen Deck, *The Second Wave: Hispanic Ministry and the Evangelization of Cultures* (New York: Paulist Press, 1989); Virgilio P. Elizondo and Timothy Matovina, *Mestizo Worship: A Pastoral Approach to Liturgical Ministry* (Collegeville, Minn.: Liturgical Press, 1998); Joseph P. Fitzpatrick, *One Church Many Cultures: The Challenge of Diversity* (Kansas City, Mo.: Sheed & Ward, 1987); Shane P. Martin, *Cultural Diversity in Catholic Schools: Challenges and Opportunities for Catholic Educators* (Washington D.C.: National Catholic Education Association, 1996).

2. Black Bishops of the United States, *What We Have Seen and Heard: Pastoral Letter on Evangelization from the Black Bishops of the United States* (Cincinnati, Ohio: St. Anthony Messenger Press, 1984); National Conference of Catholic Bishops, *The Hispanic Presence: Challenge and Commitment* (Washington D.C.: United States Catholic Conference, 1984); National Conference of Catholic Bishops, *National Pastoral Plan for Hispanic Ministry* (Washington D.C.: National Conference of Catholic Bishops, 1988); National Conference of Catholic Bishops, *Strangers and Aliens No Longer. Part One, the Hispanic Presence in the Church of the United States* (Washington D.C.: National Conference of Catholic Bishops, 1993); National Conference of Catholic Bishops, *The Hispanic Presence in the New Evangelization in the United States* (Washington D.C.: National Conference of Catholic Bishops, 1996).

3. Marcello Azevedo, *What Do We Mean When We Speak of Inculturation?* (Rio de Janeiro, Brazil: EGC, 1986), 2.

4. Anscar Chupungco, *Cultural Adaptation of the Liturgy* (New York: Paulist Press, 1982), 81.

5. See, for example, Lucien Richard, "Inculturation," in *The New Dictionary of Catholic Social Thought,* ed. Judith A. Dwyer (Collegeville, Minn.: Liturgical Press, 1994), 481–483; Aylward Shorter, *Toward a Theology of Inculturation* (Maryknoll, New York: Orbis, 1989).

6. See, for example, Lucien Richard, "Inculturation," in *The New Dictionary of Catholic Social Thought,* ed. Judith A. Dwyer (Collegeville, Minn.: Liturgical Press, 1994), 481–483; Peter Schineller, *A Handbook on Inculturation* (New York: Paulist Press, 1990).

7. Joseph Gremillion, Ed., *The Church and Culture Since Vatican II: The Experience of North and Latin America* (Notre Dame, Ind.: University of Notre Dame Press, 1985); Lucien Richard, "Inculturation," in *The New Dictionary of Catholic Social Thought,* ed. Judith A. Dwyer (Collegeville, Minn.: Liturgical Press, 1994), 481–483.

8. Peter Schineller, "Inculturation of the Liturgy," in *The New Dictionary of Sacramental Worship,* ed. Peter F. Fink (Collegeville, Minn.: Liturgical Press, 1990), 598–600.

9. Richard 483.

10. Gregory Baum, "Two Question Marks: Inculturation and Multiculturalism," in *Concilium,* ed. Norbert Greinacher, and Norbert Mette, *Christianity and Cultures: A Mutual Enrichment* (London: SCM Press, 1994).

11. Peter Schineller, *A Handbook on Inculturation* (New York: Paulist Press, 1990); Schineller 598–600.

12. Lev S. Vygotsky, *Mind in Society: The Development of Higher Psychological Processes,* ed. M. Cole, et al. (Cambridge, Mass.: Harvard University Press, 1978).

13. See, for example, Donna M. Gollnick and Philip C. Chinn, *Multi cultural Education in a Pluralistic Society,* 4th ed. (New York: Merrill, 1994).

14. G. Roland Thaw and Ronald Gallimore, *Rousing Minds to Life: Teaching, Learning, and Schooling in Social Context* (Cambridge: Cambridge University Press, 1988).

15. See, M. Floyd-Tenery, N. Gonzalez and Luis C. Moll, "Funds of Knowledge for Teaching (FTK) Project: A Replication and Update," On-line, *The Electronic Bulletin Board,* November 1993, Available Gopher: National Center for Research on Cultural Diversity and Second Language Learning, 128.111.206.1, GSE Information and Resources; Norma Gonzalez, et at., *Teacher Research on Funds of Knowledge: Learning from Households,* (Educational Practice Report: 6) (Santa Cruz, Calif.: National Center for Research on Cultural Diversity and Second Language Learning, 1993); Luis C. Molt and James B. Greenberg, "Creating Zones of Possibilities: Combining Social Contexts for Instruction," in *Vygotsky and Education,* ed. Luis C. Moll (Cambridge, London: Cambridge University Press, 1990), 319–348; Luis C. Moll, et al., "Funds of Knowledge for Teaching: Using a Qualitative Approach to Connect Homes and Classrooms," *Theory Into Practice* 31.2 (1992): 132–141; Luis C. Molt, Carlos Vélez-Ibáñez and Norma González, "Funds of Knowledge for Teaching," On-line, *The Electronic Bulletin Board,* September 1992, Available Gopher: National Center for Research on Cultural Diversity and Second Language Learning, 128.111.206.1, GSE Information and Resources; Carlos G. Vélez-Ibánez, "Networks of Exchange Among Mexicans in the U.S. and Mexico: Local Level Mediating Responses to National and International Transformations," *Urban Anthropology* 17.1 (1988): 27–51; Carlos G. Vélez-Ibáñez and James B. Greenberg, "Formation and Transformation of Funds of Knowledge Among U.S.-Mexican Households," *Anthropology & Education Quarterly* 24 (1992): 313–335.

16. Shane P. Martin, *Cultural Diversity in Catholic Schools: Challenges and Opportunities for Catholic Educators* (Washington D.C.: National Catholic Education Association, 1996).

17. Robert Rueda and Luis C. Molt, "A Sociocultural Perspective on Motivation," in *Motivation: Theory and Research,* ed. Harold F. O'Neil, and Michael Drillings (Hillsdale, N.J.: Lawrence Erlbaum Associates, 1994), 117–137.

18. James L. Empereur and Christopher G. Keisling, *The Liturgy That Does Justice* (Collegeville, Minn.: Liturgical Press, 1990).

19. James L. Empereur, *Models of Liturgical Theology* (Nottingham, England: Grove Books, 1987); James L. Empereur, *Worship: Exploring the Sacred* (Washington D.C.: Pastoral Press, 1987); James L. Empereur and Christopher G. Keisling, *The Liturgy That Does Justice* (Collegeville, Minn.: Liturgical Press, 1990).

SHANE P. MARTIN is assistant professor of intercultural education at Loyola Marymount University, Los Angeles. He is author of *Cultural Diversity in Catholic Schools: Challenges and Opportunities for Catholic Educators.*

Cultural Anthropology and Creative Inculturation of Liturgy in the South Pacific

Tom Splain, SJ

The Pacific Regional Seminary sits on a bluff above the entrance to Suva Harbor on the Pacific island of Fiji. There are presently 120 seminarians here from twelve Pacific island countries; men from many different cultures who study a liturgical tradition which was shaped by the cultures of Israel, Rome, and France. Do we then import Eucharist like we import other Western products, marketing systems, and educational techniques? How can we have a liturgy that is authentically Christian while also being truly Fijian, Tongan, Samoan, and Micronesian? Anthropology can help us answer this question because the study of culture is what defines anthropology as an academic discipline. Anthropology is more than ethnography, the descriptions of specific cultures. Taking a broader perspective, it endeavors to understand the ways symbols mediate meaning for a people, how ritual dynamics work, how societies are structured, and how parts contribute to the functioning of a whole. Cultural anthropology has evolved as a social science and its history is marked by different understandings of what culture really is. Reviewing these understandings can be a great help in our approach to inculturation. Understanding culture can also allow us to use it as a common base and framework for our approach to education and creativity.

Definition No. 1:
Culture is what is produced
and some cultures are higher than others.

Darwin's paradigm of natural selection and evolution held a strong grip on the scholarly thinking of the last century. He was to the nineteenth century what Einstein is to the twentieth. Academics saw culture against this backdrop. Culture was primarily artifacts; it was evaluated in direct proportion to progress, was largely synonymous with civilization, and had its roots in race. (How far we can go depends in large part on our genes.)

Lewis Morgan posited a progression from what he called "savagery" through a "barbarian" stage and on to the summit of "civilization." Edward Tylor saw ancient peoples confronting the mystery of dreams and death. Religion becomes our effort to explain the world beyond appearances and our explanations progress from animism to polytheism before reaching a zenith in monotheism. James Frazer took things a step further and framed the movement in terms of a process going from magic to religion and finally finding pure air and the broadest perspectives on the mountain of "science." The evolutionary paradigm achieved its most blatantly racist expression when cultures were ranked on an ascending scale. The Australian Aborigines were on the lowest rung and people were seen as ascending as their cultures corresponded to Tahitian, Aztec, Chinese, Italian, and finally British.

As the twentieth century began, the evolution paradigm began to lose some steam as a way of understanding culture. There were several factors which contributed to this. Ethnographic accounts were coming in indicating that things were not so neat. There were cultures that went from monotheism to polytheism. There were complexities and variations that could not be put in neat stages on a progressive continuum. The work of two anthropologists contributed to the movement away from evolution.

Bronislaw Malinowski did some incredibly thorough studies in the Trobiand islands showing how sophisticated, intelligent, and complex "primitive" cultures really are. He and Franz Boas created the concept of "cultural relativity" which stresses that the elements within each culture function to adequately maintain and support the people of that culture within their unique environment. Things make sense when seen in the context of the whole. Therefore, there should not be a single scale of values for all cultures. Each should be understood within its specific context.

Yet in subtle and powerful ways, the "supremacy" concept of culture is still with us. The Pacific is filled with churches, old and new, which have Gothic arches. The Gothic arch was developed for the high walls and stained glass windows of medieval Europe. They have nothing to do with the environment or cultural context of the Pacific. There is an underlying premise in U.S. foreign policy that democracy American style is an absolute for everyone. Evangelization American style is sweeping over South America, Eastern Europe, and the Pacific with the message that salvation rests on a personal choice for Jesus and that material prosperity is an indicator of the depth of one's sincerity. The Vatican position on eucharistic prayers sees the only hicit prayer as one that rigorously reflects a Latin original.

A Transitional Reflection

Each year, on the weekend after Easter, thousands gather in Hilo, Hawaii for the Merrie Monarch Festival, named after King David Kalakaua, the man who restored hula after missionaries had tried to suppress it. The festival consists of three days of hula competition with *halaus* (hula schools) from all the Hawaiian islands participating. It is seen as a major celebration of the Hawaiian culture. But on the surface it might appear that a polished dance production would fit neatly into the high culture definition of the evolutionists or the culture-for-consumers position of the hotels on Waikiki. The festival happens only once a year. Shouldn't there be more to culture than this? There is!

The halaus that participate spend the better part of a year preparing. They research the chants, costumes, and movements. They practice and prepare in established, commonly understood, and traditional ways. What we see after Easter is the tip of an iceberg. It is the structure underneath that became the focus for the second definition of culture.

Definition No. 2:
Culture is the way we think.

In the 1950s and '60s, the definition of culture did a 180-degree turn from the artifact-focused idealism of the nineteenth century. Working with techniques modeled on linguistics, anthropologists sought to understand the taxonomies and categories that people use to order their universe. They called this new emphasis the "new ethnography" or "ethnoscience." Linguists use phonemes, morphemes, and grammar to describe a language. We need to decode a culture like we decode a language. The aim is to seek a larger framework by looking at the units of classification.

In Western medicine, we classify illnesses within the categories of viruses, cancers, and genetic defects. Another culture might distinguish sickness in terms of the colors of skin rashes or where on the body the ailment occurs. We distinguish natural-supernatural, magic-science, logical-illogical. Many cultures would divide their world differently and not use these distinctions. in Polynesian languages, there are no words for "uncle," "aunt," and "cousin." Everyone is a father, mother, sister, or brother. They are certainly aware of the hereditary distinctions, but with a strong emphasis on the extended family and not the nuclear family, the distinction is not that important.

Charles Frake points out that culture is our socially acquired and shared knowledge. It is what allows us to behave in ways deemed appropriate by others in our social unit. The ethnographer aims to record not what someone did but to specify the conditions under which it would be culturally appropriate to anticipate that a person in the same position would do exactly the same thing. Culture is what the natives judge to be correct. It is not behavior but how people evaluate behavior. Culture here is not things, people, behavior, or emotions. It is rather the mental organization of these things. Culture is learned. it is knowledge organized in a particular way.

Ward Goodenough approached his ethnographic work in Chuuk by asking questions like, "Where do children go when their parents die?" and, "Where does a couple live after their marriage?" The answer to this type of question would reveal a social order and allow one to predict appropriate behavior.

The work of the cognitive anthropologists was a major contribution and provided significant data on culture and cultures. But it wasn't enough. The picture it paints is static. It doesn't allow for individual variations and personal idiosyncrasies. We live more by emotion than logic and cognitive structures don't explain emotion. The approach works in understanding different social structures and categories but it doesn't work well in understanding aesthetics and religion. Many important qualities are contained in metaphor and cognitive analysis doesn't work well with metaphor.

Critics also point out that we can simultaneously belong to several different cultures. A group of Jewish, Catholic, and Protestant liturgists gather every January for a two-day seminar. We sit around a table with a designated leader, speak a common language, and proceed in implicitly understood ways. But on Friday nights and Sunday mornings, we are all in different cultural configurations. Here at the seminary, I find that during the Eucharist, servers and lectors are bowing to the altar and lectern whenever they move in the sanctuary. I pointed out that we reverence the altar at the beginning and end of the service but not each time we pass in front of it. They reply that it is "in their culture" to bow often. In the definition of culture provided by cognitive anthropologists they are correct in saying that it "is in their culture." But I have to point out that the practice was introduced by pre-Vatican II missionaries who did not fully understand that during Eucharist, there is nothing more sacred than the *action* we do together. Bowing to objects at this time is distracting. We need a fuller understanding of culture before we can build an adequate approach to inculturation.

Definition No. 3: Culture is created.

The Maori of New Zealand and the Hawaiians who are Polynesian have been most impacted and damaged by westernization but since the mid '70s, both cultures have been experiencing and creating a major renaissance. In 1971, there was only one course in the Hawaiian language at the University of Hawaii with a handful of students. In 1994, there were more than twenty courses and most of them filled out early. The renaissance also includes political activity focused on regaining ancestral lands. The dynamics of the renaissance reveal how cultures are created.

About the turn of the century, an anthropologist in New Zealand took a series of oral traditions and tried to extrapolate and determine that the first Maoris arrived in New Zealand in a "great fleet" of canoes about 1350. His methodology was crude, much like Archbishop James Ussher's efforts to place the creation of the world at 4004 BCE by using genealogies in the Old Testament. Modern scholarship tells us that there was no "great fleet," *but the Maori themselves have incorporated the great fleet into the myths they use to create their own sense of identity.* (Allan Hanson, "The Making of the Maori, Culture Invention and Its Logic," *American Anthropologist*, volume 91, 1989, 890 ff.).

In Fiji, British colonial rulers and Fijian chiefs codified a particular regional variant of Fijian political structure to cement their domination. Since the coup in 1987, a rising Fijian middle class has been using the created myth to dispossess the Indo-Fijian minority (Roger Kessing, "Creating the Past; Custom and Identity in the Contemporary Pacific, *The Contemporary Pacific*, Spring and Fall 1989, 21–22).

When I visit the States and tell people I live in Fiji, their reaction is shaped by the images they have from *South Pacific* and a host of tourist posters. But as I sit here on this muggy afternoon, the mosquitoes are biting; I'm looking out my window at a pile of rubbish they promised to haul off six weeks ago and I am not looking forward to tonight's dinner of cassava and some spinach-like vegetable cooked in coconut milk. A tropical beach of white sand set against deep blue water seems far away. Both the people themselves and their visitors can create myths that may or may not correlate with the facts of history or the lived reality of the people.

Geoff White has done some fascinating work recounting how the people of Papua New Guinea remember the Second World War. Their memories bear little resemblance to the work of Western historians. Their memories are guided by different values, images, and myths.

Each fourth of July, speeches and celebrations in the United States try to remember, create, and re-create what it is to be an American. We create our cultural identity by what we choose to remember and how we choose to remember it. In this postmodern age, we realize that our present and our past are much too vast, complex, varied, and mysterious to fit into neat categories. Human beings are emotional and unique. We move too fast to be captured on film. But the culture as creation theory does offer us a point of reference in creating a future in consonance with our past.

Several years ago, I spent a month on a remote atoll four hundred miles from the island of Yap in the Federated States of Micronesia. Three hundred people live on a series of small, flat islands that circle a lagoon. They live a traditional lifestyle and consciously try to maintain their culture. This culture could be traditionally characterized by a high degree of interdependence and cooperation. When a man went fishing, he would return to the beach and give a fish to every child who came up to his canoe. He would then share his whole catch with family, relatives, and neighbors. But the coming of the motor boat has damaged some of this cohesiveness. Now, the owners of motor boats are not sharing the catch. They can catch more fish quicker but also need more income to cover overhead.

Another cultural feature of the people is that women are topless and the chiefs insist on maintaining this practice as a symbol of the culture. A religious sister from a neighboring atoll needed permission from the chiefs to wear a blouse on a home visit.

One June day while I was there, the teenagers went on a picnic to an uninhabited island in the lagoon. A youth minister and I were the only adults along. What was interesting was that the girls put on t-shirts while on the island and everyone listened to rock music on their portable stereo. At the end of the day, the music was tucked away, the t-shirts came off, and everyone went back home.

When my sister was thirteen, she and her friends would experiment with makeup. But as dinnertime approached, she would say, "I'd better get this lipstick off or my father will kill me!" In this remote part of the Pacific, the girls would have a variation on this theme that went, "I'd better get this t-shirt off or my father will kill me."

The point of the story is that here and elsewhere we need to make informed and sometimes difficult choices as to what is important in our tradition; what is the best thing we can do to preserve and build our identity. A tradition of cooperation is more important than what people wear or don't wear.

A medical student must be knowledgeable and skilled in many areas to be an effective physician. He or she must know how the body functions, how diseases act and interact, and how medicines work. Each patient, each case, is unique and calls for experience, knowledge, and good judgment in its treatment. A doctor cannot heal by simply applying a pat textbook treatment. We cannot effectively pray by simply going through a sacramentary.

Someone working in liturgy needs to be as informed as possible in semiotics (how symbols work), liturgical history, and the culture of the people they serve in order to create a liturgy which can shape a people and be in resonance with the deepest values of the liturgical tradition and the specific culture. Calendars are the way we order chaos and give shape to time. Liturgy and the liturgical year are the ways we sanctify time.

Liturgy Is a Creative Act

Rollo May, in his wonderful little book *The Courage to Create*, tells us that creativity is a process of making, of bringing into reality. It is a new way of seeing, the discovery of new forms or the rediscovery of old ones which form a pattern on which a new society can be built. The disciples in the inn at Emmaus during the eucharistic act recognized the presence of the resurrected Christ. The early church found in liturgy the vision and courage to create a new society. We create ourselves through the stories and myths we live by.

Creativity is not the prerogative of artists in garrets. It is the vocation of us all. And creating liturgy is not reinventing the wheel. It is a form of efficacious remembering. Creativity rests on an encounter. It is in the encounter with the reality of our times that we can either withdraw in despair or remember

our past and turning to our liturgical forms, celebrate them with intensity thus entertaining the vision and entering the process of building the kingdom.

The Framework of Inculturation

A Samoan Methodist who is married to a Catholic says that he is often brought to the point of tears when he sees his Samoan culture inculturated in a Catholic mass. The symbols, rituals, idioms, and ethos of our own culture are the richest resource for the encounter and transformation that liturgy and the kingdom calls for. Adapting a scheme from Anscar Chupungco, OSB, we can put inculturation in a spectrum with four points: radical inculturation, acculturation, adaptation, and ritualism.

Radical Inculturation

At Pentecost, the assembly was virtually all Jewish. When they went forth to live and preach the Good News, they did it entirely within a Jewish culture. None of their symbols, rituals, or idioms came from outside.

We can imagine a missionary coming to Fiji before other Europeans and initially doing no evangelizing. After learning the language, he shares the stories and teachings of Jesus in an entirely Fijian way. There is no Eucharist with bread and wine. The people celebrate by sitting around a kava bowl and singing traditional *mekes* (song-stories) about Jesus. In their daily life, they strive to live the message and life of Jesus, they strive for peace and reconciliation, but there are no symbols and rituals other than their own.

In this day, it is questionable that this model would work, but it is helpful and interesting to state it in order to better sense the importance of the cultural context out of which Christianity grew and to appreciate the potential that lies in all culture.

Acculturation

Acculturation is the word used to denote a process of exchange between different cultures. Long before Europeans came to the Pacific, Tongans and

Fijians were exchanging goods, words, foods, and spouses. Acculturation is a healthy process. Cultures are dynamic and we do not live in isolation. The danger comes when one culture dominates the other and thus either destroys or severely damages it. Native Americans and Hawaiians have suffered extensively in their encounter with American culture. But at its best, acculturation is healthy. It comes into play for us at liturgy when we take the basic structure of Christian liturgies and "enflesh" them in specific cultures. Here a eucharistic prayer would have the anamnesis, epiclesis, and doxology of the rite but be written in a local language with all the imagery and rhythms of that culture. Vatican II called for this degree of inculturation, but, as yet, Rome has not let it happen.

Adaptation

At this level, the exact words of the liturgy are given in Latin to each culture. The translation has to be as accurate as possible with little concession to the genius of the local language. This is basically Rome's position now. It's a restrictive place to be but Robert Frost defined genius as the ability to move easily in a harness.

Ritualism

This was basically what we had in the Latin mass. *Everything* is imported from outside the culture and everything is the same wherever one goes in the world; there is a complete divorce of rite from culture.

Summary

As Christians, we are called to conversion and to the task of building a new earth. The liturgy is the source and summit of our vision and liturgy gives us the strength to engage the task at hand. Like the disciples at Emmaus, we need to recognize the resurrected Christ to be with us. Like the disciples on the mountainside, we are called to bring bread to the world.

There is tremendous power and meaning for us in the symbols, rituals, rhythms, and idioms of our own culture. We need to carefully reflect on, choose, and use those elements in our culture which are most conducive to the core meaning of the Gospel. This act of prayerful reflection, choice, and use is essentially creative. *Liturgy* literally means "the work of the people." We create the liturgy and the liturgy creates us.

TOM SPLAIN, SJ, teaches in the social science department at the Gregorian University in Rome. He has worked in Paraguay, Hawaii, and Fiji and has written a dozen articles in the areas of liturgy and spirituality.

Sensual Liturgy As Hispanic Worship

Arturo Pérez Rodríguez

Introduction

Coming from a priest, it was an unusual request. It had come through an intermediary who the Tigua native people trusted. The Tigua discussed the request and acceded to holding a purification sweat for the priest.

Many of the Tigua who led and participated in the sweats had left the official Catholic faith in which they had been brought up, and now had returned to their ancestors' "old ways." That decision was made at great cost. Some other members of the tribe thought them to be divisive. The tribe should stay with the new ways of the Catholic faith. Decisions on how to live one's relationship with God were taken seriously by everyone. The leaders of the sweats were not the elderly but rather the middle-aged and young adults who had been schooled in the language, customs, rites, prayers, and ceremonies of their ancestors. Their teachers were native peoples from both sides of the El Paso, Texas, border. These leaders were among the converted that now experienced God speaking to them through their native practices. For good reasons they were distrustful of outsiders. Having a priest, who de facto represented the colonist, conquistador church that historically deprived them of these faith expressions, request a sweat was unusual. Yet if they were to be faithful to their traditions, I, the priest, by virtue of being Mexican-American, was ancestrally related and therefore one of the native peoples. I would come and learn from them.

The leaders requested an interview on the day the sweat took place. They wanted to see for themselves who I was rather than know why I had made my petition or what I wanted to learn. I had no questions for them, only openness to whatever would happen. Per their request, I accepted the tobacco and different-colored cloths provided and removed all my personal religious symbols. In their description of what would take place during the purification sweat, it became obvious that it was done in complete and utter darkness. It would be the kind of darkness where eyes, open or shut, would make no difference. The thought of ten to fifteen people cramped into a small dark space, a ceiling only inches above our heads, with heat intensifying the air, sent last minute doubts into my mind and initiated a feeling of panic into my body. I am claustrophobic. "Could I do this?" "Do I want to do this?" I silently thought to myself.

My mentors would be the leader of the sweat and a young warrior. They would sit next to me. I was assured that nothing in the sweat lodge could harm me. "You are returning to your mother's womb where everything is safe." The womb of mother earth was inviting me home. The words calmed me. I would trust not only the words but also those who spoke them.

After the initial preparations were completed we entered into the sweat lodge with our ancestors. The cloth door was drawn shut and light crept away. Almost immediately sweet sage and other burned herbs filled the darkness. The rhythm of the water drum filled our bodies. Each person took a turn and spoke their heart in Spanish, Tigua, Aztec, and English. The heat, intense as the prayer, provoked sweat to run down bare chests in rivulets of water. Prayer was my body's experience in this moment. Face to face with my claustrophobia and other fears that were its companions, I had nowhere to run.

After the first almost hour long session, a break was called. The cool night air and moonlight rushed in as the door was opened. "How do you feel?" asked the warrior. "It feels like I have been here before," I answered. "It feels like you have," he echoed back. We were connected to one another in ways unknown to me. Three more sessions followed. The night's purification sweat ended close to midnight with the food and drink that I had provided. I returned home feeling the God of the night as I have never known before.

I have nowhere to place this experience in my life. I have no adequate interpretive categories in which to explore its significance. I have only the experience that for one moment, my body came home to me. It was not an "out of body experience" as much as it was a profoundly sensual *in body* encounter of prayer. It initiated me into a way of learning beyond explanation or articulation. It provoked feelings more than thoughts of what Hispanic liturgy is: a mother's womb where nothing can harm us; where we meet and feel God's embrace; where the darkness of our lives becomes a source of revelation. I view the sweat as a filter for seeing the gift of sensuality that Hispanic worship offers the liturgy.

From the outset the use of the word "sensuality" is intentional. Casually it implies a use of the fives senses, yet the more popular understanding makes it a word loaded with images, fantasies, open to distortions and side issues. This coincides with the standard Webster dictionary definition that defines sensuality as "of the body and as distinguished from the intellect; connected or preoccupied with sexual pleasures."[1] This simple phrase speaks volumes about the way body and intellect are viewed; how they are categorically separated from one another. There exists a bias toward the intellect over the body. This is a basic Western philosophical perspective that underlies not only the definition of sensuality but also emphasizes its preoccupation with sexual pleasure.

In short, sensuality is primarily related to sexuality in the U.S. culture. This is very limiting especially when we consider it in respect to the liturgy of the church, which depends on sensuality to communicate its message. It cannot be denied that sexuality is part of sensuality. No liturgy is asexual. Certainly the sweat lodge was also very sensual though not preoccupied with sexual pleasures.

When a definition becomes an attitude separating the senses from the intellect, cloistering sensuality only with sexuality, violence is done to the human person. In the Hispanic historical context this was part of the colonization mentality of the conquistadors who sought to impose their definition of life on the native peoples of this continent: The body is bad, the soul is good; sensuality is evil, spirituality is blessing. In many ways the conquistador bias exists within the Webster definition.

This definition and approach is not necessarily pertinent for the Hispanic community whose philosophical understanding and approach to life is more Eastern than Western. The Hispanic tradition is rooted in the indigenous mentality that sees harmony within the body, sexuality, intellect, and nature. The four great elements—fire, earth, wind, and water—are connected through the fifth element, the Spirit that links all of life. There is no separation between creation. Humanity, and all that makes up a person, is part of creation. The sensual nature of our body is the bridge of connection with the Creator. Sensuality forms the language of prayer that unites the human person. This is our starting point in speaking about the sensual nature of Hispanic worship.

In this chapter I seek to affirm the sensual nature of Hispanic liturgy for us as a community as well as orient non-Hispanics who minister among us. The adage that "you cannot see the forest through the trees" is true. We, as Hispanics, do not often see or recognize the positive values and gifts our culture offers the liturgy. The larger culture in which we live often doubts our approach to life and questions our ways of prayer. In particular reference to sensuality, the stereotypic "Latin lover" shadows the standard U.S. definition that distorts and clouds our self-image of what it means to be a passionate people. We, as a Hispanic community, need to recognize and affirm our gifts. The liturgy, by its nature, depends on the full use of the senses in order to transform the paschal mystery from a theological theory into a human event. To appreciate sensuality as one of our Hispanic cultural gifts helps us to live the mystery passionately.

It is presumed that culture is learned from both family and community. It is formed through our life experiences. It should be acknowledged by Hispanic and non-Hispanic alike that there exist different perceptions of sensuality's contribution to the liturgy. Communion is found in the harmony of sharing these perceptions with one another. My hope is to share also with those who are non-Hispanic and live closely with us, who by ministerial conviction or curiosity seek to appreciate the Hispanic experience of worship. In their openness to new experiences and willingness to learn, they encourage and help us to see the beauty of the "trees in the great forest."

Finally, and quite personally, I, as a Mexican-American priest, a man of color, whose mixed blood ancestrally unites me with both sides of the a geographical border, as well as with both great traditions of worship (the Roman Catholic and Hispanic popular religion) seek to bring the body home to liturgy in a way that reflects the sweat lodge experience. Sensuality is a link, a connection to the nature of our prayer. It is like an extended hand that seeks another.

This chapter is divided into three parts: liturgy and the body, the sensual nature of Hispanic worship, and challenges to the practice of U.S. liturgy. Understandably this is more a sketch than a detailed study of this subject. The task of detailing and coloring in the sketch is left for another time.

Liturgy and the Body

The *Constitution on the Sacred Liturgy*'s statement that "the Church earnestly desires that all the faithful be led to that full, conscious, and active participation in liturgical celebrations called for by the very nature of the liturgy" has always been a pivotal phrase (14). It implies that the nature of the liturgy is to be a fully human event. The use of everything that is human—emotion, intellect, spirituality—all find their expression in and through the body's five senses, in other words, through liturgy being sensually experienced. This is what allows us to live the liturgical moment consciously. In this way active participation not only keeps people from being bored but also engages them in the actual celebration.

> The body of the individual believer
> has a symbolic place within the body
> of the Church and the senses are used
> in taste smell, and touch as well as
> sight and hearing. The liturgy is not
> a matter of 'ideas' but of 'bodies' or,
> better, or corporeality.[2]

As true as this statement obviously is, it cannot brush aside a tendency, an inherent attitude that diminishes the sensual nature of the liturgy to discrete, simplistic, stylized gestures often experienced in worship

The Latin Catholic Church has been
influenced by disembodied ideologies,
which have minimized the
understanding of gestures and
expressions of the senses in favor
of intellectual expression. This has
affected the liturgy since the Middle
Ages.[3]

For this reason the U.S. bishops' document *Environment and Art in Catholic Worship* notes that

liturgy has suffered historically from
a kind of minimalism and an overriding
concern for efficiency, partly because
sacramental causality and efficacy
has been emphasized at the expense
of sacramental signification. As our
symbols tended in practice to shrivel up
and petrify, they became much more
manageable and efficient (14).

The bishops' concern is that the symbols be opened to their fullest extent so as to let them breathe their spirit into the community. Through a physical encounter with the symbols, the paschal mystery is not only proclaimed, it is also physically felt.

When it comes to the liturgy for people of color,[4] minimalist bodily involvement runs against the grain of life experience. In a thoughtful and pertinent way Elochuku E. Uzukwu, a Nigerian theologian, states that the Christian church holds suspect the body. "It was fallen and an instrument of sin. Any display considered immodest or excessive was removed from the liturgy."[5] Pablo Ricard states that the liturgy has at times come to be used as an instrument of colonization in the Americas as seen in stressing word over gesture, reason over appetite.

The Spaniard, the man, the adult,
and the human represent the spiritual
(soul) and the rational (reason);
the Indian, the woman, the child and
the animal are only body and appetite.
Spirit and reason are consequently
not present in the Indian, the woman,
the child, or nature.[6]

This attitude today still causes tension when minimalism wins out in Hispanic liturgy. An example of this tension is found in funeral liturgies. Though acknowledging the emotional pain, loss, and sorrow, the funeral liturgy's focus is on the glory, happiness, and life as found in the resurrection. Wake services are word services with little or no gestures. White funeral vestments vest the resurrection message. Catholic interment services held in cemetery chapels speak of returning our deceased to the earth while standing in an antiseptic environment.

Without the expressions of Hispanic popular religion, the funeral liturgy clashes with the Hispanic sensitivity that sees death as an experience of life. Death is caricatured on November 2, the Day of the Dead when children and adults alike invite death to come home. The deceased members of the family are remembered through home altars raised in their honor. At Hispanic funerals, people still pray the rosary in traditional ways at wakes, dress in black, request a graveside internment even though it costs more, and throw dirt or flowers into the open grave. The Hispanic family gathers for the *novenario* (novena) after the funeral with friends. These practices coincide with the Hispanic community's emphasis on the crucifixion of Jesus as one of its vital symbols. Death and crucifixion do not emphasize the pain or the hopelessness of the moment, as is so often misinterpreted by those outside the Hispanic cultural experience. Pain and sorrow are embraced so that life might also be enriched. The death of Jesus is the promise of the resurrection already fulfilled. Death is a member of the family who has a place at the table. Death brings us into physical contact with our mortality. It also contains the promise of a greater life.

The paschal mystery embraces the death and resurrection of Jesus as a human event. They are intimately connected to one another and therefore to the people that come into contact with them. "The broken bruised body that experiences death is the one that is transformed. Bodiliness is integral to the resurrection story."[7] The body's vehicle of communicating this mystery is through sensuality. We come into physical contact with the death experience in order to be touched by the hope of the resurrection. Anne Kelly's comment on the body's connection with spirituality can easily include the liturgy.

If we are to imagine abundance of life
for all of creation we must begin
by restoring the body to its central place
in spirituality (liturgy) ... This will
enable us to move beyond dualistic
patterns of thought which separate
body and soul, male and female,
heaven and earth, thought and action."[8]

The problem lies in the way that the sensual nature of the liturgy is perceived and then acted out in the United States. The philosophical underpinnings and the theological basis for the liturgy's dependence on the symbols being fully experienced through the senses is shadowed by a suspicion that the body must be held in check. The sexual preoccupation of the sensual overrides its importance. This hesitation, to fully experience the liturgical event through a full-bodied encounter of the mystery, is not part of the nature of Hispanic liturgy. More detail on this follows.

Sensual Nature of Hispanic Worship

It is clear that the cultural starting point for Hispanic liturgy is different from non-Hispanic. The indigenous sense of body is grounded in its harmony with the earth and expressed through the symbols of nature. This is communicated through the vehicle of sensuality as it is felt in the gestures of the body. Cultural anthropologists have offered us the concepts of high- and low-context communication. For our purposes we can say that this is the way that the body is viewed as a vehicle of communication. This is in fact high- and low-context body language.[9]

Low-context body language cultures stress word over gesture. Emphasis is placed on speaking and hearing for communication to be successful. In general, northern European cultures such as German, Scandinavian, and English, and their U.S. descendants, including American WASPS are low context. These cultures are more interested *in what is said* rather than the way it is said. Articulating one's message clearly and logically allows the person who hears it to understand. Explanations, descriptions, analysis, and directions fit into this category.

High-context communication cultures such as Italian, Spaniard, Greek, Arab, and Latin American place more emphasis on *the way* the message is communicated. The message is embodied in tone of voice, facial and body gesture, and the expression of feelings. The words used are poetic, metaphoric rather than analytical. The message's meaning is intuited. The word in and of itself is not sufficient to convey the message. The word does not have to bear the full burden of the message.

Because of its Semitic origins and its variant cultural adaptations through the centuries, the liturgy is a high-context form of communication, dependent on the sensual nature of the body to communicate its message. As it is interpreted and celebrated through low-context communication cultures, it is transformed into a word service. Words take precedence over actions and gestures.

Hispanic liturgy is grounded in high-context cultural communication where the senses interplay with the word. The expressions of Hispanic popular religion form the dictionary of high-context liturgical communication. The sweat lodge brings home the body's harmony in the experience of prayer in its own way. The expressions of Hispanic popular religion perform the same function for the Hispanic community when they are inculturated into the liturgy. These expressions sensually stimulate the body's active participation, which helps create a fully human event of the paschal mystery. These expressions create a fully human experience of the moment by carving it into the body's memory. This is a living memory that is never lost but is constantly renewed. What is said is not as important as what is done. An example may help to clarify this.

In many Hispanic parishes Sundays are days when all the connections of the week come together. It seems that everyone has a question, a need, and a request. Sunday is punctuated with blessing of cars, rosaries, medals, and children that are *asustados* (frightened). On one particularly long Sunday when the requests seemed to have doubled, a *viejita* (elderly woman) came up to me asking for a special blessing for her granddaughter. The child had a speech difficulty and a blessing with the front door key of the church into the child's mouth would be beneficial. I would learn again from this event.

I felt caught between two traditions, the native old ways of popular religion and the liturgy of the church. In speaking with the woman, it was clear that the child was under medical treatment that included speech therapy and regular doctor visits. What was being asked for was a spiritual healing to also take place. The liturgy of the anointing of the sick seemed appropriate but the woman's request stressed that a key be used. I was caught in a dilemma that I didn't need or want at the end of a long day. When I mentioned that our church had no front door key, we used chains and padlocks, the elderly woman responded without a moment's hesitation that the key of the tabernacle would do fine. I was caught. No explanation would be sufficient. Something had to be done.

Once inside the church, I began an adapted form of the anointing of the sick bringing to mind the Scripture phrases in which "keys" are used. The images of the key of David, keys of the kingdom of God formed the nucleus of the message. The key of the tabernacle was placed alongside of the child's mouth as a way of petitioning God to heal and open her mouth. May God's praises be heard from her. The anointing was done in the traditional manner with a final blessing being given by myself and then by the child's grandmother. They left with their request fulfilled. I sat down to reflect on the meaning of keys, oil, the laying on of hands, and this grandmother's prayer of faith. As she had been taught, she had just "preached" eloquently to her granddaughter about trust in God. Through these gestures she had handed down to this child a physical experience of prayer that would not be easily forgotten.

Through the sensual nature of Hispanic liturgy the mystery of God's presence is touched. The living memory of Jesus is made present in a way that physically places us into contact with him. This contact is enacted in simple human ways such as greeting the saints by touching statues as we enter church; blessing various parts of the body with holy water; processing into church on our knees; kissing the hands of people we revere; lighting candles before our home altars. These practices shatter a synthetic experience of God. Our starting point in liturgy is the body and everything that the body has to offer.

For non-Hispanics whose pattern of communication is low context, this starting point is not easily understood. Like the sweat lodge, one must first experience the body in the liturgy in a new way. Hispanic liturgy is not learned by just speaking Spanish or appropriating the rites of popular religion. It is learned by physically experiencing a different form of communication that places the sensual nature of the body in the center of the liturgical experience. This can offer the U.S. church a challenge to its understanding of liturgy as well contributing to making the liturgy a full, conscious, and active human experience of the paschal mystery.

Challenges to U.S. Liturgy

The sensual nature of Hispanic liturgy offers many challenges to the practice of U.S. liturgy. Following are three examples.

The first is found in the U.S. cultural attitude toward the body. The notion of "body beautiful," having a perfect body in order to be attractive is enacted in commercial ways that people buy into. The importance of a youthful image maintained through dieting, a regular regime of physical exercise, body-sculptured fashion designs, all stress this same theme. It is interesting to note that although the body is the focus of attention few people ever achieve the desired results. The diversity of diet programs, health clubs, and new clothing fads offer the hope of becoming "body beautiful." The body becomes a superficial object of attention that yields little in achieving satisfying human relationships. In stressing the perfect, an impression is made on the liturgy that it is part of this same regime. The "designer liturgy" that exaggerates the beautiful becomes the ideal by overly emphasizing punctuality, correct order, mistake-free celebrations, elaborate environments, and vesture. "Those who have no need to struggle for existence live in a kind of luxury which estranges them from the elemental. Fire, water, wind, earth are no longer perceived as essential."[10] Stress is placed more on the way the liturgy is perfectly viewed rather than on the way liturgy is lived as a critique of the superficial.

Hispanic liturgy is an experience of the imperfect. Life is not perfect for the family struggling to live within the immigration constrictions that the majority society has placed on them. The practices of popular religion are constant sources of misinterpretation when they are treated as folkloric instead of as a source of spirituality. The old ways, enfleshed in the rites of popular religion and celebrated in Hispanic liturgy, touch the reality of pain, suffering, joy, and passion of daily life.

Secondly, the sensual nature of the body in the U.S. culture is reduced to the sexual. Television soap operas, talk shows, and late night comedy routines trivialize the notion of the erotic. Eroticism forms a necessary part of the sensual by provoking the creative instincts of the human person. There is a desire for connection, relationship, and in liturgical terms, for communion. The mystics have offered us insights into this. But the erotic becomes pornographic when it is reduced solely to physical sexual pleasure. The sexual is then mistaken for intimacy.

In this day and age the word "touch" has also become a loaded word. In actuality it is often a euphemism for sexual abuse. This casts a negative shadow on physicality and raises, if not fear of the body, at least ambiguous feelings about the sensual nature of the body. This influences the sense of communion that is expressed in the liturgy. Communion is the passion to be intimately connected with God through the liturgical action. This is "enfleshed" in the members of the assembly who touch one another not only spiritually but also physically. The joining of our lives is not an abstraction but the practical reality of touching one another's lives. "Christianity is a religion of incarnation and not of abstraction. Even the most abstract theory of knowledge will tell us that we know nothing intellectually that has not first entered into our minds through our senses."[11] Touch is primary to the experience of communion with another.

Jean Vanier has made touch the centerpiece of his work with people with mental handicaps.[12] He would state that communion is founded on vulnerability and openness that comes through the body. This intimate relationship is founded on trust between people who offer each other that which is most fragile in their lives. They trust that their gift will be honored and respected. This allows people to face their fears, to free themselves from their internal handicaps. It is through the body that the inner life is revealed and the Spirit is celebrated.

The experience of Hispanic liturgy is a crowded, organized chaos experience of prayer. The sensuality of the body is the main vehicle of communication that brings the nature of the liturgy home to both mind and heart. The Gospel message that we are people in communion with each other is expressed in the liturgy. The glory or shame of one member of the family is the glory or shame of us all. The unwed teen mother continues to come to church with her family. The gang member stands with the recent high school graduate in a *Quince años* celebration. Civilly married adults wed surrounded by their children. Grandparents embrace and bless the newly baptized. In the liturgy we are pushed up against one another's life. We remain intimately related with one another around the Lord's table.

Thirdly, the U.S. notion that life is to be free of pain, that we are to avoid suffering at all costs influences our understanding of the body's vulnerability. This is seen in the stress for convenience and comfort in all aspects of life. The desire to live in pleasantly odorous environments has produced a market for scented candles, incenses, and house fragrances. We can control the way life smells. This is what makes hospital corridors and homes for the aged so difficult to visit. There the reminder is that life is not only unpleasant but that we are likely to be in the same position one day. We are reminded that our bodies are limited, mortal, and vulnerable.

Hispanic liturgy does not celebrate our vulnerability only in the sacrament of the anointing or in funerals. Liturgy's challenge is to integrate the body's limits into our prayer. Ascetical practices have never lost their meaning or place within the experience of Hispanic worship. There is a need for enacted practices of penance that remind us of our body's ability to live our prayer. Words are not necessary here. The living Stations of the Cross become the great Good Friday processions for the entire community in walking the path of suffering that brings forth new life. This is further personalized in such practices as processing into church on one's knees; by walking long distances on pilgrimage; by touching the wounds of the crucified Christ; by striking one's breast while saying *"por mi culpa, por mi culpa, por mi gran culpa"* ("through my fault, through my fault, through my great fault"). It is interesting to note that this gesture is found in the sacramentary's rubric though it is not generally done in non-Hispanic liturgies. "An aesthetic that embraces thick, ambiguous, multivalent, sensuous forms seems to hold more promise for Catholic worship than a liturgical aesthetic of clarity and pure form."[13] Ascetical practices united to the liturgy celebrate our imperfection and integrate the body's vulnerability into the liturgy.

The paschal mystery as proclaimed in the liturgy is not a theory as much as it is an experience of the presence of God in this time and place. The sensuous nature of the Hispanic liturgy in making full use of the body brings this mystery home. There is a physical contact with the living person of Christ in this celebration. The sense of Christ's presence is felt through the ways that the expressions of popular religion are enacted and included in the liturgy. Through these practices sensuality is not reduced to the sexual, the harmonious connection of the body with nature is fostered, and the embrace of the imperfect vulnerable character of human life is lived. The Spirit that unites all of creation is found in the paschal mystery that transforms Hispanic liturgy into a life-giving event.

Conclusion

The sweat lodge became an experience of communion in a way that I had not known before. I was ushered into a small dark tent that contained not only my fear of enclosed places but also my inner darkness. This fear was not rational but emotional. In order to have this experience I had to not only face these fears but also place my trust in people who were unknown to me. They, for their part would also place their trust in me, that I would respect and honor their ways. We were physically vulnerable to one another. This became a liturgy of communion.

The sensual nature of Hispanic liturgy sees the body as the fundamental instrument of communion. The body brings us once again into harmonious communion with the earth. The expressions of popular religion act out this connection through blessings, healing, and prayers that are grounded in the full and maximum use of the five senses. These signal the inner life that unites us all. This is an experience of the Spirit that is contained in the paschal mystery. This is the womb of God where nothing can harm us.

Notes

1. *Webster's New World Dictionary* (Warner Books: New York, 1987).

2. *Liturgy and the Body.* Eds. Louis-Marie Chauvet and Francois Kabasele Lumbala (Maryknoll: Orbis, 1995), viii.

3. Marc Metzger, "Liturgy and Cosmos," in *Liturgy and the Body*, ed.Louis-Marie Chauvet and Francois Kabasele Lumbala (Maryknoll: Orbis, 1995), 45.

4. Eric H.F. Law in *The Wolf Shall Dwell with the Lamb* (St. Louis: Chalice Press, 1993) helps define the term "people of color" in reference to power. In Spanish, "trigueno" or "moreno" means dark skinned whereas "color" signifies "black."

5. Elochukwu E. Uzukwu, "Body and Memory in African Liturgy," in *Liturgy and the Body*, ed. Louis-Marie Chauvet and Francois Kabasele Lumbala (Maryknoll: Orbis Books, 1995), 73.

6. Pablo Ricard, "Inculturation defends human, cosmic life," *National Catholic Reporter*, 34, 8 (19 December 1997): 14.

7. Anne F. Kelly, "To 'Reconstitute the World,'" in *The Candles Are Still Burning*, ed. Mary Grey, Andree Heaton, and Danny Sullivan (Collegeville, Minn.: The Liturgical Press, 1995), 18.

8. Ibid. 19.

9. See Archdiocese of Newark, *Presencia Nueva (Newark, N.J., 1988), 258* for how this principle works in the Hispanic context.

10. Jyoti Sahi, "The Body in Search of Interiority," in *Liturgy and the Body*, ed. Louis-Marie Chauvet and Francois Kasasele Lumbala (Maryknoll: Orbis, 1995), 88.

11. Adrian Nocent, *A Rereading of the Renewed Liturgy* (Collegeville, Minn.: The Liturgical Press, 1994), 132.

12. This is Vanier's term. For a fuller appreciation of his work see *Our Journey Home* (Maryknoll: Orbis, 1997).

13. Mary Collins, OSB, "Beginning Again" in *The Renewal That Awaits Us*, ed. Eleanor Bernstein, CSJ, and Martin F. Connell (Chicago: Liturgy Training Publications, 1997), 36.

ARTURO PÉREZ RODRÍGUEZ is director of the Hispanic liturgical certificate program in El Paso, Texas, an adjunct faculty member of Catholic Theological Union, and a parish priest of the Archdiocese of Chicago. He is co-author of *Asi Es, Stories of Hispanic Spirituality*, *Primero Dios: A Hispanic Liturgical Resource*, and *La Navidad Hispana at Home and at Church*.

How Can the Church Worship in Postmodern Times?

James L. Empereur, SJ

The twentieth century was characterized by those various movements which culminated in that singular religious event of the Second Vatican Council, and we can celebrate with a sense of accomplishment. However it must be tempered by the realization of the task that lies ahead of us. What we can rightly celebrate is the implementation of the reform of the liturgy promoted by the pioneers of the modern liturgical movement and made official policy of the church at the time of the Council. Despite the falterings and the resistances to this undertaking, it has been successful.[1] What lies ahead is far more difficult because it must move beyond the determining principle of the Council which was to rediscover the liturgy in its pristine form and make it pastorally relevant for today. There is no map for what lies ahead. It is not merely a matter of putting the tradition of the church in dialogue with modern culture. Rather we must first allow the basic evangelical message through its symbols, metaphors, and images to find a home in the many cultures of this planet so that the dialogue is between contemporary cultures and the ritual expressions of a contemporary faith.

In the previous dialogue, that of Vatican II and modernity, the partners came to the conversation from relatively well defined positions: the church, with its tradition ever struggling to update itself and the modern world with its emphasis on the enlightened autonomous self at the center of an ordered universe. In the second dialogue, that of our post–Vatican Council period and contemporary societies in which the Gospel is being preached, we have the new phenomenon in which both partners are pluralistic in nature. While in fact, pluralism was always a more accurate way to describe the lives of Christians, in Catholicism the Council of Trent had at least created the illusion of uniformity in doctrine, liturgy, and life. But the specificity of liturgical reforms easily swept away that illusion. As Anscar Chupungco, OSB, has pointed out:

> It (Vatican II's liturgical reform)
> was a rediscovery in favor of liturgical
> pluralism. For one, it meant that
> the doctrinal and spiritual riches
> of the liturgy needed to be shared
> with every person in the worshiping
> assembly and with peoples of every
> culture and tradition .... Pluralism
> is one of the more conspicuous
> consequences of inculturation.[2]

This movement for the inculturation of the liturgy contributes to and is stimulated by the need for greater dialogue between culture and faith. This dialogue has always taken place in some sense in the history of the church. The point is that we have arrived at a stage in our church life where we need to re-image this dialogue, reactivate it in such a way that it corresponds to contemporary questions, and then apply this conversation in a particular way to our life of worship. Why the dialogue now takes on a new form has been articulated by Dermot Lane:

> There are elements surrounding
> the issue today which were not present
> previously. These elements include,
> for example, the emergence of an
> Enlightenment shaped historical
> consciousness which is quite distinct
> from earlier times, the collapse of a
> unified and single metaphysical system,
> and the growing presence of cultural
> pluralism. These developments
> influence the way we understand
> culture today.[3]

Lane draws out several characteristics of this new mode of conversation. This encounter is transformative. It is mutual in the true sense of a dialogue where there is a movement back and forth between faith and culture. There is a real conversation where the subject matter takes over[4] rather than a kind of "co-existence of faith alongside culture."[5] Inculturation still presupposes a theology of incarnation.[6] But more is needed. There is more to making

liturgy and culture interact than putting their particularities in conversation, although that is a *conditio sine qua non*. Something transformative must happen as a result of the conversation. And what this is will be something creative, something which mobilizes both the culture and faith (and in particular, liturgy) to show forth more clearly their sacramentality. Lane speaks about it in terms of a liberating praxis.

> Ultimately, the goal of conversation
> must be the liberation of the
> participants in a way that affects
> not only their individual differences
> and otherness, but also transforms
> the structures and institutions
> that perpetuate such alienation
> and separation.[7]

The fact that our liturgies have been insufficiently transformative is evidence of the fact that we have been engaging in a kind of inculturation which is best described as adapting the liturgy to modernity. The task for the next century is the kind of inculturation of the liturgy which corresponds to a postmodern world. There is not a great deal of evidence that this is now happening. There are movements to restore the liturgy to a kind of classicism and there are those, mostly springing from the Second Vatican Council, which are trying to place the liturgy in conversation with the *modern* world. To the latter belong those who are of the opinion that we have not yet had a true dialogue between the liturgy and modernity (the Post-Enlightenment mentality) and that the church still needs to transform the negatives of modernism so that we can begin to transform modernity itself of those elements which diminish human dignity."[8]

Perhaps, in the larger context of faith and culture Lane is correct in that we must complete the task of dialogue with modern culture before we launch into the postmodern context. But in so many ways the modern liturgical movement, both before and after the Council, has been engaged in that conversation. That conversation, it seems, is no longer transformative and has lost much of its energy. It is no longer a conversation in which the subject matter takes over. The "post-Enlightenment world view which emphasized individual subjectivity, interiority, and self-subsistent autonomy"[9] has been the approach upon which so much of present practice and theology of the liturgy is based. The calls for a new liturgical movement[10] indicate that this strategy is no longer viable and that we must seek for something beyond it.[11]

In another place I have written that in recent years there have been calls for a new liturgical movement because there is a growing sense that the powerful energies which culminated in the liturgy of the Second Vatican Council have petered out.[12] We are experiencing a loss of nerve. The abiding question for those who belong to the first world, especially the United States, is: Why is it that in a country which has more liturgical resources than ever before, more workshops, more training programs, more homily commentaries, more masters of liturgy programs, more RCIA programs, more liturgical and musical organizations, and greater emphasis on the study of spirituality under the guidance of the scriptural and ecumenical gains of the last century as well as a greater integration of the humanistic sciences in practical spiritual practices, that we have not yet fulfilled the immediate aims of the Second Vatican Council's reforms? Why is there such discrepancy among liturgical assemblies as to the degree to which these reforms are implemented? Why is the parish with a good liturgy considered something exceptional so that everyone in the city or state knows about it? Why is there less interest in liturgy among those who in the past (for example, sisters, seminarians) were most devoted to the renewal? Why is liturgy less and less considered important in a theological and spiritual renewal program? Why is there not more passion about liturgy? In other words, why are we starving in the midst of plenty?

Or to put it in a more folksy way: Why does the Advent wreath have no chance against Santa Claus so solemnly enthroned in all the major department stores? The easy, although true, answer is that we do not live in a Christian world and our symbols no longer interpret us because we have to interpret them. This for many reasons influences the liturgy and removes it from the public arena. If the liturgical pioneers of the past could have seen the influence of these more clearly, they would have been less san-

guine in what they thought the liturgical movement could accomplish.[13]

What, then, can we say about liturgy in a postmodern age? In Michael Downey's brief description of postmodernity, he points out that "it is the shock of historical events that has shaken modernity's certitude and called into question the ability of modernity to make good on its promise for order, cohesion, coherence in self, community, history and world.[14] He stresses that it is suffering which has subverted this modern belief in an "ordered, coherent, unified purpose.[15] Downey highlights three aspects of the postmodern mentality: 1) since it understands reality as something which is not simply given, but is actually constructed, it is suspicious of "universal and normative claims"; 2) it moves away from modernity's tendency to compartmentalize and specialize; thus, it embraces a more holistic approach, especially in regard to the human person, in which the person is integrated in "relation to others in community and tradition;" and 3) that wholeness is not the opposite of particularity (so strongly embraced by modern thought), but rather both are complementary and even inseparable. What this means for something like spirituality is that the person cannot be treated as an autonomous intellect. Rather, all the dimensions of the self become relevant in articulating a spirituality, for example, the person's relation to community, and the concrete human traditions.[16]

In terms of the first aspect, the suspicion of universal and normative claims, the celebration of postmodern liturgies will be more tentative in character, less based on certain theological presuppositions. There will be fewer claims that liturgy is the summit of Christian spirituality except in a very carefully nuanced sense. In postmodern understanding liturgy is not the most important thing in religious living. It acts like art does. We could not live humanly without these symbolizing moments in our lives, but neither do they have an absolute character in the order of what constitutes our humanity.

The unchanging elements of the liturgy from a postmodern point of view will be even more ambiguous than they are now. We hear a great deal about these unchanging elements but few are willing to draw the line between those that change and those which are permanently enduring. That the liturgy should celebrate the mysteries of Christ, be integrated into the Gospel proclamation, be sacramental in character might be seen as unchanging elements. But in themselves these are not concrete elements. Rather, they are principles which underlie the actual concreteness of Christian ritual.

In the process of liturgical inculturation we must begin somewhere and so a specific liturgical order will be involved. But to claim that in inculturation the Roman rite must be maintained is to undermine the process of inculturation itself.[17] That the mysteries of Christ be celebrated, that the word of God be proclaimed, and that the Christian life be sacramentalized does not require the Roman rite, even in a highly adapted form. That liturgy be Christian cannot be denied; but that it need be Roman can hardly be maintained. As Gordon Lathrop has pointed out:

> It is not sufficient to know only
> the nature, purpose, and laws
> of Christian liturgy.[18] Culture,
> like the liturgy, has its nature,
> components, and laws .... Culture
> has its own requirements which need
> to be respected, if dialogue with it is
> to be honest and fruitful.[19]

From the point of view of the second aspect of postmodernism, the embracing of a more holistic approach, liturgy will not follow the pedagogical model that the reforms of the Second Vatican Council have done. Those in charge of the revisions did not intend to adopt the classroom model, but strong emphasis on intelligibility inevitably moved them in that direction. The usual area in which points of connection have been made between liturgy and holistic practice is that of the importance of the body. But the connections often still reflect modernism's separation of matter and spirit. Dualism has been and is the abiding heresy in the Christian churches. Embodiment in the liturgy usually implies singing, gestures, fuller use of symbols such as oil, water, bread, and wine. But often the line is drawn when it comes to dance or movement or to something sensual such as full touch. Part of the postmodern task is the development of a theology of the sacramentality of the body. Even feminist theology has not been able to contribute one appropriate for our time.[20]

The holistic emphasis of postmodernism implies considerable plurality in liturgical forms. But even more it presupposes pluralistic communities. There is no methodology of liturgical reform that can succeed in the future without a more pluralistic structure in parish leadership and membership. And yet Christian pluralism only makes sense if there is also unity. Chupungco suggests that:

> Whereas the theological content,
> particularly the sacraments, requires
> unity, the liturgical form encourages
> cultural diversity. We may thus
> define liturgical pluralism as unity
> in theological content and diversity
> in liturgical form.[21]

But that position very much comes from a modernist mentality. Postmodernism's holistic viewpoint cannot so easily separate form from matter or external from internal. A change in form will also mean a change in belief. It is not simply that we all believe the same about the resurrection of Christ and that we can then engage in different forms of the Easter Vigil. Rather, it is that all of us standing around the same Easter candle singing our paschal praises may well have divergent beliefs about what the resurrection of Christ means. Although we cannot fully agree about the resurrection of Christ on the discursive, rational, self-autonomous level, we can enter into the same symbol because it addresses us more completely, and it is not limited to speaking to only our rationality.

Downey's third characteristic of postmodernism is that wholeness and particularity are not only not antagonists but demand each other. This means that postmodern liturgy will probably develop along the lines put forth by Jozef Lamberts when he speaks of two liturgies existing alongside each other, the official liturgy and a more popular liturgy.

> [T]hat in the Catholic Church there
> exist two forms of liturgy next to one
> another, two forms which sometimes
> obviously act separately and on other
> occasions interact. These occasions
> especially occur when the so called
> "seasonal Christians" or "marginal

Christians" come to celebrate
the sacraments at the key moments
of their lives and on the occasion
of the solemn feasts which coincide
in a certain sense with the seasons,
although their expectations do not
always coincide with what the "official"
church is offering them [22]

In this case the particularity is represented by the official liturgy of a particular tradition and wholeness is represented by those "unofficial" liturgies and the life they represent as they engage the worshipers more fully and more completely. The point is that postmodern liturgy does not exist in itself and connecting it with life is not simply a matter of improvements in the official liturgy (although these might be helpful). Rather, it is that the official liturgy in order to serve its purpose must be accompanied by, surrounded by, and immersed in a second liturgy that lives alongside it. Sometimes it is more subtle as when there is an official rite such as confirmation with its attendant official meanings as put forth by church documentation and theological argumentation, but in fact "the celebration of confirmation has a quite different meaning than that which the Church wants to express by it."[23]

Sometimes this parallel liturgy is more clearly defined as in the case of Hispanic *Posadas*, *Pastorelas*, or public ways of the cross. Official recognition and presence of clergy is not necessary, and, at times, not even desirable, for their vitality and nourishing qualities. Attempting simply to integrate these latter celebrations into the official liturgy is wrong headed. Rather, they need to be promoted so that they can be the nurturing ambience of the official worship of the church. Perhaps, it is more a matter of bridge building between liturgy and popular religion than making popular religion liturgical. Mark R. Francis, CSV, illustrates this bridge building in his example of the feast of Our Lady of Guadalupe, a singularly important celebration for Mexican-Americans, and the season of Advent during which time this feast falls. He makes some parallels between Mary's pregnancy and the pregnant Virgin of Guadalupe. He finds in both experiences the unqualified "yes" in the midst of oppression, and the symbols of hope and of dignity and worth for the lit-

tle people of this world.[24] This bridge building is appropriate as long as one side of the tension is not co-opted by the other. The nonofficial liturgical Guadalupe experiences must be preserved if the more official liturgical experience of Advent, enriched by the presence of Guadalupe, is to maintain its force and energy. The power of the Advent liturgy to transform can be enhanced when the justice oriented imagery of Advent is combined with the liberating images of Guadalupe.

Liturgy in a postmodern world cannot make it on its own. Liturgy probably never did, although it may have tried by narrowing the world of liturgical prayer whether it be to post-Tridentine rubrical fixity or to post-Vatican II rationality. The inculturation of the "core" liturgy of the church cannot take place unless it is allowed a garden in which to grow. The liturgy needs a garden because inculturation is not a matter of transplanting the plant of the Gospel from one garden to another, but rather that of taking the seed of the Gospel and placing it in the local soil so that the plant of the Gospel is both born and takes it nourishment from the garden in which it is planted. Exhortations that the daily Christian life, what Christians do on the other days of the week, should provide this rich ground have been tried and have failed. The next stage of liturgical renewal has more to do with the liturgies outside of the official rites than with these rites themselves.[25]

So what chance does our poor liturgy have in a world enveloped in this postmodern sensibility, especially when this sensibility is defined negatively as in the words of Paul Lakeland:

> Postmodern sensibility is
> nonsequential, nonescatological,
> nonutopian, nonsystematic,
> nonfoundational, and ultimately,
> nonpolitical. This postmodern
> human being wants lots but expects
> little. The emotional range is narrow,
> between mild depression at one end
> and a whimsical insouciance at the
> other. Postmodern heroes and heroines
> are safe, so far beyond that we
> could not possibly emulate them,
> avatars of power or success or money
> or sex—all without consequences[26]

Of course, as with everything else, there is a middle, left, and right to postmodern sensibility. The characteristics of postmodern thought are not always clearly and consistently distinguished from those of modernity. I think Lakeland is right when he notes that it is in the fields of the arts and architecture that we find the clearest delineation between postmodernity and its predecessor. But then in the arts you have something to see, touch, and hear and not just think about. Charles Jencks, in his *What is Post-Modernism?* makes an imaginative comparison of modernity and postmodernity with the Protestant Reformation and the Catholic Counter Reformation. In his study of modernity in architecture of the early twentieth century he says it has a Protestant spirit, namely, "the idea that living in pure, white washing machines can improve life."[27]

What does he mean when he sees Walter Gropius and the German Bauhaus, the exemplar of the international style in architecture, making a creed out of the relationship between design and industrial techniques or when he sees Mies von der Rohe who embraced the spirit of industrialization in his designs as forms of modernity having a Protestant character? He means that the leading architects of modernity practiced a Calvinistic style for they "believed that if their faith were to govern industrialization, then it could change the world for better, physically and spirituality."[28]

Modernity's seminaries were the major universities of Cambridge and Harvard who taught the purest doctrines of Corbusier, Gropius, and Van der Rohe so that:

> [T]heir white cathedrals, the black
> and white boxes of the International
> Style were soon built in every land ....
> Ornament, polychromy, metaphor,
> humor, symbolism, place, cultural
> identity, urban context and convention
> were put on the Index and all forms
> of decoration and historical reference
> were declared taboo.[29]

Modernity's architecture, the zenith of rationalism in the arts, the triumph of the autonomous building with its disregard for its context, brings us back to Calvinist Geneva where the only music was unaccompanied psalmody and the only decoration in the central dominating pulpit was the minister himself. Modern architecture had an overpowering faith in industrial progressivism and believed that its translation into the pure white international style would transform society both in its sensibility and social make-up.[30] I can think of no better concrete symbol of what modernity is all about. But modern architecture died with "its ideology of progress, which offered technical solutions to social problems.[31] It should need no comment that the liturgical reforms of Vatican II were more in the spirit of these protestantizing tendencies: intelligibility, no repetition, clean lines, no liturgical clutter, minimal devotional objects that might distract from a few key sanitized symbols. When Catholics and others come into some of what have been called modern churches and decry the lack of beauty and lament the missing sense of the holy, it is not simply because they are reverting nostalgically to a former but no longer existing world. It is also because they are not Calvinist in their spirituality.[32]

Postmodern architecture restored much that was banished by the modernists: wit, ornament, polychromy, metaphor ... symbolism, expressive technology, new ambiguous space, urban contextualization."[33] In liturgical architecture we see this in the reintroduction of devotional spaces, the return of decoration, more interesting and engaging sight lines, attention to the play of light and color in larger gathering spaces and symbolic pluralism. Most important of all is the principle of postmodern liturgy: That worship is context, not text.[34]

Jencks sees the return of symbolism, ornament, and the former taboos of the modernist period as a kind of Counter Reformation. In speaking about this movement's response to the Protestant Reformation in architectural terms he has this to say:

> The real Counter-Reformation resulted
> in the Baroque style (then called
> the Jesuit style) and the building
> of many splendid churches replete
> with exuberant polychromy and
> narrative sculpture. All this was sign
> of new spirituality and the new
> authority of the church.[35]

The postmodern agenda is surely more pluralistic than the faith of the Baroque period, but postmodernity's acceptance of "history, symbolism, narrative, pluralism, and the role of memory, place and local culture"[36] was anticipated in the earlier Counter Reformation's architecture. In summary we can say that the spirit of the Counter Reformation lives in the postmodern agenda with its:

- intense concern for pluralism
- respect for the local culture
- acknowledgment of difference and otherness which the feminist movement and others have brought to the forefront
- acceptance that culture is evolutionary
- recognition that knowledge is power where in an electronic age information moves quickly
- belief that the universe is the measure of all things.[37]

But if only a fraction of this summary of postmodernity is on the mark, the implications for the liturgy are overwhelming. What happens to liturgical theologies when they are deprived of anthropocentric language about God? What role can the official statements of the church on the liturgy play when the concepts of God's action in the world and the past reigning understandings of immortality, grace, salvation, and redemption can no longer be presumed? So many of the current liturgical theologies are narrowly ecclesiocentric and based on Christologies which not only do not imagine Christ as cosmic but have not even broken out of the mold of the Western world (and I include the Third World). These are all assumptions rejected by postmodernity. Already a postmodern eschatology in which the spiritual never leaves the realm of the material has invaded our funeral celebrations, although many priests and congregants would be shocked at its realization. And will the pope's latest encyclical in praise of rationality be strong enough to summon enough rescuers of metaphysics as it sinks below the waves of suspicion, contextualization, and cultural conditioning?

What will become of liturgy which is supposed to supply the larger incorporating story in which we insert our own meager—full of holes—personal story in a time which has grown suspicious of these larger metanarratives? Is liturgy which symbolizes the Christian story to end up as some kind of ideological

museum piece? The only ones who care about the story are the Christians who fight among themselves about the meaning of the story itself. The postmodern world does not even consider it worth the trouble to stop and see what is taking place in our liturgical assemblies although the admission is free.

It seems clear to me that even a mild interpretation of what is happening in our world from a postmodern perspective demands a reordering of the mission of the church. This, of course, will cause a refocusing of liturgical worship. The mission of the church is not so much to tell its treasured story as it is to awaken the world to divinity found within itself, while understanding that the church itself is not "the only avenue to the divine into history, the only manifestation of the spirit.[38] It is reminiscent of what the Latin American bishops did years ago at Medellin when they placed liturgy not as the summit of Christian spirituality but under the category of the church's mission of bringing justice to our world. For Medellin, "the liturgical celebration crowns and nourishes a commitment to the human situation, to development and human promotion."[39] Elsewhere I have written about this changed perspective:

> This (Medellin) is more centrifugal
> and takes the uniqueness of the
> historical situation more seriously.
> Liturgy at the Vatican Council is still
> seen from a dualistic perspective
> where the church is the subject of a
> sacred history alongside of secular
> history. In Medellin, liturgy is the
> climax of the efforts for development,
> promotion, and liberation, albeit,
> in Latin America specifically. Liturgy
> is that stop along the way where we
> celebrate our history and its meaning
> in terms of the Easter event. There
> is no question of moving back and forth
> from one history to another, but
> of recapturing the profound meaning
> of the only history we have.[40]

Liturgy will not and cannot be immune from the issues with which the postmodern church will be preoccupied: A world perspective in which we humans are no longer at the center, one for which there is no reigning story to bestow unqualified meaning, and most traumatically of all, a world in which the Christ of the pantokrator, resplendent in glory in the domes of Byzantine churches in a space with no artistic beginning and no artistic end, proclaiming his omnipotence and his timelessness, his gaze not looking but all seeing, has been dethroned and dismissed leaving us only with pristine Christianity's young shepherd boy carrying home on his shoulders one of his straying sheep.

Concluding Note

So, many of us continue to starve while so much effort and money is poured into new ways of preparing for and celebrating liturgy whether it be a lectionary based catechesis or computer programs for liturgical planning. But those are for what goes on in church. And in this area we have done much. More can always be done. But there is a deeper urgency and that calls for a new liturgical movement, one founded on a spirituality whose confines are not the ritual and theologies of the rites. This must be a spirituality which provides a cultural context for the rituals. This spirituality will not even begin with liturgy and its theology, but rather with the larger world wherever humans connect and come together with a sense of commitment. And this commitment will not be first of all to the religious faith, although it will be that, but to those who find themselves marginal for whatever reason.

Since our culture has made it difficult to experience sacrality in a public forum, another cultural context must be supplied. This will take different forms depending on the cultural situation, It will be more difficult for those groups whose lives are not supplemented by a micro cultural experience. What I mean by micro cultural support is this: One evening I was celebrating the Eucharist in a Hispanic parish in San Jose, California. It was the feast of *El Señor de los Milagros* (Lord of the miracles). There was a celebration going on outside and around the church while the Eucharist was being celebrated inside. At the conclusion of the Eucharist as I moved to the outside to greet the people, I was caught up in the swirling crowd and it became impossible to distinguish the celebration inside from the celebration outside. In that moment I experienced the kind of context in which liturgy can work. Certainly, there was continuity of liturgy and life, there was a community to which liturgy is intrinsic, there was a sense of liberation, there was a nondualistic spirituality, and there was a continuity of celebration present. It is such an experience that the second liturgical movement must work toward. We can only be fed by the marvelous symbols we have prepared inside the building if we are also fed by equally marvelous ones outside.[41]

Notes

1. For those interested in the American liturgical movement I recommend the thorough and fascinating book by Keith Pecklers, SJ, *The Unread Vision: The Liturgical Movement in the United States of America 1926-1955* (Collegeville, Minn.: The Liturgical Press, 1998).

2. Anscar Chupungco, OSB, "Liturgical Pluralism in Multiethnic Communities, *Worship: Beyond Inculturation* (Washington, D.C.: The Pastoral Press, 1994), 158–159.

3. Dermot Lane, "Faith and Culture: The Challenge of Inculturation," *Religion and Culture in Dialogue: A Challenge for the Next Millennium* (Dublin: The Columba Press, 1993), 11. This chapter is a good introduction to the question of the relation of faith to culture.

4. As Hans-Georg Gadamer has so well developed in his book, *Truth and Method* (New York: The Seabury Press, 1975), 330. "To conduct a conversation means to allow oneself to be conducted by the object to which the partners in the conversation are directed."

5. Lane 21.

6. We see this incarnational basis applied specifically to the liturgy in such works as that by Chupungco in his *Cultural Adaptation of the Liturgy* (New York: Paulist Press, 1982). This has been the major approach taken by people who address the issue of the inculturation of the liturgy.

7. Lane 27.

8. Ibid. 35. Lane does not think we are ready for the faith/postmodernism kind of conversation.

9. See the article on postmodernity by Michael Downey in *The New Dictionary of Catholic Spirituality*, ed. Michael Downey, (Collegeville, Minn.: The Liturgical Press, A Michael Glazier Book, 1993), 746.

10. See my article "Starvation in the Midst of Plenty" in *Liturgical Ministry* 3 (Summer 1994). The entire volume is devoted to a "Second Liturgical Movement." See also "A New Liturgical Movement" by Lawrence Madden, SJ, in *America* (September 10, 1994): 16.

11. The previous paragraphs as well as many to follow in the chapter are taken from a chapter from a festschrift in honor of Jacob Vellian, an Indian liturgist. The festschriff is entitled *Tuvaik: Studies in Honour of Rev. Jacob Vellian*, edited by Fr. George Karukaparampil (Kottayam, Kerala: Wigi Offset Printings, 1995). My chapter is entitled: "Liturgy and Culture in Dialogue: A Challenge for the Twenty-First Century." The material included in this article is used with permission to give it wider diffusion.

12. I have detailed this in an article which appeared in *The National Catholic Reporter* (December 11, 1992).

13. Empereur, "Starvation in the Midst of Plenty" 82–83.

14. "Postmodernity" 746.

15. Ibid. 747.

16. Ibid. 748–749.

17. On this point I am not in agreement with Chupungco. See his *Liturgical Inculturation: Sacramentals, Religiosity, and Catechesis* (Collegeville, Minn.: The Liturgical Press, 1992), 51.

18. "Worship and Culture in Dialogue," in *Worship and Culture in Dialogue* (Geneva: The Lutheran World Federation, 1994), 164.

19. Ibid. 154.

20. See "Feminist and Sacramental Theology on the Body," by Susan Ross in *Horizons*, vol. 16:1 (Spring, 1989). For a more recent discussion by Ross on this matter see her *Extravagant Affections: A Feminist Sacramental Theology* (New York: Continuum, 1998). I find her notion of grounding embodiment not in espousal terms but in the context of the family particularly rich and exciting.

21. Chupungco 1994, 162.

22. "Who are our Guests? Some Considerations about Liturgy and Popular Catholicism," in *Questions Liturgiques*, vol. 74 (1993/2).

23. Ibid. 83.

24. See his unpublished article, "Building Bridges Between Liturgy, Devotionalism, and Popular Religion," which was given at the meeting of the North American Academy of Liturgy in Boston, January, 1995.

25. Some of the previous paragraphs are taken from my article, "Liturgy and Culture in Dialogue."

26. Paul Lakeland, *Postmodernity: Christian Identity in a Fragmented Age* (Minneapolis: Fortress Press, 1997), 8–9.

27. Charles Jencks, *What is Post-Modernism?* (London: Academy Editions, 1996), 22.

28. Ibid.

29. Ibid.

30. Ibid.

31. Ibid. 30.

32. I am aware that there are those who would want to make a case that Calvinism is not inimical to the aesthetic dimension and that there is a holistic aspect to that form of spirituality which embraces the arts. I trust the reader will understand that I am only trying to carry through on the example provided by Jencks.

33. Jencks 35.

34. For a development of this notion see *Context and Text: Method in Liturgical Theology* by Kevin Irwin (Collegeville, Minn.: The Liturgical Press, 1994).

35. Jencks 39.

36. Ibid.

37. Ibid. 77.

38. Lakeland 105.

39. Medellin, "Liturgy," 4; English translation, Consejo Episcopal Latinoamericano, *The Church in the Present-Day Transformation of Latin America in the Light of the Council, vol. II Conclusions* (Washington, D.C.: Latin American Bureau, USCC, 1968).

40. James Empereur, SJ, and Christopher Kiesling, OP, *The Liturgy That Does Justice* (Collegeville, Minn.: The Liturgical Press, A Michael Glazier Book, 1990), 27–28.

41. These last few paragraphs are taken from my article "Starvation in the Midst of Plenty."

JAMES L. EMPEREUR, SJ, was professor of liturgical and systematic theology at the Jesuit School of Theology at Berkeley for two decades before going to direct liturgies at San Fernando Cathedral in San Antonio, Texas. Among his many books are *Models of Liturgical Theology* and *Worship: Exploring the Sacred*. He is co-author of *The Liturgy That Does Justice*.

Discover the most effective way to catechize!

Here is a resource that could effectively form the faith of everyone in your community—babies, grade-schoolers, teenagers, adults, and seniors.

Liturgical Catechesis shows you how to use a tool you already have—the liturgy.

Six times each year this information-packed magazine will give you background, ideas, tips, and the expertise you need to make catechesis come alive for everyone in your community. Each issue makes the attempt to connect catechesis with real life and offers articles dealing with pre-catechesis, classroom rituals, and specific examples of liturgical catechesis in action. The church has mandated that all catechesis should be modeled on the baptismal catechumenate, so you can't afford to be without this valuable aid to your ministry.

Request a risk-free subscription to *Liturgical Catechesis* by phone, fax, mail, or email. If you like what you see in the first issue, return the invoice with a check for $30 and receive the next five issues. If you choose not to subscribe, just mark "cancel" on the invoice and return it within 15 days.

Liturgical Catechesis

160 E. Virginia Street, Suite #290

San Jose, CA 95112-5876

(408) 286-8505 (phone)

(408) 287-8748 (fax)

Orders@rpinet.com (email)

www.liturgicalcatechesis.com/ml (internet)